Dear
G-Spot

Dear G-Spot

Straight Talk about Sex and Love

ZANE

ATRIA BOOKS

NEW YORK LONDON TORONTO SYDNEY

ATRIA
BOOKS

A Division of Simon & Schuster, Inc.
1230 Avenue of the Americas
New York, NY 10020

First Atria Books trade paperback edition June 2008

ATRIA BOOKS and colophon are trademarks of Simon & Schuster, Inc.

For information about special discounts for bulk purchases,
please contact Simon & Schuster Special Sales at 1-800-456-6798
or business@simonandschuster.com

Designed by Joseph Rutt

Manufactured in the United States of America

1   3   5   7   9   10   8   6   4   2

The Library of Congress has cataloged the hardcover edition as follows:
Zane.
Dear G-spot / Zane. —1st Atria Books hardcover ed.
p.   cm.
1. Sex.   2. Sex customs.   3. Sex instruction.   I. Title.
HQ21.Z36   2007
306.77—dc22
2006101285

ISBN-13: 978-0-7434-5705-7
ISBN-10:   0-7434-5705-6
ISBN-13: 978-0-7434-5706-4 (pbk)
ISBN-10:   0-7434-5706-4 (pbk)

To all the women—young, middle-aged, and elderly—who still believe that we were placed on this earth to "service" men. May this book liberate your pussies, free your minds from the chains of sexual oppression, and make you realize that you are entitled to fuck your way.

WARNING
If you are sexually oppressed, sexually repressed,
or have any sexual hang-ups whatsoever,
please put my book down and slowly walk away from it.
It is too damn hot for your ass.

Contents

Dear
G-Spot

Introduction

This is a book about fucking. This is a book about love. This is a book about what love has to do with fucking and fucking has to do with love. Do not read it from cover to cover and then start whining about the contents. Do not email me saying that I should be ashamed of myself and that I am wasting my talent. Do not pen negative articles about how I am keeping "literary" authors from selling books. Do not start protests at your local library to ban me from the shelves. I have no regrets and make no apologies for writing this book.

It is hard to believe that nearly ten years have passed since I began giving sex and relationship advice via the internet. Nothing about my commitment has changed. I believe . . . actually I know . . . that there are many women (and men) who are completely lost when it comes to understanding and expressing their sexuality. Contrary to the beliefs of some, being sexually uninhibited is not a criminal act.

What surprised me most when I first started writing erotica was how afraid people were of me. There were tons of novels on the market about people being gunned down in their own homes, people being chopped to pieces and thrown in Dumpsters, aliens landing and eliminating everyone on earth, men fucking each other behind their women's backs, and just about every other damn thing. A lot of the books were critically acclaimed and award-winning bestsellers. Most of them deserved it. But heaven forbid, do not let a black woman start talking openly about sex! It was like an earthquake had struck, like a volcano had erupted in the middle of publishers' row in New York City. Everyone was convinced that I would be the laughingstock of the book industry, that I would kill my career before it started, and that I would be blackballed from ever writing again. Now everyone is either looking for or masquerading as "the next Zane." Like Maxwell's "This Woman's Work," the real Zane has a little life left in her. In fact, I am ready to kick it up to the next level and keep them guessing about what I will do next. Try as they might, they will never figure it out. Thus, this book.

In all actuality, it was way back in late 2001 or early 2002 when I initially came up with *Dear G-Spot* as the title for my first nonfiction book—a manual on sex. I submitted four or five concepts to my editor at the time, Tracy Sherrod, and even started a couple of different versions of the book. Then I got sidetracked with some other books. Yet this book rarely left my thoughts and I remained determined to one day write it. I did not follow any of my original concepts—all of them intriguing—but one day they may become my nonfiction books two through five. I am not going to say what they deal with because "the hills have eyes." If you know anything about my imagination, then you realize that, if nothing else, they will all be unique.

I have never been one to sugarcoat anything, so why start now? *Dear G-Spot* is an in-your-face, straight up with no chaser book about fucking. How to fuck, how not to fuck, and knowing whether or not you have any business fucking in the first place. While there have been countless books written about sex, in the tradition of my erotic short story collections, I seriously doubt you will ever read another one quite like this bitch here. I am "coming hard" so you can "cum hard" later. Some of the parts of this book are very graphic, and they were meant to be. Once again, if you don't think you can handle the heat, stay out of my kitchen.

Do I profess to be the ultimate source of sexual knowledge? Hell to the fuck no! Do I think that porn stars have nothing on me? That's debatable and it depends on the porn star! Do I think that I am serving a purpose by writing this book and offering my outlooks and opinions on sex? Absolutely!

I see this as a comprehensive guide to fucking. One that will not put people to sleep and that I hope will entertain as well as inform. It is as simple as that. Some experts will surely say that a lot of my views are incorrect. They need to go write their own books. This one is mine. Some readers will brag to their buddies and say, "I done all that shit in Zane's book already! I've been blowing out backs for decades!" To that, all I can say is, "High five and more power to you! Go on with your bad self!"

In all seriousness, this book is really for "the lost and confused," for the tens of thousands of people who have reached out and asked for my advice over the past ten years. By doing this book, I hope to accomplish many things. Most of all, I hope to open up the lines of communication between men and women, parents and children, etc. Communicating is the first line of both the offense and the defense in any healthy relationship. People write to me because they feel as if they have no one else to discuss their feelings and concerns with. That is a travesty in itself. I will touch upon that more in the communication chapter, but please let your loved ones know that you are there for them, no matter what.

Welcome to *Dear G-Spot*. I hope you enjoy it. If you are not on my email list, please send a blank email to Eroticanoir-subscribe@topica.com. That way I can keep you informed about my new books, events, films, television shows, plays, etc. You are much loved and appreciated. Also, come check out my increasingly popular blog at http://myspace.com/zaneland. Talk about venting; I am a hot mess and should have never gotten started with the blogging action. Last, if you want to host a Zane Adult Toy Party or become a sales representative for my adult toys, books, or body products, please email StreborBooks@gmail.com or visit me at www.eroticanoir.com.

Peace and many blessings,
Zane

Sexual Addiction

*S*exual addiction is a topic very near and dear to my heart. When I first decided to write my novel *Addicted*, nearly nine years ago, it started out as a short story. At first, I was simply going to write a quick sexcapade about a woman screwing three people other than her husband. But the Zoe character fascinated me. I put the short story aside and decided it would be my first full-length novel. I wanted to study and find out what caused sexual addiction and not merely concentrate on her being a freak. I wanted to open the floodgates, so to speak, on why women cheat and the underlying causes of cheating. I also wanted to explore the difference between a nymphomaniac and an addict.

At the time, I had a male friend who confided in me that he slept with numerous married women. He knew that I was writing erotica, had read a few stories that set his boxers on fire, and wanted my opinion. He asked why women would be willing to do explicit things with him that they were not willing to do with their husbands. I did not hesitate when I answered, because it was obvious to me. They did it with him because they did not fear being judged by him, nor did they care what he thought. Their husbands and serious mates were there at home with them, the fathers of their kids, and men who could hurt their feelings if their sexual behavior was taken out of context.

I want to share a brief, real-life sex experience that someone recently emailed to me. Then I am going to ask you a question afterward.

Dear G-Spot:

I realize you must receive a ton of emails from people who believe that their lives portray parts of your books. Well, here is another one. *Addicted* is exactly like my life. I married my childhood sweetheart, had two wonderful kids, and I am cheating. Unlike Zoe and Jason, my husband and I live paycheck to paycheck. So do my three lovers—two men and one woman. They have all fallen in love with my sex, and even though they knew from the onset that I was married, none of them want to share me with my husband. I made it clear that I was only seeking sexcapades with them. Only one of them truly knows me in the respect that I share my heart, my thoughts, my truth, and my lies with him. My husband loves me more than Jason could ever love Zoe, but I do have a sexual addiction. The sex is not good, but I am all that he knows because I was his first. Sex is too predictable for me when I have to instruct a man on what to do. That is my only reason for cheating on him. Other than that, I am fine, he is fine, and our lives are fine. Can you suggest anything? Possibly a sex therapist for us both or something?

Misery

Dear Misery:

You need therapy in the worst way, but I would hold off on pulling your husband into it unless you plan to tell him about your three other lovers. Like Zoe, you are playing a very dangerous game. Any law enforcement official will tell you that the most treacherous scenario for them to enter into is a domestic one. Emotions run high; no one is thinking clearly, and that entire "If I can't have you, no one will" mentality often kicks in. You say all three of your extra lovers are sprung. You need to get them the hell unsprung and leave them all alone. I do believe you have an addiction and it will not be easy for you to walk away. That is why you must get help. Even though funds are tight, does either one of your jobs offer mental health counseling? Most group health insurance policies do offer it, with limitations. Check into that, and if that does not pan out, research your local agencies. You cannot give up on your quest to get help.

While you may not want to instruct your husband because of the sex ending up predictable, you have to do what you have to do to make things work. You could possibly rent or purchase some porn movies and watch them together to give him ideas—ones that you are personally feeling and would like to live out in your own bedroom. That way it is not obvious that you are saying he is lacking. First things first, though. Go get help and let me know what happens.

Blessings,
Zane

Most of the emails that I receive are from women who I do not think are sexual addicts, like the ones below. However, the woman above does appear to have a serious issue with her sexuality and it could very well be an addiction. Like most addictions, sex is used to take away pain or to temporarily ignore it. If you are not in control of your life, but your life is controlled by your sexual urges, then you need to seek help. Many addicts—to drugs, alcohol, gambling, or sex—have to reach an all-time low before they admit to even having a problem. Sometimes that can be deadly and too late. That is why it is essential to get immediate help as soon as you recognize the symptoms.

What are the symptoms of sexual addiction? Experts vary in their opinions about this, but some things seem agreed on by most. One, when a person's sexual behavior gets out of control, whether that means actually engaging in intercourse or watching pornography. If every waking moment is spent thinking about fucking, or actually fucking, it all means the same. Two, if your fascination with sex has started to trickle over into your family life and you are not spending time with your kids and mate. If you are constantly cheating on your mate for no apparent reason, other than fulfilling an actual need. Three, if your sexual activities have gotten you into trouble at work or, heaven forbid, with the law. Four, if you have tried to stop doing it and cannot or your sexual urges constantly grow in intensity.

Here are some common examples of how addictions relate to one another:

A crack addict does not go home for days at a time but lies up in a crack house doing drugs and not thinking about his friends and family members or the possibility that they are worried sick about his whereabouts, wondering if he is alive or dead.

A sex addict does not go home for days at a time but lies up in the bed with a lover or goes from house to house of various lovers to satisfy her sexual urges. She does not call home or worry about what her husband and kids are thinking.

A gambling addict goes to Atlantic City and spends his entire paycheck on the slots or trying his luck at poker. He takes out a loan inside the casino and loses all of that as well. He has no idea how he is going to pay his mortgage because he does not even want to go to work; he just wants to be there gambling.

A sex addict calls in to work sick for days on end; instead she stays at home and leaves only to go to the local adult shop to purchase new sex toys. She cleans out her savings account to purchase pornos or she runs up a tremendous cable bill by ordering pay-per-view pornos. She lies in bed all day, playing in her pussy with a rabbit, a dildo, and working anal beads in and out of her behind. She has orgasm after orgasm but still feels a tremendous need no matter how many times she climaxes.

An alcoholic drinks in private, trying to hide the fact that he is drinking at all. He sits in his car or office after hours and turns the bottle upside down, searching for that ultimate feeling from an external source. He goes to a bar one night and drinks for three hours straight. When the bartender refuses to serve him anything else but coffee, he becomes irate and attempts to punch the bartender's lights out. The police are called and he is arrested. He is ashamed to have to call his wife to come bail him out.

A sex addict hides it from her family. She might not even have a regular sex life with her husband because he cannot give her that rush, that chemical stimulation to the brain that having sex with strangers does. She goes out to a club one night, in this really skimpy dress she changed into in her car. She grinds her ass against a man on the dance floor for an hour and then asks him to fuck her out in the alley. They are out in the alley, fucking against the brick siding of the building, when suddenly they are blinded by a flashlight and then red swirling lights from the top of a police car. They are both arrested for committing a lewd act and she is too embarrassed to call her husband to come bail her out.

All of that is sad, but it happens every day throughout the world. Addiction is when you know you should stop something and you want desperately to stop but you cannot. This applies to drugs, sex, gambling, shopping, overeating, smoking cigarettes, alcohol, and many other things.

What causes sexual addiction? Most times, there is more than one contributing factor. Often something tracing back to childhood is the root of the addiction. Some of it traces back to being exposed to pornography at a young age, or being molested or somehow sexually traumatized. It is a "progressive disease" and not something that pops up overnight. After I wrote *Addicted*, having zero experience with sexual addiction myself, I was stunned at the number of women who approached me via email or by falling into my arms crying at book signings. Women who had ignored their issues for a long time—sometimes decades—and who now planned to get help before they turned into my main character, Zoe. Women who loved their husbands but could not stop what they were feeling and/or doing to self-destruct both themselves and their marriage.

There is nothing wrong with being sexually healthy and craving to be active on a regular basis. However, if you find yourself masturbating three times a day; putting sex before work, family, and responsibilities; living on the internet on porno sites or watching pornos the first thing in the morning and the last thing at night; having numerous affairs; or engaging in dangerous or illegal behavior, you might be an addict. You should get help immediately.

Dear G-Spot:

I truly believe I am addicted to sex. I was married for four years and separated for two of those years. During the end of our relationship, the thought of having sex with my husband disgusted me. After we separated, I dated here and there. We are now officially divorced. I am constantly fantasizing about sex, especially sex with complete strangers. When I meet an interesting man, I don't know how long I should wait before having sex with him. Part of me says that I'm a grown-ass woman—I'm twenty-six—and I shouldn't be ashamed of anything. I think it would be better to determine sexual compatibility up front. The other part of me says I need to wait and refrain from acting like a slut.

I haven't mastered the art of masturbating, but I'm working on it. Sometimes a woman needs the real thing: some meat; flesh against flesh; some weight on top of me, behind me, or underneath me. To a degree, I consider myself sexually free. I'm willing to experiment but haven't found the right person to experiment with.

Shouldn't a person live out her fantasies? If she doesn't, then she'll always have them, right? My mother was and is still very promiscuous. I have witnessed many of her experiences and she has gained a reputation. I'm afraid of becoming the person she is because of my sexual desires. Can you give me some advice? Thank you and continue to do what you do.

Sex-on-the-Brain

Dear Sex-on-the-Brain:

Tomorrow is promised to no one, so yes, you should live out your fantasies as long as you do it safely and use protection. Nothing is more disappointing than to spend a lot of time getting to know a man only to discover that you are sexually incompatible months later. While sex is not everything, it is something.

Masturbation is wonderful, but a real person in the bed beside you takes it to another level, especially if that person is compassionate and understanding. I don't think you are addicted to sex. I think you are normal but simply falling into the paradigm that society has instilled in so many young women that men can do what they wish but women must refrain. That is bullshit, because we have as much right to fall asleep at night sexually content as they do.

By no means am I suggesting that you go out and start boning men right and left, because that is much too risky. However, you need not abstain from sex to fit into some sort of imaginary time frame to properly give it up. The bottom line is that if you were truly addicted to sex, you would not be emailing me. You would be fucking someone right this minute and not be caring about the repercussions. Do not worry about following in your mother's footsteps. Her unwise decisions should serve as lessons to you as to what not to do, but it does not mean that you are like her. It sounds like you have learned something from her mistakes.

Blessings,

Zane

Dear G-Spot:

I am a twenty-two-year-old female who is in a relationship with a thirty-six-year-old man. Don't get me wrong. I do love him but, at the same time, I am still in love with my oldest daughter's father. I have an okay sex life. I say "okay" because I recently started reading your books, which I find to be very sexually liberating. There are a lot of things that I have in common with your characters. I really felt connected to Rayne from *Afterburn*. I felt like my situation and hers were exactly the same, except that I have yet to find my Yardley. To get to the point, I find myself wanting to experiment with different positions, but I am afraid to because of my weight and what my three lovers might think. Yes, you heard me right: I have three lovers. Not only am I having sex with my daughter's father and my current flame, but I am also sexually active with a married man. To tell the truth, if I was approached by another man who turned me on, I would probably start fucking him also. I really want to just find one man and settle down, but it seems that plan is not even about to happen. What should I do?

Confused Sex Addict

Dear Confused Sex Addict:

I cannot totally fault you for having three lovers, because a shitload of men are fucking multiple women at the same time and are proud of it. It seems like you are using several men to make a whole person. Of course, you need to leave the married man the hell alone. That goes without saying, because nothing good can come from that and karma will always return and bite us all in the ass. You are still young and I get the feeling that you have a high sex drive, but I would not say it is an addiction. You want to find one man and settle down, but it doesn't sound like it will be with any of the men with whom you are currently involved. If one of them was the one, you would know it and not need the other two. I often tell my friends that they cannot expect to find or attract another man when they already have one lounging on the sofa and, more important, causing drama in their lives. You probably need some "me time" to discover yourself, love yourself, and then regroup and map out the traits you want in a lifelong mate. Here is the thing, though: you have to possess those same traits. Thus, if you want a man willing to make a commitment and not fuck around, you cannot be whoring like you are. Your daughter's father will always be a part of your life, but I suspect that he has a new woman. That's just nasty, and why should you share? Same goes for the married man, because trust that he is banging his wife, whether he denies it or not. You have a chance to start over since twenty-two is very young. But victory begins with you, so please dump all of those zeros and reinvent yourself for a hero.

Blessings,
Zane

Dear G-Spot:

I am the wife of a Southern Baptist preacher. It may sound right, but to be totally honest, it is not the marriage of my dreams. When I met my husband, he was a virgin at twenty-two and I was a sex fiend at eighteen. It was difficult trying to instruct him on pleasing me because I was still learning myself. I have attempted to be creative, but he thinks that I am too freaky. Nine years into our marriage, I stepped out on my own and into the world of S & M with older, more experienced men. I have done some truly explicit things and can't get that type of freedom with my husband. I love him, but being a preacher's wife is so difficult. I have cheated on and off for two years. Sex with my husband is rare and not satisfying at all. I am afraid that I may fall weak to temptation and begin to prowl to the dark side of S & M again, something I have not done in about a year. It is a scary thing. I am alone a lot and sometimes a woman needs a good dick. Sometimes a woman needs a dick in every hole at the same time. I am a kinky freak; always will be. I don't have anyone to talk to about this. I have the public face, the church face, and the family face. I am a long way from my hometown, with no one who has a common situation that I can reach out to. This secret is killing me. My urges are killing me. Is there any hope? Who can I talk to?

Preacher's Wifey

Dear Preacher's Wifey:

If your husband is truly spiritual, he will be able to deal with your issues and seek counseling with you to fix them. The only way you will be able to save your marriage is to come clean. Otherwise, your situation will fester inside of you like a knot and lead you to do things that can cause irreversible damage. Because of your husband's profession, word of you doing such things could literally cost him his career and, thus, his livelihood. When you ask whom you should talk to, you need to talk to him. If you feel uncomfortable doing it alone, reach out to someone else—a close friend, a relative, or a therapist who can initiate the conversation for you. You can turn this around, if you have faith, but going out and engaging in S & M is not the solution.

Blessings,
Zane

Dear G-Spot:

I am your number one fan, literally. Girl, I feel like I know you because I can relate to at least one character in your many "great" books. Zane, you are truly holding it down for all of us NYMPHS out here. I never thought anyone in the world could relate to me. After reading so many of your books, I realize that I am not the only one reading Zane. Many others began to inform me that they also read you. On the flip side, you know there are those ladies out there who label us as freaks. That is because they have not had a "good fix." Zane, you have taught my best friend and me not to be afraid to express our sexual tension with our men. We have men on us like gravy on rice, but there is one issue: I am addicted to it. What should I do? Is it a problem to want some all of the time? Please write me back.

Dick Freak

Dear Dick Freak:

It is a problem only if you are suffering from an actual addiction. That would mean you exhibit reckless behavior, give it up on the drop of a dime to strangers who may not even appeal to you, and practice unsafe sex on the regular. Being sensual and aware of your sexual desires is a good thing because many women go through their entire life never once experiencing sexual gratification.

Wanting sex all the time is cool if you have one lover who reciprocates what he receives from you. However, do not allow sex to cloud your common sense or prevent you from doing the appropriate things to further your education or career. Sex is like the cherry on top of a sundae, but you need to make the sundae first, if you get my drift. I applaud you and your friend for being sexually liberated. That is why I write what I write—to let other women know they are not alone. As for the ladies out there labeling people as freaks, that is all a matter of opinion. Some women have no problem with allowing men to leave the bedroom more satisfied than them. After all, they cannot miss something they have never had. Once a woman experiences that "first high," a mind-blowing orgasm, anything else seems substandard.

Blessings,
Zane

Virginity/ Young Love

*I*n the introduction to this book, I stated that it is about how to fuck, how not to fuck, and knowing whether or not you have any business fucking in the first place. This is the section that covers knowing whether or not you have any business fucking in the first place. Virginity is something special because you can lose it only once and who you choose to do that with—whether male or female—can have a positive or negative effect on how you view sex from that moment on. Some people decide to go ahead and get it over with as quickly as possible, not giving careful consideration to the outcome. They want to become sexually active so they can begin their lifelong journey of seeing how freaky they can be. They listen to their peers—rarely their parents—and think that sex is an essential part of growing up and that they are nerds if they do not participate. That is not true. There are many people who do not lose their virginity until much later in life. It is all a matter of preference.

Many people—mostly for religious reasons—do not believe in sex before marriage. Again, that is a personal preference and I give them many kudos if they can hold out for marriage. But what happens if the right person never comes along? Should a person be celibate her entire life? In the old days, chances were that people would get married, have a bunch of children, and stay married until one or both of them died. In today's age, more than half of the marriages end in divorce, and a lot of people do not get married in the first place. So where does that leave them?

I am not encouraging everyone to have sex, but I do think that people—in particular parents—need to be realistic. Parents can have these sexual urges that are out of this world, fuck each other like it is going out of style night and day, and yet expect their offspring never to think about it. The apples do not fall far from the tree, and sooner or later, hormones will kick in and our children will have sex on the brain. It is inevitable and we cannot protect our children from that. It is important that they be able to discuss it with people older than them and more experienced instead of relying on children their same age for guidance.

I get a lot of letters from people—mostly young ladies—who are considering losing their virginity but want to know how they can tell if the person is the right one. There is no surefire way to tell, because people have mad game and will lie their way into a girl's drawers without thinking twice. However, there are those who are sincere and legitimately want that closeness. My suggestion is to hold off and see if the person sticks around and is willing to wait. If he is not, then he is not the one. How long should he have to wait? Until you are completely comfortable with the situation and are deeply infatuated, if not in love.

I was having a conversation with a few women my age a couple of days ago and we were talking about how older men tend to date younger women. One of the women, in her early forties, said that a male friend told her that young girls do not hesitate for five seconds to give oral sex or fuck altogether. That they do it without even knowing you at all. The same is evident with these reality dating shows, where people meet and are tonguing each other down in the space of thirty television minutes. Soaking in hot tubs and feeling and humping all over each other. That is not a good sign but not a surprise either. When the people involved in sexual activities are really young, I do not consider that being sexually uninhibited; I consider that confusion about both sex and love.

At first I was going to divide "Virginity" and "Young Love" into two different sections but decided that they are basically the same thing. While I think it is important for people to express their sexuality, I do find it equally important that they share themselves only with people who care. In this age of diseases and crazy people running rampant on the internet, we have to be more careful than ever.

As you will see from the numerous emails below, about both virginity and young love, our youth are more confused than ever when it comes to sex. Some think they are experts when they are not, some are facing the demands of peer pressure, and some are downright scared of sex and what might happen if they have it. Parents really need to guide their children when it comes down to all aspects of their young lives, including being honest with them about sex when and if they ever address it.

Dear G-Spot:

I am eighteen years old and I am still a virgin. To me there is nothing wrong with that. Seventy percent of my friends are not virgins and most of them tell me not to lose it because I would regret it. I masturbate almost nightly, but I quit after five minutes because I cannot take the pressure or the feeling. Does that mean that I am not ready for sex? I think I am ready to experience sex, but I fear getting pregnant, contracting HIV or other STDs, and my friends say it hurts. One of my friends said it only hurts for five minutes and feels like medium to heavy menstrual cramps.

I am talking to this twenty-year-old guy right now. We met about two weeks ago and he is so fine. If our relationship grows and I do decide to have sex with him, how do I ask him to get tested? He might take it as a sign of mistrust, but I am just trying to protect myself.

Zane, how do I know—for sure—when I am ready to have sex? Am I going to bleed? I want to try it to see how it feels, but most of my friends swear that once I get started, it will become an addiction. Most of the boys these days get bored without sex and do not want to wait—like this other guy I used to talk to. I told him that I was a virgin and he badgered me constantly about when I was going to give it up. Eventually he stopped calling me altogether. One day I played a mind game on him and told him that I would have sex with him. He called my phone at least twenty times the next night. That is when I realized that all he ever wanted from me was sex and that he was not right for me.

How do I know who the right person is? Is it normal to enter college as a virgin? Ms. Zane, please tell me what to do. I really need to hear this from you. Does sex really feel as good as people say that it does?

A Virgin

Dear A Virgin:

You are so sweet and innocent, and while I wish some little girls could always stay that way, hormones will not allow it for long. Thus I am going to try to guide you in the right direction. You are in a common situation:

relying on people your own age for sexual information when, in all actuality, they know as little or barely more than you do. Their suggestions are not those on which you should base your life decisions. You did the right thing by not sleeping with that other boy. His intentions were obvious. If he cared about you, he would have been calling you twenty times a day without the promise of a sexual encounter. This new one you just met two weeks ago is not worthy of anything from you. You have to make him earn your goodies, and in two weeks, instant infatuation is still there. Two more weeks from now you might think he is the scum of the earth.

Plenty of people enter college as virgins and plenty of them graduate from college as virgins. Giving up your virginity is not a prerequisite for an education. In fact, you could probably concentrate on your studies more without sex and the ultimate drama usually attached to relationships.

When you do have sex—or contemplate having sex—you should ask the man to be tested, even if he claims he is a virgin himself. They sell kits at the local drugstore that you can purchase and send in via snail mail. You call in three to seven days and punch in a code to get your results. To make him feel comfortable and not make it seem like you do not trust him, test yourself as well. That way you can both start with a clean slate. Always protect yourself from disease by using a condom and double protect yourself from pregnancy by using a backup method such as birth control pills.

Sex might hurt at the very beginning, but that is normal. You are doing something that you have never done before. Your hymen must be broken, and it takes some pressure to make that happen. There is no reason to speculate that you will become addicted to sex. Your friends do not mean that in the literal sense anyway; they simply mean that they want to do it a lot. Addiction is something totally different altogether.

Sex does feel good—possibly even great—when you are with the right partner. However, without feelings, it is just sex and not a spectacular feat to accomplish. Any woman can spread her legs and any man can stick his dick inside her. Making love is so much more special—a time when you feel a closeness that no one can interfere with.

By no means am I encouraging you to take the plunge and lose your virginity. The inevitable will happen, but it seems like you are trying to keep the pace of your friends. Do not allow the peer pressure to get to you and cause you to make rash decisions. You will know the right person when he comes to you. The sun will seem brighter. Your heart will flutter when he is around you. It will be an unmistakable feeling, one that you obviously have not yet experienced.

Blessings,
Zane

Dear G-Spot:

Here is my problem. I started having sex earlier this month. I enjoy sex with my love, and just like every other girl's first time, it hurt. I figured that after a couple of times, I would loosen up. It turns out that I was wrong. We have had sex countless times and I am extremely tight. It hurts so bad that the last time I had to stop. It was worse than my first time. What should I do? Is there something that I am doing wrong?

Tight Fit

Dear Tight Fit:

You might have vaginismus, which is involuntary muscle spasms. Or you might just still be kind of stressed out about being new to sex. Are you using contraceptives? Condoms and lubricants can cause the vaginal walls to tense up as well. You might also need to see your gynecologist to make sure you do not have a yeast infection or an STD that is causing your vagina to tighten up. Many items such as tampons, soap, and even laundry detergent can irritate you down there. It might not be noticeable until the friction of sex occurs. I would go see a doctor.

Blessings,
Zane

Dear G-Spot:

I have a problem and I am seeking your advice. I have been dating my boyfriend for about a year and he is twenty-six years old. I love him dearly, but I am not sexually satisfied and he is simply not doing it for me. I am used to guys with big dicks; he is not one of them. I don't want that to be the issue. My sex drive is extremely high. When I try to communicate and tell him what I want and how I want it, he does not seem to be listening. I told him a long time ago that I was not satisfied and he promised me that he would try. I guess that I am just sick of the guys always "getting theirs" when I am not getting mine.

Two months ago, I met someone. He is eighteen and wonderful, not just in bed but the total package of emotional, physical, and spiritual satisfaction. I really want to be with the eighteen-year-old, but since I am twenty-two, it feels weird. People say that age is nothing but a number and he does not act his age at all. He is always there for me. When we have sex, it is great. He has opened me up sexually in ways that I could not imagine and has me doing things that I would previously never do. For example, the other night I gave him oral sex in the park, with a parked car beside us watching. Usually, I would be nervous, but I loved it and wanted more. Not to mention that he is the first person ever to give me an orgasm. I could not believe it but he did. There is something about him that I cannot let go of. He drives me crazy. When we are not having sex, I still enjoy spending time with him watching television or going to the movies.

I realize that what I am doing is wrong, but my current boyfriend has caused some pain in our relationship. Plus, there is nothing thrilling about our sex life. What do I do?

Torn

Dear Torn:

As long as the young man you are dealing with is of legal age, age is truly nothing but a number. It is not like you are robbing the cradle, since you are less than five years older than him. The bottom line is that he treats you well, makes you feel special, and seemingly is everything you have ever desired. Do not front and stay with the other man because it looks better. At some point, you have to begin to live your life for you and not for others or what they think. Personally, I wish you the best, but you have to cut the other man off because it is the right thing to do. I read someplace that relationships tend to overlap for up to 250 days while people try to decide between two lovers. That is crazy and surely a setup for failure if found out. Be yourself, love this young man, and keep fucking him in the park if it makes you happy. But before you do any of that, let the other man go find someone who can love him back.

Blessings,
Zane

Dear G-Spot:

How are you doing, Zane? I am a twenty-two-year-old virgin and I do not want to die. I have a wonderful man but I am scared of being with him sexually. I do not know if he will look at me the same as eight months ago, when we first met. We have tried to do it but it is so painful and we can never go any farther. What can we do? I am in need of some serious help.

Ready but Not Altogether Sure

Dear Ready but Not Altogether Sure:

I am not sure if you are afraid to die because you might catch a disease or if you think this man might actually fuck you to death. I do not think you have to worry about the latter. The pain associated with first-time sex is perfectly normal, just as normal as the pain associated with childbirth *each and every time.* Trust me, that is a thousand times worse. Taking in a dick is a lot less strenuous than pushing out a six- to eleven-pound human being. I am not trying to make light of your situation, but listen, maybe eight months is not enough time to determine if he is the one. You have maintained your virginity for twenty-two years. What's the rush? If this man was the ultimate turn-on, you would be so wet that your body would be yearning for him to the point that it would try to suck his dick inside like a straw. I am not saying never try to have sex with him again, but take your time and do it right. Make him treat you special. If you are already thinking that he might throw you by the wayside—or misjudge you—once you do the nasty with him, that means you have reservations about his sincerity. Think it through and make a clear-headed decision.

Blessings,

Zane

Dear G-Spot:

I am a nineteen-year-old virgin. I have an extremely conservative roommate who doesn't approve of one-night stands. She also doesn't believe in sex before marriage. I completely respect her and therefore I followed her wishes. One of my other friends decided that I could use her sex toy box for a while. I refused because it is nasty to have someone else's cum and pussy juice all over something that I stick into myself. I really want to have sex, but I am going to wait until marriage. Thus, I decided on self-arousal. What types of toys do you recommend?

Ready to Jill Off

Dear Ready to Jill Off:

I commend you on making the decision to stay a virgin until marriage, your roommate as well. I hope that your decision is yours alone and no one else's, because everyone has the right to live her own life. I am elated that you refused to use another woman's sex toys. You are correct; that is downright nasty and a practice of poor hygiene. As far as toys I would suggest, vibrators never fail. To me, dildos take a lot more work than necessary, but some women love them for their girth and size. You could get away with purchasing a little bullet or fingertip vibrator that will give you immense pleasure. Ultimately, though, your greatest sex toy will be within you—inside your head. Many women can place a towel or pillow between their legs, play with their nipples, and fantasize themselves to an orgasm. It may take a minute for you to understand your body enough to recognize your trigger points, but once you do and master the art of masturbation, you will be leagues ahead of many women having sex who can't even experience a single orgasm. Once you do begin to have sex—whether it is before or after marriage—you will be able to instruct a man on how to get you off. That is something special and unique—just like your virginity.

Blessings,

Zane

Dear G-Spot:

First I wanted to say that I think that your website is all of that. It is so reassuring to see stories and advice from African-American individuals. After reading your Q & A section, I have a situation that requires good advice. Since you have given good advice to the individuals I have read, here goes my situation:

I recently turned thirty and had been a virgin up until two months ago. I was raised in a family that practiced religious beliefs that banned sex before marriage. I have dated several men but, when it got to those intimate moments and I did not put out, the relationships went sour.

I met this Jamaican man two months ago (I guess you can see who I gave my virginity to) and he is a very sexual Scorpio. I did not tell him that I was a virgin right away for fear of two things. One, he would be too anxious to pop the cherry, and two, he would run away. Finally, after nights of him trying to perform oral sex on me, I allowed him. I enjoyed it a great deal. However, it was not at all like I thought it would be. He was about to make love to me next when I stopped him and told him that I was a virgin. He sat back on the couch in a complete daze. He looked at me and started to massage my legs. He said, "I've never had a virgin before."

After that night, he tried endlessly to sleep with me, coming later and later to my house, conveniently not showing up on time to avoid going to the movies or dinner. I decided I was tired of being a virgin and was sexually frustrated. I agreed to have sex with him but at a nice place for my first time. We went to the Inn of the Dove. It was very nice. I was looking forward to a beautiful night. However, that did not happen. He quickly took a shower and then told me to go get into something comfortable.

I had a nice silk gown with a slit up the side that accented all of the right places. I lay next to him and he dimmed all the lights except for the one over us (I was mortified). He got right on me and started to enter me. No foreplay or anything. The music channel had a rock song playing or something; he didn't even change the channel. He had a hard time entering me because I was so tight. He pulled me to the edge of the bed and entered me. I was in such pain and felt such great pressure, but I endured it because I knew this was how it was supposed to be my first time (little did I know). He came right away. He came out with a wet washcloth and handed it to me afterward.

Fifteen minutes later he was in full form again. This time he positioned my legs in the air and deep-thrusted me. I was in extreme pain and asked that my legs be put down. I got comfortable and started to enjoy the sex, but he quickly put my legs up again. He lasted for what seemed to be hours (ten minutes to be exact) and he came hard and screamed. I lay there, frustrated and unsatisfied. I refused to let him touch me the rest of the night.

The next morning, he woke me up by grinding his penis up against my buttocks. We had sex twice before leaving. I forgot to mention the little details like him holding me all night and each time we made love (if that's what you want to call it), but I could not stand for him to touch me.

I did not call him for a while afterward, although he constantly called me. I did not like the sex and thought this was how it was going to be with everyone else I decided to be intimate with. We had sex one more time but, before we did, I told him how I felt. I told him that I was not satisfied and I did not climax. When we had sex again, he took it slow this time and did what I told him, but lasted only one minute. I was mortified. I do not want to have sex with him anymore, because I think he is selfish.

Am I the one being selfish, or am I doing something wrong? Is it me? Did he use me? Are all men like this with sex?

Confused

Dear Confused:

Stay away from him! I am so upset that you waited for so long to lose your virginity only to end up with an insensitive dog. I wish that I could get hold of him and beat his ass myself. No, not all men are like that with sex. Unfortunately, quite a few of them are. I implore you not to give up on finding the right man for yourself, but proceed with extreme caution.

If this man is still calling you, tell him in no uncertain terms to stop. Anyone that selfish with you, knowing that you were a virgin, will continue to be selfish both in and out of the bedroom. I wouldn't give his ass the time of day from here on out.

You need a real man who is capable of giving you the type of love, tenderness, and reciprocity in lovemaking that you deserve. You gave him a very precious part of yourself and he took it for granted. No foreplay? No orgasm? You do not need a man like that in your life. Your body is your temple and you have to be extremely careful about who you allow to commune inside of it.

I would suggest meeting men from your church, since you come from an extremely religious family. You need a man who mirrors your beliefs, one you have something in common with, and one who will treat you like the Nubian queen that you are. The Jamaican fool is not him.

I cannot tell you how much something like this upsets me. Men do not realize that making love is not fucking and that they are not the only ones who are supposed to leave satisfied with the experience. I wish you the best. I really do. I hope that you will stay in touch and let me help you celebrate when you do find a man worthy of your affection.

Blessings,
Zane

Dear G-Spot:

I have mad love for your stories. They give me new ideas. Anyway, I have this problem that I hope is unique enough to make it onto your site. I am an eighteen-year-old brother with what I feel is a kind of unique problem . . . I KNOW EXACTLY WHAT I'M DOING WHEN IT COMES TO SEX!!!

I know a good many of a woman's hot spots—her whole body. I love the taste of a woman . . . all over. I even dipped into Tantra and can safely say that I have the techniques of male multiple orgasms down pat. You might call this a gift, but in my situation, it truly is beginning to feel like a curse.

I've been amassing knowledge about how to please a woman sexually since the age of fourteen. Back then, I thought it was like learning to drive and that every man learned how eventually. But now I'm at a point where every stage of a relationship has an underlying sexual tone that I can't ignore. While most dudes my age fantasize about sex, I'm sure it's not about sex that literally could last for hours, with slow massage . . . whispering dirty thoughts in her ear . . . treating her body like a piece of mango fruit . . . or a slice of deep chocolate cake. I have only one male friend who even knows what the G-spot is. And trying to convince them that slower can sometimes be better . . . forget about it! It might sound like I'm trying to brag or something, but really I just need you to feel my situation.

See, despite this knowledge, I'm not all that experienced. So far I've had only one sexual encounter. It went very well and only cemented my belief that I knew how to treat a lady right. I even tried that thing you always talk about . . . taking both nipples in my mouth at once. Thanks for the tip! But I think that my number of partners is low because I feel a huge sense of guilt over my sexual needs. Once I got older and learned that MANY men never learn how to please a woman and don't even think that sex is important—beyond bragging rights—I started to feel like I was putting unnecessary strain into new relationships.

Whenever I meet a new woman now, I feel like I'm taking advantage of her by simply just being around. Sometimes I feel like not only will I be so deep in "sex mode" that I will hurt my partner, but I am also truly afraid that if they ever saw how much I really want them that women will think I'm an animal. I am half West Indian and a native of the DC area, so I think I'm above average looking. Not overly tall . . . but with an athletic build. I don't have trouble meeting women; I just can't allow myself to get close. I must also confess that I have a passion for the sistahs that borders on a fetish. Each of the different skin tones is like another flavor to me . . . which adds to my guilt. I'm sure other brothas with what I call old soul skillz feel the same way as me . . . Could you please post this and give some advice?

P.S. Please don't tell me to find someone as sexual as me 'cause believe me, Zane . . . I'm looking. I just need some guidance about this in-between time.

Woman Pleaser

Dear Woman Pleaser:

Honey, I appreciate your self-evaluation of being a man so in tune with the needs of women that you feel it is unfair even to subject them to your sensuality. However, I am confident that the sisters can hold down their end. You have so much more to experience and you are basing your statements on the tip of a big iceberg. The only thing that can come from your "vast knowledge" is mutual gratification once you find the right female to settle down with. Do not be afraid to speak your mind and express your emotions. If you are all that you claim to be, the young sisters of the world are waiting for you, the proverbial knight in shining armor.

Blessings,

Zane

Dear G-Spot:

I have known my friend since high school. One day we made the mistake of sleeping together. I am not saying it was actually bad, because—truth be known—the shit was good. Lately we have been enjoying each other on a more sexual level, but he does not want to make a commitment. At least, that is what he says. However, his actions say something altogether different. We lie together afterward; he holds me and makes me feel like the only person in the world. He makes sweet and tender love to me. He gives me what my body craves without taking too much. I am wondering if I should keep doing what we are doing and wait to see if he comes around. Or should I leave him alone and move on with my life?

Young and Full of Cum

Dear Young and Full of Cum:

Leave him alone if the two of you are seeking different things in the relationship. You obviously want a commitment while he does not. Why should you settle for anything less? As sweet and tender as his lovemaking is with you, he might be making two or three other girls feel just as special. Some people have that "talent," the ability to make everyone feel like she is special and appreciated. Do not wait for him to come around. Tell him exactly what you want, and if he is not willing either to meet those demands or even consider them, move on. He will not understand what he has until it is gone.

Blessings,

Zane

Dear G-Spot:

Last year there was this boy—a new student. The moment we saw each other, it was like, "Damn! I want him!" and you could tell he was thinking the same thing. He tried to holler at me a few times, but I hesitated. He is the popular type while I am more of a quiet girl. Most of the time popular boys want to turn quiet girls into wild girls and mess up their reputations.

I stayed away from him for about a year and, finally, one night I talked to him for almost ten hours. Once I got to know him, he was not the way I had expected. I did not expect him to talk to me in such a way. He told me that I was everything he wanted, and we discussed everything from our backgrounds to sex to marriage. He was a lot more experienced than me, but I liked that. We would see each other at the park, and I started to get more comfortable around him. We held each other while we talked and sometimes we would kiss for thirty minutes straight—just tongue tying. He would ask me to go to his house, but since I was a virgin, I did not want to seem easy. He respected that and assured me that I did not have to do anything that made me feel uncomfortable.

After a particular weekend, when I returned to school, all my feelings had vanished and I did not like him anymore. He returned to Ohio, where he was from originally, and called me all the time. I was reluctant to call him after hearing rumors that he had gotten some girl pregnant and was not coming back. I asked him about it and he told me the truth. He claimed that the baby was not his, even though he had been with the girl some time earlier. I asked how he could be so positive that the baby was not his but he had no reasonable reply. I felt betrayed, even though their sex had preceded our relationship. In fact, we were not officially dating, just talking friends with benefits.

He did say he was coming back and that I should not believe everything that I hear. Later on, he found out that the baby was not his, just like he said. It did not matter to me because I had grown sick of him. I suggested for us to be merely friends and he got mad. He said that he was not coming back if I did not want to be with him, and he did not come back. He has called me a few times. Now I am starting to like him again. Is this normal? This is really starting to get on my nerves, since I keep having mixed emotions.

Searching for an Answer

Dear Searching for an Answer:

Young love can be a tough pill to swallow. What is amazing about all this is that about ten years from now, you will more than likely not even remember the name of this young man who has your heart in limbo right now. You will fall in and out of love numerous times, thinking each time it is the real thing. You will consider a man to be everything you ever wanted only to discover some months or years later that he is not all that he was cracked up to be. Do not be deterred by this, my young sister. Life's curveballs are what makes it interesting. This young man from Ohio is a stepping-stone, a man in your path who will help you recognize the real thing when it comes along.

While it is a good thing for him that he was not the father of the baby, his immediate response showed his immaturity. You should consider yourself lucky, because if he had gotten you pregnant, he would have said he was not the father of your baby either. Boys are quick to drop their pants but run away scared when the proverbial shit hits the fan. Women do not procreate by themselves. Yet we are the ones blamed for not protecting ourselves when unplanned pregnancies happen.

I am glad that you found a special time with him, but that time needs to find closure. Sure, if he calls, be pleasant to him, but move on with your life. I guarantee you that his hormones are raging and someone is fulfilling his immediate needs in Ohio. What is scary is that he might even be sleeping with the same girl who just had a baby by someone else. Crazier things have happened. You cannot afford to get caught up in that drama, and you are much too young to try to carry on a long-distance romance.

Concentrate on your schoolwork, bettering yourself as a person, and taking care of your health. Everything will happen exactly when it is supposed to.

Blessings,
Zane

Dear G-Spot:

Hey again, Zane. How are you doing? Last time I had asked you for advice on this boy, I used your advice and it worked very well, so I just wanted to say thank you. Now that I have moved on and stopped affiliating with him, I am talking to another guy. I have known him for about four years but we never expressed our feelings for each other. About three weeks after I took your advice, he called and said that he had always liked me but could not find the words to say it. I was shocked because I never thought my feelings for him might be mutual, only one-sided on my end. I was mad happy when he wanted to hang out with me. Take a deep breath, Zane, because here comes the bad part. I am sixteen and he is twenty, about to be twenty-one. He is dating one of my best friends but they do not chill that much lately because she is in college. She is my girl and I feel like I am betraying her. I asked him, "What about you and my girl?" He claimed they were not in contact as much, that he had strong feelings for me, stronger than the ones he had for her.

My friend was telling me on the phone that she was about to go meet some guy at a club that she had met a while back. She claims to be dating but she was going to check out another guy. I did not call her on it because it was none of my business. Then I thought about his honesty in telling me his true feelings for me. He is not the player type who sits at home all day, plays Nintendo, and sleeps. He works hard, has his own car, and even though he still lives at home with his father and little brother, he is wise when it comes to making decisions and taking things seriously. He is far from immature and the type of guy any girl would want.

My father is a teacher and had him in his class a couple of years ago. Dad said he was a good person and very bright. Let me get to the point. We have been hanging out as much as possible and keeping in touch. In fact, you could call it dating. I am still a virgin and he asked if I am ready to have sex with him. He assures me that there is no pressure, to just let him know when I am ready. Since it would be my first time, he said he would be easy and that I should not worry about a thing. Zane, I adore him and part of me wants to know what sex feels like. Another part of me is not prepared. Then I keep thinking about the feelings of my girl away in college. If you were in my position, tell me what you would do. God bless.

Betrayed

Dear Betrayed:

I am glad that my advice helped you before and I hope it will help you again. If you are truly a friend to the young lady you mentioned, then you should leave him alone sexually. It seems apparent that they are not connecting the right way, but they need to split on their own terms and not because of you. If he was really over her, there would be no confusion on either of their parts about a continuing relationship, no matter if they are both seeing other people.

   Then you have to ask yourself if he would flirt with you behind your friend's back, what is he likely to do behind yours? Men with certain traits will have those same traits no matter what woman they are dealing with. The good part is that he is not pressuring you for sex—and don't ever allow him to. Still, I think your first time should be with someone who cares for you unconditionally and has no feelings whatsoever for anyone else, rather less one of your close friends.

Blessings,
Zane

Dear G-Spot:

   I am a young teenager who is going out with a guy who wants a blow job, plus he wants me to ride him. I really love him, but I cannot get up the nerve to tell him that I can give him a blow job whenever he wants but cannot ride him because I have my period. Half of the time, I do not have my period. I am afraid to tell him that I am scared. I do not want him to ram me hard; I want it gentle. I am afraid he will not like that. Thanks.

In Love but Afraid

Dear In Love but Afraid:

   Let me say this right off of the bat. NEVER do anything sexually that you feel uncomfortable with. When you say young teenager, how old does that mean exactly? I know you do not want to hear this, but you might not need to be having sex in the first place. The mere fact that you feel uneasy about talking to him about something that bothers you so much shows that there is something wrong with the relationship that you are in. How old is the male you are having sex with? Is he around the same age as you, or older?

   If you are giving him blow jobs, you need to make sure that he is wearing a condom and *always* practice safe sex, whether vaginal or oral. Since you are scared, you need to seriously reconsider what you are doing. You really love him and I understand that, but that love should be reciprocal. If it is, then he should be able to understand any and all of your feelings. If he truly loves you, he will stay by your side and make love to you the way that you want—gently—and only when you are ready. You are going to have to discuss this with him, because you should never fear the reaction of a person that you are intimate with. Please email me back and let me know what is going on with you. I am extremely concerned about your welfare.

Blessings,
Zane

Dear G-Spot:

My man—or whatever you want to call him—has been acting funny. We break up, then make up. Last time we made up, he acted like he did not want to be with me. He is always saying he loves me, but I do not believe he means it, which is why I feel like leaving him. There is something holding me in this relationship. He has been acting so funny lately. Does it mean that he does not trust me because I do not trust him? Zane, he is always pulling the "I love you" card, and I fall for it every time. Please, girl, give me some advice.

Lady D

Dear Lady D:

Lack of trust in a relationship is like the kiss of death. I sense from your email that you are rather young and, thus, your man might simply have a maturity issue. You need to weigh the pros and cons of your relationship and decide whether you want to stay on the roller-coaster ride or get off. It does not sound like the two of you have a viable future, but I could be wrong.

Blessings,
Zane

Dear G-Spot:

I have a question that has been weighing heavily on my mind. I have not found the right person to address it to, so I figured maybe you would be able to understand my situation better than anyone in my social circle. I am eighteen years young and, up until recent months, I have had sex only with two partners in my entire life, which is saying a lot considering that I began having sex at age thirteen. The thing is that about six or seven months ago, I began having what most would call "casual sex." I left a relationship seven months ago. Immediately after the breakup, I had sex with someone I hardly knew. Now that those seven months have passed, I have had more than seven new partners.

When I sit calmly and think about it, I feel dirty inside, but it is only momentary guilt. After that, I have no regrets. In many ways, I think that I did exactly what my body, mind, and heart wanted me to do. Still, my question remains: Is my newly changed lifestyle wrong, dirty, or whorish in any way? Before I was so exclusive and serious about sex. Then I let my walls come down and began to view sex as merely that. In many ways I am simply looking for a man who can satisfy my sexual needs. I happen to be an extremely needy person. If you can give any words—good or bad—I am eager to hear your thoughts/opinion on my situation.

Confused by
Society's Standards

Dear Confused by Society's Standards:

You are searching for the man who can make your toes curl and make you feel special. He is out there, but I do feel you are going about it the wrong way. We live in the age of AIDS, and casual sex is no longer something to toy around with like it used to be. These men you are sleeping with obviously view you as nothing more than sex as well. That is the first problem. The man who will ultimately be "the one" will want to make love to you both mentally and physically. He will care about your needs, your wants, and your desires—not as much as he cares about his own but more. You will come first.

Unfortunately, at such a young age, most of the men in your age group will still be all about seeing how many notches they can get on their belts. My suggestion to you is that you stop having sex for a few months, concentrate on getting yourself together, and see if someone unexpectedly pops up in your life—first as a friend without wanting to get in your drawers at all. That man has potential.

I am also concerned that you may be using sex as a way to increase your self-esteem. Nothing you wrote alludes to that, but a lot of young ladies go through that "validation stage" where they want to feel like they are a sexy, desirable woman. Be careful not to allow too many people into your temple, and that is exactly what your body is: a temple. Please, please, please practice safe sex. You want to be here and be healthy when Mr. Right does come along.

Blessings,
Zane

Dear G-Spot:

Why do I think sex is the answer to get a man? I'm a twenty-two-year-old college student who has had her share of men. I am really feeling this football player from Jackson State University. I'd like for him to be my man. I totally like him so much that I sucked his dick one night while we were riding in his car. I simply couldn't help myself. I needed it in my mouth. I want to be with him but not merely to fuck him. What should I do? I don't want to be a whore, fuck him for a while, and have things not work out. What do I need to do to get his attention besides having sex with him?

Unable to understand,
Devastated Diva

Dear Devastated Diva:

I am assuming when you say "besides having sex" that you do still intend to have sex with him but are searching for a way to make it last. Even though you have not actually let him partake of the goodies, you have given him head. Backtracking from that might prove difficult because he is more than likely going to expect at least that much and, ultimately, he's going to want to fuck you straight up.

You have a dilemma as old as time. Women throughout the ages have attempted to separate sex from love—opting for a love that lasts. Unfortunately, most younger men (like your college ballplayer) opt for the sex. He could be different, one of the rare breed who are ready to make a commitment if the right woman should come along. I don't have all the facts in your case, but your standing with him relies on many things. If you sucked his dick without even talking to him at length, he probably already thinks you are a whore. I realize you don't view it that way. You cared for him, desired him, and wanted to please him as well as yourself by letting him fill up your mouth.

The bottom line is, if you like the man, and you apparently do, there is nothing wrong with having protected sex with him. In order to evolve from a friend with benefits to his woman, you are going to have to stimulate his mind as well. You need to make suggestions for the two of you to spend quality time together. Determine his favorite pastimes and hobbies and share those adventures with him. When it comes down to it, most men want the same thing: a woman who can satisfy their physical and mental needs, one who can get along with their friends and family, and one who doesn't display a lot of insecurity and low self-esteem issues to the point where they feel like they have to constantly reassure her or prove their fidelity.

You need to sit the man down and be honest about your feelings, see if he is even in the same neighborhood as far as what he wants and expects, and try to open an honest line of communication. That is the first essential need for any long-term relationship.

Hope this helps you out, my sister!

Blessings,
Zane

Dear G-Spot:

Thanks for the advice about my male friend. I have known him since he was a freshman; he is now a junior and I am a senior. We knew of each other but never took the time to get to explore one another except one day in a September class. He finally took my number and we then started talking.

We always discussed football and school-related things, never getting truly personal until last week. We began "sex talk" and our goals after college. I also met his sister before he came to school and we are now associates. I really like him, even though he is younger. He just does something to me whenever I see him. After I tasted him, the question running through my mind was: Is he going to tell someone what I did? I am not ashamed but I also do not want to be labeled. He is the first person I have given head to at my school.

I expressed that I was feeling him; he said he was feeling me also, but he was not ready for a relationship. Even with that said, I still gave him head. Was I foolish for doing that? Do you think I should give up on him since he stressed that he does not want a girlfriend right now? Immediately after giving him head, it seemed like he wanted to be with me because of the way he was acting. I do not know; I am so damn confused. I am a grown woman wanting to be with a twenty-year-old sexy-ass young man. Given that you know a little more about the situation, should I continue to attempt to be with him or not?

Devastated Diva

Dear Devastated Diva:

Not! He made it clear to you that he does not want a relationship with you, or anyone else for that matter. He is still at the stage where he thinks getting various women in bed defines him as a man. You made one mistake by giving him a blow job *after* he told you he was not trying to settle down. I understand you have no regrets and you should not. However, it was what it was: head for him and a fulfilled desire for you. Now you should make it a memory and find a better match for yourself or concentrate on finishing your education and developing appealing qualities that will attract appealing men.

Blessings,
Zane

Dear G-Spot:

I met this guy about three months ago. Upon introducing myself to him, he informed me that he was involved with someone else at the moment but still wanted to get to know me. Unsure at that time how far things would go, I reluctantly agreed to give him my number. We have been chatting via phone ever since. However, he is a fraternity member, on the basketball team, a full-time college student, and holding down a job as well as having a relationship with the other woman. Thus, our quality time together is minimal. I crave to see him more often and that stresses me. He reassures me that he values our time and that things will improve soon. I am still unable to cope with it.

Although we have never actually had intercourse, we have engaged in oral sex. I have given and received but am not sure why we have not actually had intercourse. I am not sure if it is because of this other person in his life or if he does not want to go that far with me. My feelings for him make me want to explore everything, not just the oral. I want to know him both sexually and emotionally. What should I do? Wait it out and see if he comes around and gives me the things I desire of him? Or should I simply walk away from the situation? Is it a case of bad timing?

Uncertain

Dear Uncertain:

The immediate thing that jumps out at me is that he has someone else in his life; that automatically means you are the substitute player. You have invested only three months into the nonsense and you must move on, in order to preserve your self-esteem and your health. Oral sex usually involves trading body fluids without barriers. While dental dams and condoms are recommended for oral sex, realistically the majority of people do not utilize them. Correct me if I am wrong about you, but I doubt it.

The man is busy. You are someone he chats with on the phone in his spare time. Without doubting his sincerity, you might possibly be the one for him if he did not already have a woman. When two people like each other, it is often hard to see the forest for the trees. He might mean well, but it is unfair to you to be strung along like some puppet. You deserve better than that—we all do. Put yourself in the other young lady's shoes. If you were seeing him and you found out that he had been engaging in oral sex with someone else, would you accept it? No, you would not. You would be hurt, very hurt. You are inadvertently contributing to hurting another individual through your actions. Do not continue to be a contributor. There are a ton of young men out there who can appreciate what you have to offer. You will not find them as long as you stay infatuated with this man. Three months are gone. Do not waste another day.

Blessings,
Zane

Dear G-Spot:
I fell in love with this guy after I began the twelfth grade. He never paid attention to me back then, but now we are kissing and touching each other. I am afraid that if we have sex, he will run and tell all of his friends. I am in love with him. I want to do it with him, but I do not know what to do. Should I take the risk of him telling everyone? He tells me that he likes me and wants to be with me. When we are alone on dates, he treats me like a princess. When we are around other people who say something ignorant, he laughs right along with them. I do not understand this behavior. Around his friends, he has this habit of staring at me and licking his lips. I love it when he checks me out. As soon as we kiss, he gets hard. Can you give me some advice?

Hot but Not Convinced

Dear Hot but Not Convinced:
If you are telling me that he laughs when other people make fun of you, you need to leave him the hell alone, no matter how he treats you in private. That would mean that he is playing immature games. As far as telling his friends if you give it up, he probably will, but will you not tell your

friends as well if he makes you scream? That is what young people do. If you get some good sex—or even mediocre sex—you will be ready to share your coming-of-age story. He will naturally do the same. The only reason he would not tell his friends is out of embarrassment, and if that is the case, then you do not need to have sex with him in the first place. He does not see your value or appreciate you. If you are a virgin, do not come to a rash decision. Think about this. Can you see yourself married to him, with four kids, and living together happily ever after? If you cannot even imagine that—whether or not it could ever feasibly come true—then why give yourself to him? You should be only with men who you can see yourself in a serious relationship with, and vice versa.

Blessings,
Zane

Bisexuality/Lesbianism

*M*y sisters, my sisters, do not be ashamed of who you are. Let me start off by saying that right off the bat. No one has a right to judge you. My only concern is that you be totally comfortable with who you are and what you are doing with your life, both in and out of the bedroom. It has been said that 10 to 12 percent of females are lesbians. The word *lesbian* originally meant an inhabitant of the isle of Lesbos. Now it simply means a female homosexual.

No one has the right to judge you, and you can only be yourself in this life. To attempt to live your life for someone else will only lead to unhappiness, drama, and ultimately a ton of regrets. Each person is entitled to embrace her sexuality, no matter what that sexuality may be.

A lot of people assume that lesbians are "butch" or "manly." While there are many who adhere to that appearance, it is more of a stereotype, because most are soft, sensual women who look just like women who love themselves some dick. Just as it is nearly impossible to detect a male who is "on the downlow," you cannot simply look at a woman and tell which sex she prefers in the bedroom. That is a stupid thought. There are those who are flamboyant about their sexuality and love to engage in public displays of affection, similar to openly gay males. However, if you really think about it, the percentage of heterosexual couples that tongue the shit out of each other, rub all over each other's booties, and get their freak on in public is not high enough even to talk about.

The only thing that concerns me are those who are lost and confused about their sexuality or are afraid of being judged. Nothing can stress a person out more than trying to hide something from her loved ones. An added problem for many lesbians is if they have children from previous relationships. Trying to explain why "Auntie" is over all the time can get old. I recently received an email from a woman in a similar situation, and here it is:

Dear G-Spot:

Your recent blog posed a question about single mothers dating again. Well, I have a three-year-old daughter. I have not been with her father since she was born. It was the classic line: "I'll be there for you." That lasted only while I was pregnant; then he was ghost. He pays child support but we rarely get a visual of him, unless I am talking about sleeping with him.

I began to hang out with my friends, mostly to find some kind of comfort regarding my confusing relationship with him. One of my friends moved away for a while and then returned. She admitted to being a lesbian while she was away. We still hung out and I still loved her the same. My daughter loved her to death also and really enjoyed her being around. While she was being a friend and comforting me, we started feeling more for each other. We have now been in a relationship for a year.

I am sure that your mouth just dropped to the floor. I have never been with a woman before and I don't think that I ever will be again after her, if this relationship ends. How do I deal with her being there all the time, and what will my daughter think? I have fallen in love with her and we have grown so close together. My daughter still likes her to be around; they have fun together and everything. I don't know when it will be safe to say something about us being together. We don't hug or kiss or anything in front of my daughter; she just thinks that my friend is over a lot. My daughter has heard me say "I love you" to her, but since she is three, she doesn't think much of it. I really have no clue what to do in this situation. I realize that people will be looking at me crazy for being in a lesbian relationship with a child, but what is a girl to do? Please help a sistah out.

If Loving Her Is Wrong

Dear If Loving Her Is Wrong:

First, my mouth did not drop to the floor, because you are simply being you and I applaud that. The fact of the matter is that children are brilliant and your daughter has more than likely figured out that there is a special relationship going on between the two of you. That is the equivalent of a woman dating a man who is always around the house, always with the kids, and a constant presence. Even if the two people never show intimacy in front of the children, they figure it out.

I find it refreshing that you did not mention worrying about what other people think, outside of your daughter. That is none of their business and they have no right to judge you. It is not better to be with a man who mistreats you—for the sake of pretenses—than with a woman who adores you. Let me ask this: If you were not with this particular woman any longer, at this point in your life would you be searching for a male lover or a female lover to replace her? My only concern is that there may be some confusion about your sexuality. If so, you need to deal with it sooner as opposed to later. If not, I wish you nothing but the best. Just make sure that your daughter recognizes that she is loved, and everything will come up roses.

Blessings,
Zane

Dear G-Spot:

I have been thinking about sex a lot lately and I don't know why because this is a new occurrence. When I was fourteen, I first had sex but broke up with my boyfriend at age eighteen after he cheated. I am twenty-three now, and after four years, I have been thinking about my ex-boyfriend all week. I fantasize about having sex with him again. Furthermore, I am confident that I am not a lesbian, but I have been fantasizing about having sex with women, too. Zane, why am I thinking about that? Please answer me.

Lesbian Thoughts

Dear Lesbian Thoughts:

Imagining having sex with other women is a natural feeling that the majority of women have at some point in their lives. Curiosity is the cause of most of it. We are all curious about the unknown, and since we are female, have female organs, and know what pleasure we gain from things being done to us, we cannot help but wonder if another woman could please us more than a man. She has the same thing we do and thus could probably use her own personal experience to bring us pleasure. Do not make a big deal out of thinking about it, even if you think about it often. In fact, some women engage in sexual acts with other women, just to see, and then never do it again. It all depends on if you can control your curiosity. True lesbians are clear about their wants and desires; there is no confusion. Sure, they may refrain from it because of fear of judgment, but they clearly know they are lesbian and attracted only to women.

Now, as far as your ex-boyfriend, it has been four years and there is no reason to backtrack. He cheated on you once, showing his lack of respect for you. He has no reason not to do it again, especially if you get back with him knowing full well that he did it. You are thinking about him because the sex was hot and you are probably going through a dick drought. It will end and someone else will turn you out. However, a new—better—man cannot enter your life if you have Mr. Cheater occupying space in it.

Blessings,

Zane

Dear G-Spot:

I have an issue that I hope you can help me handle. It is more of a secret. I have always been a very sexual person but I tend to suppress it. I call myself a trisexual since I will try anything once. I am bisexual but there are only two people who know it. I cannot tell my family because they all seem repulsed by the entire bi/lesbian issue. Not letting the real me out is driving me crazy. What is a girl to do? I cannot be myself and I really fucking hate it.

Needing to Be Myself

Dear Needing to Be Myself:

Fear of what others might think causes so many people to miss out on life. You ultimately have two choices: either start living your life for you or keep living your life for everybody else. At the end of your life, do you want to look back and say, "I had one hell of a ride," or do you want to look back and say, "I have nothing but regrets"? People are repulsed by things they cannot relate to or understand. Hell, my writing repulses a lot of people because of their sexual repression and/or oppression. That is their issue, not mine. The fact that you made the statement that you cannot be yourself speaks volumes. If you are not you, then who the hell are you? Since you are bisexual, I am assuming that means you have been with women before. If you truly like it and want to continue, do it. If you want to be with men and women, do it, but do not be dishonest with anyone about your activities. A person who sleeps with both sexes and does not reveal it is just as bad as a man or woman who cheats on his or her mate. If you want a relationship—a serious one—you will have to make the decision to be with one or the other. Good luck, my friend, but please live your own life, not the one your parents or friends want you to live. They get to do whatever the hell they want to do; you do the same.

Blessings,

Zane

Dear G-Spot:

Zane, I guess my situation is a little different so I don't know if you can help me, but hopefully you can. I'm bisexual and have been in a weird relationship with a woman for five months. We were the best of friends before we went out, and we still are. I love her more than anything. That saying that a woman can give better head is true. We have the best sex and we have these great feelings, but I feel like something is missing. I express my feelings to her but she doesn't like expressing hers to me. Instead, she tells someone else, and that is holding us back. She's always stepping over me and making me feel bad. I feel she doesn't appreciate the unexpected, affectionate things I do. She claims to care about me and credits me with repairing her heart. Yet I can't help but think she has a dishonest streak. What should I do?

We talk all day about a ton of things, but when it comes to our feelings, I'm the only one saying stuff. Her mother and family don't know that she's bisexual. What makes the situation worse is that her mother hates me and she doesn't know me. When we mess around, we express our feelings, but then we start arguing about little things. Well, she starts arguing about little things and puts me on the spot so that makes a little thing a big thing. I don't know what to do. I love her as my friend but care more for her as my lover. I don't want to lose our friendship; she is my best friend. If you can offer me some advice on how I can give better oral sex to a female, it would be appreciated. That is, if you know from your experiences. Thank you very much, Zane. I'm waiting patiently for your next book. Once again, big ups to your success.

Ms. Bitch

Dear Ms. Bitch:

Whether it is a man and a woman, two men, or two women, when best friends become lovers, it is always a hit-or-miss situation. Many people marry their best friends because they feel that they have so much in common and love has not worked out for them with others. In your case, the attraction apparently became overwhelming and you needed to act on it.

I believe the biggest problem—and more than likely the underlying problem with all the difficulties in your relationship—is your lover leading a double life. By that I mean she has not come out to her family. Whenever we keep something from our loved ones—particularly something we feel ashamed about—it causes a great deal of stress. This can lead to arguing about unimportant things with the one person we feel the closest to. In this case, that would be you. She is confused, not about her sexuality but about her decision to express it openly or keep it hidden. This is evidenced in many ways, in particular the way she shies away from talking to you about her deepest emotions.

I have no clue how old the two of you are, but I sense that you are young since no children are mentioned and she is still deeply concerned about her family accepting her. As we get older, we realize that at some point our lives become our own and we choose how we want to live them, despite what others think. She is obviously not at that point yet. You need to tell her that you understand her conflict and are willing to help her work through it—piece by piece. However, be honest with her by saying that you don't want things to fall apart between you and the only way the two of you can make it long term is for you to form an indestructible bond. That means putting each other above everyone else.

As far as oral sex, have you spelled out the alphabet yet on her pussy? Do you finger her and eat her at the same time? Have you stuck a finger in her ass and moved it back and forth while you are going down on her? Have you made her feel like the most erotic and desirable woman in the world by dining on her off of fine china or a silver platter? The mind—and everything leading up to actual sex—is still the biggest aphrodisiac. The two of you seem like you need some time away—alone. Maybe you should plan a special getaway. It doesn't have to be anything pricey, but go someplace where you can be open and free with your sexuality. I would even suggest looking into going to a lesbian or bisexual convention or party. That way she can see that many are comfortable with who they are and that hangups only cause stress and disappointment.

Blessings,
Zane

Cheaters

The one thing that shocked me most when I started writing erotica and doing my monthly ezines was the number of women who confessed to cheating. I knew that women had sexual desires that needed to be fulfilled, but like a lot of people, I assumed that married women were happily married and had gotten married because the sex was on point. That is the case with many, but over the years, people fall into ruts and the routine sex is no longer enough. Then there are other reasons.

I want to share a brief, real-life sex experience that someone recently emailed to me. Then I am going to ask you a question afterward.

My mother and I went on a well-known cruise ship. I dated the bartender from St. Vincennes and the cabin steward from Ghana. Every night on the seven-day cruise, I had wonderful sex with the bartender. He was awesome and extremely endowed. One night, after his shift was over, I went to the ladies' room. As I was ready to wipe, he came in the door, hard dick and all. We fucked in the ladies' room next to where he worked. We almost got caught by the cleaning crew at 4:30 A.M. We also did it on the stage in the lounge, where the condom broke and got lost. We even screwed in the adults-only hot tub after it was closed. He was the perfect lover.

The cabin steward had it going on also. Not as good as the bartender but sexually satisfying nonetheless. He was working with a big dick too. While my mother went to dinner one night, the cabin steward came in and rocked my world. He ate my pussy so well.

At St. Martin, the two of them almost got into a fight about me at the beach. That was exciting to me, but I didn't want anyone to get harmed. After my cruise was over and I had given the bartender a good-bye screw, I returned home to my husband and five kids. That was the first cruise during which I had been unfaithful.

Okay, here's the question. Do you think the woman who wrote the story is a whore? Most men are probably saying, "Hell, yeah, she's a fucking whore!" Most women—particularly my regular readers—are probably saying, "Damn, I wish that had been me!"

Here's another one from a female reader:

I am so afraid that this will get out. Each year my childhood girlfriends and I go to Ocho Rios, Jamaica (should you change the city here?). We stay for five days and go buck wild, sleeping with as many men as we care to sleep with—protected, of course. We tell our husbands and significant others that we are traveling together to maintain the tight bond of friendship. But for the last four years, we have been taking a page out of your books and doing whatever we want, no questions asked and definitely no stories told. We do not talk about what we have done via email or phone. We have one major rule: once we land back at our hometown airport, nothing else is spoken about it, unless we are sure that we cannot be overheard. It keeps us close and relieves pent-up sexual frustration. Shh . . . please keep this confidential . . . I'm deleting all traces of this email right now.

Yes, groups of women do travel out of town—sometimes out of the country—to get their freak on together. This is a common fantasy of most women, but only those who have freed themselves from sexual oppression engage in that behavior. People always try to examine why men cheat. I am going to flip the script and examine why women cheat, because I get tons of emails from them, as evidenced below in the advice mails for this section. Here is the thing. Men think they are sexual giants and that women will settle for whatever "favors" are thrown out to them between the sheets. Many women do settle and live their lives in misery, wishing and hoping that their men will improve in the bedroom or start catering to their needs.

If that does not happen, eventually some will stray, get what they need elsewhere, and then return home for dinner. Women are not meek creatures, especially not in today's society where we are working to be providers, sometimes taking care of men, and more empowered than we have ever been in history. Men, you must step up to the plate and do right by your women. Being able to get a bunch of women in the sack because of your looks, "game," or whatever you choose to call it means nothing if they do not climax. I say it all the time: a real man is not a man who has made love to a thousand different women, but a man who can make love to a single woman a thousand different ways. Variety is the spice of life and that can occur right in your own bedroom.

There are "retaliation cheaters" also, women who cheat because their men have cheated. Men have double standards and think it is cool for them to get their freak on, but women are supposed to settle. Those days are over. While the above real-life experiences might seem far-fetched to some readers, trust me when I say that it is very common behavior. It is not that these women do not love their husbands; they just love themselves more. Men, if you are not asking your woman if she is satisfied sexually, do not be shocked when she either leaves you, fucks someone else, or stops fucking you altogether because she is not getting anything out of it.

Dear G-Spot:
I am thirty-four years old. I have four children and I have been with my husband for sixteen years. We started dating in high school. My husband has been cheating on me for several years, so I finally got fed up and decided to return the favor. I called up a friend of ours who was in our wedding and asked if I could go over to his house. Of course, he told me yes. When I got there, he opened the door and greeted me in his boxers. The action just kind of took off by itself, but there was a problem. During the activities, he had a difficult time staying hard. As much as he claimed to have thought about being with me over the years, he never expected it to actually happen and blamed his "softness" on me taking him off guard. He has asked me to give him another shot at making love to me. I am not sure that I should give him one. The sex was not awful, because he would do other things to me until he was able to get it up. However, I do not want to waste my time or make him feel even worse if it happens again. His dick does have a fun curve to it. What do you think?

The Horny Housewife

Dear Horny Housewife:

Do not go anywhere near that man again, unless you are completely prepared to lose your entire family behind a piece of dick. Added to the madness that he could not even satisfy you, you are not going to solve your problem with a man who is a mutual friend of both you and your husband. In fact, he is not a friend at all—a member of your wedding party or not. A true friend would not succumb to your advances, even if you showed up at his front door butt-naked with a pack of condoms in one hand and a tube of lubricant in the other. He took advantage of you in a weak moment. While he may have harbored a desire for you all these years and fantasized what it would be like, he was just as wrong as you for participating in the brief affair. Brief is exactly how it needs to stay. You need to hope and pray that your husband never finds out, either directly from this man or from someone else he might have told. Men have this serious double standard when it comes to cheating—among other things. They can sleep with dozens of women outside the marriage, but let them find out their woman has cheated and you would think the sky had fallen.

On the flip side, you do need to do something about your husband. He should not be able to continue to cheat. Point-blank, you must issue an ultimatum to him. He needs to either keep his dick in his pants or move the fuck on. If he chooses to leave you and the kids, then, and only then, should you find someone else. However, it needs to be someone who has not broken bread in your home. He cannot be trusted any more than your husband.

First, ask your husband what his damn problem is and why he feels the need to bed other women. If you value your marriage and can see it in your heart to forgive him—some women cannot ever do that—then try to fill in the blanks of what he feels is missing in the marriage. If possible, the two of you should seek counseling. The one and only reason I am not telling you to pack your shit and scatter is because the two of you do have four children and have been married an awfully long time by today's standards. That does not mean that you should be mistreated. He either needs to step up to the plate and be a real man—meaning limiting his sexual activities to your bedroom—or he needs to set you free. But that decision-making process comes with a time limit. Give him one last chance and if he still throws it all away for a quick lay, life is too short and you should move on.

Blessings,
Zane

Dear G-Spot:

I am a married mother of two and my husband and I have not had sex in more than two years. We have been together for five. Lately I have been fantasizing about other men. To make matters worse, I have been hooking up once a month with my college sweetheart. We have "our special place" where we meet, about halfway between our two states. I realize two wrongs don't make a right. He is married also, but I need something to fill the void. When I try to talk to my husband, his usual response is, "Just let me know when you want to do It." That's not what I am looking for and I tell him as much. I want to ease into sex and let it happen naturally. There are no sparks and I am not sexually attracted to my husband anymore. Let me put it out there: he is twenty years my senior. What should I do? I will patiently await your response.

Creeper

Dear Creeper:

You are playing with fire, but I am sure that you know that already. That "once-a-month hookup" can only lead to disaster. Sooner or later, your husband will figure it out. You are like a young sex kitten compared to him, since he is twenty years older than you. He might be ready to shut it down because of age, stress, or lack of desire. However, cheating is not going to solve your problems. Is that other man willing to leave his wife for you? I seriously doubt it. The last thing you want is to be ass out at the end of the day. While I agree that your husband needs to be more spontaneous, are you putting any effort into seducing him? Probably not, since you are no longer attracted to him. What should you do? Make a decision. Either love your husband, or let him go and find a man who is not cheating on his wife but is willing to make a commitment to you. You are not being fair to any of the parties involved, including yourself.

Blessings,
Zane

Dear G-Spot:

My man, and the father of my son, cheated on me. I cannot stand to look at him and I will not even let him hold me. I discovered his infidelity one day when I checked his voice mail. She was asking why he had disappeared and stated that she was pregnant. I love him with all my heart and we have been to hell and back together. However, when someone cheats on me, I feel like there is no working it out. Since I have not gone back to work, we still live together. Once I go back to work in August, I plan to move out and I have informed him of my intentions. He pleaded for another chance, saying that he still loves me and will never cheat on me again. I do not believe him. Something tells me that there are other women as well. Out of his numerous female friends, I think he's slept with at least half of them. I gave this man four years, as well as his only son, and this is how he repays me for my efforts. He claims that he slept with the girl only twice and the excuse he gave for even being around her was the stupidest thing that I have ever heard. Every time he walks out the door, I ask him where he is going and when he is coming back. Trust is the number one necessity for a healthy relationship and my trust in him is gone. I feel like damaged goods. I actually thought that he would love me forever and that we would grow old together. I wanted to marry him, but who isn't looking for Mr. Right? I am not sure what advice you can give me, but even a hello would be appreciated.

A Heart-Broken Woman

Dear Heart-Broken Woman:

He claims that he slept with the girl only twice? That is not acceptable. It is a good thing that you are not married, even though you share a child. You cannot force a person to show you respect, but you can refuse to be disrespected. I am glad that you are doing the right thing and getting your own place. He will never change. If you stay, you are basically saying that it is okay for him to fuck up, and five years, ten years, twenty years from now, he will still expect you to deal with his cheating ways. You are better than that and his dick is obviously guiding him, instead of his brain. He can bring all kinds of diseases—and extra kids—home, and men do it "because they can." You said it yourself: the trust is gone, and rightfully so. Your heart is broken but it will mend, especially when you move out on your own and explore a world of possibilities outside of that idiot.

Blessings,
Zane

Dear G-Spot:

I am thirty-eight, married, and just read "How to Really Fuck a Man: The Bottom Line." Due to my husband's low sex drive, I went "fishing" and met a man whom I see mostly at his house or at motels. He has asked to come to my home some mornings, but I have been hesitant to do that. Since we met, I have done things that I never thought I would do. I shave my pussy for him and whatever else he asks. He appears to like spending time with me and I love being with him. At times, I feel guilty, but I don't want to cut off the affair. My husband's lack of desire for me has made me angry, and I blame him for my extramarital relationship. All my husband wants is a blow job in the morning and, even then, he makes it seem like he is doing me a favor. I am not trying to go through a nasty divorce, but I do plan to keep seeing my friend. Would it be wrong to let him come to my house some mornings? He is not pressuring me, but I realize that he wants to fuck in my house. When he asked me to shave my pussy, I was eager to do that. To tell him that I don't want him at my house seems like I'm telling him that I am not eager to please him. Please give me some advice.

Risky Behavior

Dear Risky Behavior:

You are playing a very dangerous game, because crimes of passion are one of the top emergency calls that police officers get, and people will quickly become violent in such situations. For example, if your husband comes home and finds another man fucking you in his house, heaven help you. Fuck trying to please this other man; you'd better not let him come over there. He will just have to be offended. It seems like he is playing a game by seeing how far you are willing to jump for his dick action. Your husband's lack of sexual desire could be due to many factors, but rarely do men stop fucking because they want to. It could be stress, medications, or a physical illness that he is not aware of. Since you do not want to go through a nasty divorce, which is exactly where you are headed if this affair continues, I suggest you end it and start trying to please your husband. Ask him how you can make him happy. Ask him if he wants to go to counseling. Put the same amount of effort into your marriage that you have been putting into shaving your pussy for someone else.

Blessings,
Zane

Dear G-Spot:

I am a thirty-year-old woman who has been married for five years. I have been in love with a man who is not my husband for seven years. We had a mutual split and we never told each other how we felt until recently. I wanted to ask you: How do you extinguish a fire? This man used to set my soul, my shit, and everything on fire. He had me so sprung that I showed up at his door in nothing but a trench coat. That may not sound wild, but we were overseas at the time and it was twenty degrees outside.

I have tried to forget him but I cannot. Every time I think of him, I get wet. On the other hand, my sex life, and the marriage itself, have their problems. Should I go to my past lover and try to get him out of my system by having one last fling, or should I wait on faith? Help me! I am so sexually frustrated that I cannot even think straight. Masturbating only makes me crave him more because he used to love to watch me play with myself.

Sprung for Life

Dear Sprung for Life:

Part of me wants to tell you to stay true to your marriage, but since I am in the middle of a bitter divorce myself, I will say that sometimes people are simply not compatible and a relationship can become unhealthy. Since you are saying that your marriage has many issues anyway and you two have been married for a relatively short period of time, you should really think about what—and who—you want to be with for the rest of your life.

Do not base it all on sex, but the entire package—love, respect, support, the total enhancement of your being. You obviously married your husband for a reason. He may have changed up on you like mine did on me. If that is the case, then maybe it is time to leave and start anew. Sometimes we have to move on and seek out true happiness. It is not often that people get a second chance to right a wrong. The first thing you should do is see if you can rekindle or ignite a new fire with your husband. He is the one you made a commitment to. However, if you come to a point where you feel all efforts have been exhausted, then have a heart-to-heart with the man you have not been able to get over. Realize that if you have an affair, morally you are wrong, and karma will come back and slap you in the face. If you are going to be with the other man, you should already be working your way out of your marriage.

Blessings,
Zane

Dear G-Spot:

You are not only a great author, but an inspiration. You are like the long-lost sister that I never had. Anyway, to the point. I need a little advice from you. I have a boyfriend and we are in love; at least, I am. I hear a lot of stuff about him, not as much as I used to but I still hear it. I get angry and confront him, but when it comes down to breaking up, I cannot let him go. I am not sure if it is the sex or pure love. I am only fifteen and I do not know what to do. When we are in public, he respects me and everything. Other girls are invisible when we are together and we are rolling a lot. When he is not around, it is still all about him, but I hear things about him and other females. He is my first and I cannot go there and mess my body up like everyone else does. I am not a whore, and no one other than him can say that he kissed me or sexed me or anything like that. I can only claim two real boyfriends in my entire life. I do not have children, I am a straight-A student, but I am stuck on this one boy. Help me out because I do not want to be just plain stupid. So, big sister, please help me out.

Little Sis in Need

Dear Little Sis in Need:

You are like a lot of women twice, three times, or even four times your age: you are in denial of the obvious. Wherever there is smoke, there is also fire. People are telling you that this boy is unfaithful and you believe it, but you clam up when it comes time to do something about it. You would rather let him continue to play you than be alone and have to find someone new. My suggestion is that you break up with him, concentrate on school, keep getting those great grades, and wait for a young man to come along who can appreciate you. I know what you are thinking, that it is easier said than done and you are used to being around him. Again, women in their eighties are still letting men play them if they started out that way in life. You still have time to learn a valuable lesson. Please do so.

Blessings,
Zane

Riding Dick

If someone ever were to ask me what kind of advice email I receive the most, hands down it would be emails asking how to ride a man's dick. It is amazing to me, but the more and more I have thought about it, the more it dawned on me that there is a logical reason behind this phenomenon. Women have traditionally been considered missionaries, vessels for the man's pleasure. Think about it. Way back in the day they used to literally put pussy on lockdown with chastity belts. What kind of perverted shit was that? They had to unlock your coochie before a man could blow your back out. The entire "Me caveman, you woman" shit was a trip too. Men have always been made out to be superior in society, even when they were still barbarians, and women have always been undervalued. Most people still cannot grasp that. All of you need to read *God in the Image of Woman* by D. V. Bernard. It is about a future society where there are no women and men lose their fucking minds. The book is a great research guide for men who think women are unimportant unless we are sucking their dicks; then we are essential needs.

The term "missionary position" speaks volumes in the sense that it is saying that the men are not simply on top; they are in control. Thus, when some women even think about actually controlling a sexual encounter, they freak out. Women are firefighters, go defend our country in Iraq, birth ten kids, hold political offices, and are movie stars, but ask some of them to ride a dick and they will freak the hell out, as if you asked them to commit murder.

Their hearts will start beating faster. They will break out in cold sweats. They will be afraid to answer their cell phones because their men might ask them to get on top. First, let us examine why people would want a woman on top. Men crave it from time to time because it gives them something different and, after all, variety is the spice of life. They also want it because it gives them an opportunity to lie or sit there and damn near relax while the woman does all the work. Ladies, put yourself in the position of our men. If you were a man and had a woman, would you always want to have to feel like you have been to a twenty-four-hour Nautilus after sex? Hell to the fuck no. Men want—and expect—us to get on top some of the time.

Now for the basics. The best way to learn is to have him sit in a chair so that your feet can remain planted on the floor. That will give you more leverage. Whether you are riding him while facing him or with your back to him, just take your time and experiment with different variations of movement until you get a steady rhythm. Most important, ask him what feels so-so, good, or great. He will tell you and more than likely guide you as well. Men aren't shy when it comes to asking for what they want, so they are going to set you straight if they need you to move another way for them to get off. Women can have incredible sex and not necessarily have to reach orgasm but, to be blunt, men want to bust a nut.

Relax and have fun with it. Rome was not built in a day and you will not be able to ride a dick like a cowboy rides a bull in a day. The fun part about experimenting with sex is that both parties can find out what will or will not get them off.

There are a few positions that are great for the woman on top. The woman can get on top, facing the man, and recline backward while he is lying back in the opposite direction. Her feet are on the sides of his shoulders and positioned near his head. She can use his knees as handles to move herself around on his dick. The most basic of all positions is for her just to sit right on top of him while he is lying down and hold onto his hands while she moves up and down and around on his dick. A woman can also get on top of the man with her back to his face and recline back in the same direction, with the back of her head dangling on top of his, her back on his chest. This position can lead to a greater sense of intimacy than other positions, and he can whisper sweet nothings in her ear. For freakier people and for men who like to see a lot of ass in their face, they can get with the doggy-style position. The woman can lie on top of him in the regular sixty-nine, with her face toward his feet and her feet near his face. She can grab onto his ankles to help her maneuver up and down on his dick. Then there is the edge of the bed (or chair) position, where he can sit and she can be on top of him with her legs wrapped around his back. They can have a lot of intimacy that way and can kiss and cuddle. The last position that I would recommend is the woman lying on top of the man in the reverse missionary position, where they are lying chest to chest, and she can look him dead in the eyes as she rides him. If you are going to take the position of control, make sure you go all the way and talk dirty to him. Ask him, "Do you like this pussy? You love this pussy, don't you?" If you are too shy to talk dirty, then you are probably too shy to be riding a dick in the first place. Below are a few of the typical dick-riding questions that I receive day in and day out. I did not include my responses for this section because goose is goose and guinea is guinea and one answer is the same as any when it comes to riding a man's dick.

Dear G-Spot:

I am a seventeen-year-old female dating a nineteen-year-old male. My sexual past is not what you would consider normal. When I was younger and in a scary relationship, I was raped. My current boyfriend and I decided to take it to the sexual level. Considering the fact that I was raped, he did not want to hurt me and made me do it all, as far as putting him inside me and things like that. Once I did, he worked it and work it he did.

What I want to know is "how to put it on him" without him wanting to explain things to me. In the bedroom, he is the teacher since he is my first, minus the fact that I was raped. Spiritually he is my first. He and I are engaged and I am not looking to get out of it or change the situation that we are in.

His favorite is doggy and I have no problems with that. I do know that he wants me to ride him, but I cannot, or I am unable to, at the moment. I would like to know from another sexual female how it is done. From the book of yours that I have read, girl, you are the queen at it! I need to learn how to do it with him actually inside of me. When we are on the dance floor, I can get with it and he gets excited, as do I. When it comes to actually doing it, I am unable to. Any advice would be greatly appreciated. Thanks.

Fear of Riding

Dear G-Spot:

This is kind of embarrassing for me to talk about, even with someone who has never met me. I am twenty-three years old and have had the same boyfriend for six years. My problem is not oral sex, because I think that I am very good at it. My problem is not anal sex, because I am willing to experiment. My boyfriend thinks that I am lazy in bed, but the truth is that I am not. I am just not sure how to ride his dick the proper way. This has been an issue for a long time. I want to be able to knock his socks off, and I need to know the right way. We are going away soon and I am really, really worried that I am not going to be good. I want to surprise him and be on top for once. I am scared that I will never learn and I am embarrassed as well. Can you tell me all that I need to know? I am not sure if I am supposed to go up and down or what? Can you please help me? Is there a video or something? Please get back to me soon, before it is too late. I do not want to hop on top and not know what comes next.

Please Help

Dear G-Spot:

I wanted to know if you can give me some pointers on riding a man. Well, not just any man. I have a friend who is big-boned and I am a bigger person also. I can't seem to get the hang of it. I have pretty much mastered everything else, but riding his dick is aggravating. I really like this person and want to give him as much pleasure as possible.

Anonymous

Dear G-Spot:

I would like to know how to ride a man without my legs getting tired. I always get cramps or something. Am I doing something wrong? Also, I need expert step-by-step advice on how to ride a man in order to keep him coming back. I really need details.

Detail-Oriented

Dear G-Spot:

I was reading your website and I have a general question. How do you master riding your man's dick? I mean, there are several ways, but I can only go so fast or slow. How do I know it is the speed that he wants? I want to please the guy, but I do not know how to *master* it.

I Wanna Be a Master

Dear G-Spot:

I am desperate and need help badly. I am a twenty-something female, 5'7", 210 lbs., with a strong, solid frame. I need help learning how to ride a man. When it comes to sex, I can roll with it . . . until I am asked to get on top. I do not know what it is, but I cannot ride my man good at all. I have been on your site and have not found anything in detail. Can you please give me some advice and techniques on how to position myself to make my man happy while I am on top? You are my only hope!

Can't Ride

Dear G-Spot:

Well, I am pretty experienced in all aspects of sex, but I am not sure how to ride a dick. I can't get the motion/rhythm of it. Are you supposed to go up and down? I am curious, so please help me.

Motionless

Dear G-Spot:

In your opinion, what would be the best/proper way to ride a dick—a nice-size dick at that? I understand that there are many ways to do this and different guys have their favorites when it comes to having their dick ridden. Could you please school me with everything that you know when it comes to riding dicks? I want to make their toes curl even better.

Student Rider

Dear G-Spot:

Hello, Zane. I need some help and I know you can help a sister out. I was on your website and I was reading "How to Really Fuck a Man." I cannot ride a dick for shit. I've watched pornos to see if I could learn, but that's not helpful at all. I would appreciate it if you could tell me how or give me some tips. You didn't go into detail on your page so, if it's not a problem, could you email me back in detail? I know you are busy and all, but it would be truly helpful. I don't want my man to leave me for another sister. Feel me? Thanks.

Milks

Dear G-Spot:

I am nineteen and I have been with only one person until now. My new boyfriend is *so* sexually experienced. My ex was 7.5" and my new boyfriend is 12.5". When he goes too far inside of me, it becomes painful and I have to ask him to stop. I realize that I should grin and bear it, but it hurts! Ouch! I tried to ride him, but that hurt also. I want to show him how good he makes me feel inside and out. I want to ride his dick so good that every time he thinks about me, he'll get hard. I need some dick-riding tips so that I don't hurt when I get on top of him. I love him and want him to feel my love.

                                             Aching but Willing to Please

Oral Sex

*O*kay, here we go. People have finally started admitting that they suck dick and eat pussy, but some of us still have a long way to go. At some point in time, someone came up with the idea to start performing oral sex—kind of like someone inventing the lightbulb and penicillin. Do not think that this is a recent thing; it clearly is not. I am not sure how far it goes back, but let's just say that I would not be surprised if the dinosaurs were inhabiting the earth.

I am not going to write a dick-sucking or pussy-eating manual, because that is another book. However, I will simply say that like opera, some people hate it and others love it. Oral sex techniques vary like regular sex; different strokes for different folks. I know of many women who hate for a man even to eye their pussies like a buffet. Honestly, I have never heard of a man who didn't want his dick waxed, but I have heard rumors of their existence.

If you have a hang-up about performing oral sex yet expect your mate to go down on you, shame on you and shame on it all. That's not fair, so if you don't want to sucky sucky or licky licky, don't be surprised when your situation gets tricky. For those who have mental hang-ups about it, oral sex is no more of a sin than fucking. If you feel that it is degrading to have to service a person's private parts, don't do it, but make it clear from the beginning of a relationship that you are simply not into it. Then the other person can make an informed decision.

I will say this. I have gotten a lot of emails—mostly from men—complaining that their wives won't suck their dicks and they are considering stepping out. The thing that pisses me off is when they knew that before marriage and all of a sudden—several years and a few kids later—they want to talk shit and threaten to cheat.

If you do have oral sex, use protection unless you are *clearly* in a monogamous relationship and get tested on a regular basis. Other than that, have fun and don't do anything the majority of the rest of the world is not doing. Yes, I am being sarcastic. People are sucking all over the planet; believe that.

Dear G-Spot:

I am not overly interested in receiving oral sex. I am wondering if I am the only woman out there with that mentality. There are many times when I stop my partner as he heads "there," and this seems to frustrate him. I love giving him oral sex. As a matter of fact, it is one of my biggest turn-ons. Why do you think that I am one-sided in this issue and what can I do to overcome it?

SSS

Dear SSS:

You didn't specify whether or not you have problems with your current lover going downtown or everyone who has ever been there. My initial reaction, and this is not a rare situation, is that you may have a bad oral sex experience lurking in your past. Some men are so bad at performing oral sex that they have been known to turn a woman off of the idea for weeks, months, and sometimes even years. However, if that is not the case and you just don't like it, then you just don't like it. Every aspect of sex is not for everybody. People like different things. If you enjoy performing oral sex on your man and don't expect him to return the favor, there is nothing wrong with that. I sense that he really wants to go "there," as you put it, so that changes things. If it is putting a damper on your relationship and you care enough for him to want to please him, teach him how to please you. If you experiment enough with it and let him know what does and does not turn you on orally, it should lead to a sensual experience for both of you. The only thing I can stress is never to do anything that makes you feel uncomfortable. He is getting his, royally from the way you talk since you love to go down on him, so he can't be too unhappy about the whole thing.

Blessings,

Zane

Dear G-Spot:

I am a twenty-seven-year-old African-American female who is intrigued by the art of oral sex. I read on your advice page about using breath mints. If you don't mind, could you explain to me how I would try it on my boyfriend? Thanks.

Female Oral Assassin

Dear Female Oral Assassin:

You simply put the breath mints in your mouth and then suck his dick. The heat that is generated by the mints adds to his pleasure, kind of like the massage oil that you can blow on and make hot works on the rest of the body. Trust me, if you do it right, he will keep a tin can of those bad boys right beside the bed at all times.

Blessings,

Zane

Dear G-Spot:

I have a cum and deep-throat/oral sex fetish that is not being satisfied by my wife. I love watching pornos with tons of oral sex involved, but I do not feel that they are the source of my fetish. I have been this way since I was in high school. I have always craved more oral sex than regular sex. I damn near fell in love the first time that I was deep-throated to my balls. The woman could put both my hard dick and balls into her mouth, and I am far from a little dick brother. The first time that I saw a "bukkake" porno flick, I thought that it was amazing that a woman would be turned on or paid to act turned on by having damn near a gallon of cum from various men all over her face. Zane, I swear that even as I type this, my dick is getting hard from thinking about it. When I get head, I would love for my lover to allow me to cum in her mouth and then keep sucking my dick as the cum oozes out of her mouth and back onto my dick. Something creative, if you feel me. I love that fantasy and have many others that I want to be fulfilled. I want to do these things only with my wife, but she is not having it; she is not hearing any of it. What am I to do? Wait for her while my fantasies wither away? Take matters into my own hands and find someone else to satisfy the fantasies that she refuses to fulfill? I am a good brother, too. I do not cheat; I earn a steady paycheck and have great benefits from the military; I am a good father to our child; and feel that I deserve my fantasies to be granted. I would gladly do the same for her. Sometimes this makes me question why I ever married her. Am I being too selfish? Thank you for listening.

Man with Needs

Dear Man with Needs:

When I first read your email, I was inclined to get pissed off, but I re-read it and have a new perspective. My knee-jerk reaction was that you were being selfish and clearly knew about your desire for oral sex before you married your wife. Thus, that was the time to demand that she either put up or get to stepping. In retrospect, now that you claim to be such a good man otherwise, I feel that women need to at least try to do things for their man. At that point, if they are still not feeling the act, then it might come down to a compromise. There are many men who are obsessed with getting their dicks waxed; some love it more than fucking. It is what it is and you are who you are. By no means do I think that you should cheat. Whatever you do, do not confront your wife and inform her that if she does not suck it, someone else will be happy to do it. Then you might not ever even touch her pussy again. What you should do is truly stress your obsession with it and tell her that you love her to death and will do anything for her. Ask her to please do this one thing for you in return for all that you shower upon her. If she still refuses, then she is the selfish one and not you. You need to analyze the importance of this oral sex thing and understand that you may lose your marriage if you persist in getting your jollies off elsewhere.

Blessings,
Zane

Dear G-Spot:

I read your page on the web. I am kind of new to "eating pussy." I would like some pointers. If you could help me, that would be great. I would like to know what she really likes and doesn't like. If you could give me a couple of pointers on foreplay and getting her in the mood, that would be great also.

Of course, any other pointers you have would be good too. Thank you very much.

Looking for Tips

Dear Looking for Tips:

The first thing you need to do is read "How to Make Love to a Woman: Mind and Body." That will answer a lot of your questions.

Second, no one knows your woman better than her. At least, that should be the case. As much as you hate to face it, you are more than likely not her first lover. Therefore, she should be able to educate you about what does and does not turn her on. Do something most women get down on their knees and pray for their man to do: ask her what she wants in the bedroom. That may just be the opening she was waiting for.

A lot of women don't tell their men what they want because they think the man will be offended and assume she is implying that he is a lousy fuck. Not! It is simply that people must be more open with one another, in and out of the bedroom.

As far as eating pussy, just remember not to suck too roughly on her clit, because a woman's clit is just as sensitive as your balls. Would you want a woman gnawing on your balls? I don't think so. Don't stay down there too long. You are performing oral sex, not chowing down at an all-you-can-eat buffet. Ideally, you should perform oral sex on her before you stick your dick in because it will aid greatly in her being lubricated enough to enjoy the actual sex. A lot of women fake headaches because they know their men will be finished, bust a nut, and go to sleep before they are even turned on good. Why bother if that is the case?

Make sure you engage in a lot of foreplay with your woman, both physical *and* mental. Tell her why she means so much to you, but be honest. Never lie just to get sex. Most important, if whatever you are doing to her doesn't also do something for you, don't do it, because it will definitely show.

Blessings,
Zane

Dear G-Spot:

I would like to know what foods a man can eat to alter the taste of his cum. I saw an article in a popular magazine a while back but have not seen or heard anything else since. Thank you for your time.

Not Yummy at All

Dear Not Yummy at All:

The average ejaculate contains aboutonia, ascorbic acid, blood-group antigens, calcium, chlorine, cholesterol, choline, citric acid, creatine, deoxyribonucleic acid (DNA), enzymes, fructose, glutathione, hyaluronidase, inositol, lactic acid, magnesium, nitrogen, phosphorus, potassium, protein, purine, pyrimidine, pyruvic acid, sodium, sorbitol, spermidine, spermine, urea, uric acid, vitamin B_{12}, and zinc. The caloric content of an average ejaculate is estimated to be approximately fifteen calories.

If you find that his cum has an offensive odor to it, ask him to eat more fruits, sweets, glucose-based foods, and sweet wines, which will produce a sweet or bland ejaculate. He needs to lay off the spicy foods and strong dairy products, and put more organic foods in his body rather than nonorganic or processed foods. Change his diet for him. If he loves what you are about to do to him, he will comply.

> Blessings,
> Zane

Dear G-Spot:

I was giving my partner a blow job when my tongue hit a spot that tasted . . . odd. It did not have a peculiar smell or anything, and I did an inspection to check for sores, etc. He is uncircumcised. Is what I tasted the "smegma" that occasionally accumulates under the foreskin?

> Taste Tester

Dear Taste Tester:

I would say that is probably what you were tasting. Uncircumcised men have to be extra careful about hygiene, and it might even come down to you cleaning him yourself before you participate in oral or vaginal sex. If the bad taste continues after that, I would suggest you invest in some flavored oils to spread on him before you head downtown. Also, if you put a breath mint in your mouth, both of you will have one hell of a good time.

> Blessings,
> Zane

Dear G-Spot:

My boyfriend and I have been dating for a long time now. I love him very much and he loves me as well. My problem is I love sucking his dick and making him cum, but it tastes and smells nasty! Is there anything that can be done to change it?

Can't Take the Musk

Dear Can't Take the Musk:

Putting one of those tiny breath mints in your mouth before you go down on him will work wonders for both of you. It will increase his pleasure because of the heat and it will mask the taste of his cum so you can enjoy the experience. That is a short-term solution. The long-term solution is to suggest that he bathe before you make love. Better yet, get in the shower or tub together and scrub each other down in a sensual manner. Also, what a person eats does affect the taste of his bodily fluids. Tell him to eat more fruits and vegetables. I hope this helps. Let me know.

Blessings,
Zane

Dear G-Spot:

I have been with my boyfriend for two and a half years and I love him very much. He is the best lover I have ever had. I love our sex life, but ever since we have been together I have never been able to bring him to climax when I perform oral sex on him. It is not that I do not try; it is just that he does not cum. I can suck and lick and stroke until I am blue in the face, but no matter what I try, nothing works. He does not complain and it does not even matter to him, but it does matter to me. Do you have any tips you can give?

Aim to Please

Dear Aim to Please:

Believe it or not, there are many men who cannot climax through oral sex. There are many women who also have the same issue. Just because he does not cum does not mean he is not enjoying the act. In your case, it is best to use oral sex as foreplay and then let him climax from penetrating you. One good thing is that most men's dicks are never harder than right after being sucked on so it is a wonderful thing for you in the long run. I do have a manual that describes blow jobs in detail. You may just have one of those men who cannot get off that way.

Blessings,
Zane

Dear G-Spot:

I'm nineteen and I bought oral sex dice for my man, and one of them says "undercarriage." From the dictionary definition, I'm totally confused. What part of the body is the undercarriage?

Seeking Knowledge

Dear Seeking Knowledge:

The "undercarriage" is the bottom side of his dick, which might even include his balls.

Blessings,
Zane

Long-Distance Lovers

I will not lie to you. Long-distance relationships can be heavenly or they can be a nightmare. It all depends on the personalities, needs, and agendas of the people involved. If you need sex damn near daily, a long-distance relationship is certainly not for you. People with high sex drives are not going to remain faithful and will eventually cheat. They feel they have no chance of getting caught because you are hundreds—sometimes thousands—of miles away. Long-distance relationships are the best way to eat your cake and have it too. You live separate lives, talk on the phone or via the internet daily, and occasionally meet up and fuck.

In today's age, more and more people are dating long distance, mostly because of cyberspace hookups. Because of hectic schedules and being tired of hanging out at clubs or merely tired of playing the traditional dating game, people can say, do, and be whatever they want on the web. Men can be six-five when they are really five-two. Women can be a hundred fifteen pounds when they are really two hundred thirty pounds. A woman can get on the internet in her pajamas with a fucked-up weave and not brush her teeth for three days and have men swooning over her in a chat room. What a life!

Here is the catch-22. If you truly get a man sprung through email and chat, he is going to want to come and get some coochie. He is going to get to the point where he is thinking about your pussy all the time. First, there will be the daily pussy thought, then the hourly pussy thought, and finally the minute pussy thought. He is going to want the pussy that he has put so much time and effort into and he is not going to take no for an answer. If you take the plunge and meet up, either you will both be happy as shit or mad as hell. The sex might be the best thing since sliced bread or it might be the worst thing since Jheri curls. One thing is for sure, nothing is ever exactly as we imagine it.

I am not saying that the only reason people have long-distance relationships is because of the internet. Some people are not together daily because of the military or other work commitments, or because they meet in a city not home to at least one of them and want to get to know each other better after one or both of them return home. Some long-distance relationships can be lovely. For example, take two people who are career driven and do not want to take out a lot of time to date on a weekly basis. It is more convenient for them to see each other sporadically or on a predetermined schedule, and absence truly makes the heart grow fonder. As long as both parties are on the same page, it is copacetic.

Where it gets tricky is when some people take it to the extreme and set up dick or pussy action in various cities or go all out and become international lovers. I know a man who has a lady to stay with in every city he travels to. That's hot for him, because he saves on hotel rooms plus gets some pussy and probably even gets home-cooked meals. I have seen some of the women, and they all think that they are special. If they only knew.

Last, there are those in "imaginary" relationships, like one of the young ladies who wrote me for advice (see below). People who think they are in serious relationships but are only wasting time, which they can never get back, on a dream. If you are going to engage in a long-distance love, make sure that the two of you discuss parameters and expectations. Unless you do that, do not be surprised when the shit hits the fan.

Dear G-Spot:

I am so in love with this guy and I think he feels the same about me, but I won't say a word about it. The thing is that we live in two different states and we are getting along fine. We were together before, but it got too hard, so we broke it off. Now I am back to where I started with him and I know he has some feelings for me but I just don't know what they are. I am moving up there, but not to be with him. I am moving because of school. What am I going to do? I would like to settle this before I move there. I don't like feeling confused.

                                                                Hates Confusion

Dear Hates Confusion:

There is only one option. Ask him how he envisions your connection once you move closer to him. Ask him does he have sincere feelings for you and express what you are feeling as well. Ask him if there is someone else in his life who might complicate matters, and make it clear that you have no intentions of sharing his attention. Obviously, if you took the time out to write me for advice, this is really weighing heavily on your mind. You absolutely have to do something about it or face being stressed out indefinitely. My only caution: be emotionally prepared to take the news that he might not be interested or that he might have stronger feelings toward someone else. Either way, you have to find out the truth. Good luck but, most important, put your education ahead of everything.

Blessings,

Zane

Dear G-Spot:

I am an eighteen-year-old woman from New York. Recently, I met a guy online via a popular website. We have kept contact for the past four months and have held several phone conversations. He wants me to spend a weekend with him. I want the same thing, but I have never met a person from the web before. I am extremely nervous but do not want to miss an opportunity to have a good relationship. From our web conversations, we seem like a perfect match. I am not sure what to do. Should I take the chance and meet up with him, or should I stick to men that I've already met in person? Please help me.

Too Nervous

Dear Too Nervous:

You should absolutely not spend a weekend with him. What if you meet up with him and he is a maniac? I would suggest meeting him in a public place for a real date and taking it from there. In addition, you need to tell at least three people where you are going, give them his contact information and photo if you have one, and make sure that he does not accompany you home. You have invested four months into this; do not rush to the finish line. If he is sincere, he will be sincere after doing some actual wining and dining. Because you are so young, I am especially concerned that you may not recognize a game being run on you. Please be extra careful, and if you must see where this man is coming from, do it with extreme caution.

Blessings,

Zane

Dear G-Spot:

I am twenty-two years young with a very healthy sexual appetite, but I am confused out of my mind. I am in a relationship with a man who lives clear across the country from me. I stay in Nevada and he is in South Carolina. We have been together nearly a year now and I still have not been in a physical relationship with this man. My hormones are raging out of control. I have this feeling that if he does not come to me soon, then I am going to release my tension on someone else in a weak moment.

He tells me that he loves me and he really wants to be with me, but he has made zero effort to come and see me. I have tried compromising and agreed to come to him. He objects and insists that if anyone dips into their finances, it should be him. He does not have the means to make that happen at this point. I fear the worst for this relationship. I really need to see him. He claims to be making future plans for us. As elated as that makes me, I cannot wait much longer. I am an extremely needy person when it comes to attention and affection. If I cannot get what I need from the person I yearn for it from, it is sometimes easy for me to seek out someone I would see myself with if I were not attached. What do you think I should do? Thank you in advance for your advice.

Long-Distance Nonlover

Dear Long-Distance Nonlover:

Here is the ugly truth. You are not in a real relationship. You are friends with a man who lives a long way from you and one who is surely fucking someone in South Carolina. Do you honestly believe that he has abstained from sex for an entire year? Even though he has never even experienced yours? Trust me when I say that you have a better chance of winning your state lottery than finding such a man. He is giving you obvious hints, without trying to come directly out and hurt your feelings. If he really wanted to see you, he would find a way to get the money together or allow you to come see him. Plane fares are not that damn high. Then there is the bus and the train. He is lying when he says that he is making future plans for the two of you. Why would he? The two of you do not even know if you are compatible, if you can get along for more than twenty-four hours in the same environment, any of that. You are ready to get your freak on with someone else, and that is exactly what you need to do to get your mind off this long-distance nonsense. Some long-distance relationships can work, when the two people are willing to commute to see one another and one or both are willing eventually to relocate. He is not trying to do a damn thing for you or with you. Do not hop on the first dick or face you see, but start dating. Do not continue to let life pass you by, because time is the one thing we can never get back. You did not say how you met this man in South Carolina whom you have never been with, so I am going out on a limb and guessing it was via the internet. He is playing games with your heart. Do not allow it.

Blessings,
Zane

Dear G-Spot:

How are you? Thanks a lot for your lovely words. I am John and I reside in Uganda, East Africa. I have written to you to get your advice about a long-distance relationship. I have a woman outside of my country. I want her to come visit me or allow me to go to her country to visit her. I love her as much as possible but she still refuses to believe in me. I would be pleased to hear a positive response from you. Have a good day.

Love in Uganda

Dear Love in Uganda:

Long-distance relationships within one country are difficult, but across borders makes it even harder. It seems like you have never met this woman in person; maybe you met via the internet or some other way. A lot of people get caught up in loving strangers, but when it comes time to actually take a risk, the majority clam up. You are expecting this woman to go outside of her comfort zone and fly to Africa or allow you to make that long trip to be with her. You cannot force her to be with you, and if I were you, I would make one final effort to get her to oblige and then give it up. Life is short, and if she is not willing to be open, then move on. Do not fault her, though. She probably does care, but caring and making sacrifices by venturing into the unknown are two different things altogether.

Blessings,
Zane

Reigniting Old Flames

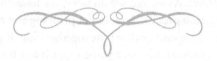

$\mathcal{M}$ost people would wonder why on earth a person would want to start again dating a person he or she had broken up with. Some people even get married twice. Others have been together all along and the sizzle has fizzled out of their relationships. This chapter is all about reigniting old flames—if you really want to do it. Determining whether or not a current or past relationship is worth salvaging is the first step. What happened the first time you were together? If it involved cheating or disrespect, he will probably still cheat on you and be disrespectful. If it involved outside influences like friends or family, you both need to make sure that you are mature enough not to let that happen again. If it was one person being lazy or a workaholic, has that changed at all?

I engaged in an old relationship, got married, and it was a complete nightmare. The person I knew way back when did not even exist anymore, but I was so caught up in thinking that he did that I was a fool and paid the consequences. I would never do it again and would rather hook up with someone I have known two months than twenty years. Familiarity can often breed contempt.

Each situation is different, but if you want to reignite those flames, remember what made the relationship so hot in the first damn place and set about trying to re-create those situations and feelings. If you used to shower each other with compliments, bathe together, sleep in the spoon position to feel secure, whatever—do it again. A lot of new couples sleep right under each other, but as time goes on, they find themselves on opposite edges of the bed, a world apart. When two people first get together, they tend to want to bathe together, spoon as they are sleeping, and communicate about life. As time goes on, they start migrating to opposite sides of the bed, bathing alone, and talking to their friends or family members instead of their lover. As we age, we do not crave tenderness any less. We tend to crave it even more. You have to put planning and effort into a serious relationship and spend quality time together. Search your soul before you make a commitment, but once you do, give it one hundred percent.

Dear G-Spot:

There is this cool guy whom I like. We have been intimate friends for a year. We are both in our forties—forty-four to be exact—and we knew each other twenty years ago in high school. We played around during those times, but the sex was not as good as the foreplay. Now it is much better. I have tried things that I would not attempt with others and our times together are nothing short of magical. We are good together. We have so much in common. My question is, do you think our passion can turn into love? I am already in love with him but cannot bring myself to admit it to him. He used to be a player and is accustomed to women chasing after him and going crazy. I am not doing that and he is eating it up. I yearn to be his wife or lover until we are too old to care. I feel that if we are meant to be, we will be without any additional prodding from me. We have great talks. We are both into politics and community affairs. We could be perfect together. Is there any hope for us?

Hopeful

Dear Hopeful:

I would say there is a lot of hope for your relationship. Even the biggest playas eventually run out of steam. There comes a time when a man starts worrying more about the quality of women than the quantity. Just like you used to think that driving a car and hanging out at clubs was thrilling, but it all changed by the time you hit thirty. The two of you seem to have a lot in common and I would venture to guess that you will not have to help the situation out much at all. Like you said, he is eating up the fact that you are not chasing after him. Most men relish it when the pressure is taken off and they can just take their time developing the feelings they need to go long term. You love him and that is a definite plus. If I were you, I would just take it one day at a time, let him know that you do care deeply for him, and wait for him to take the leap. I have a feeling it will be a whole lot sooner than you think.

Blessings,
Zane

Dear G-Spot:

I have been married for sixteen years. Our sex life is somewhat nonexistent, simply because of our work schedules. He works third shift while I work first. We rarely have alone time. We never argue because we never see each other. If we are lucky, we have sex maybe once every two weeks. What can we do to enhance our marriage, despite our hectic and varied schedules?

Seeking Quality Time

Dear Seeking Quality Time:

Your schedules are definitely the main issue. Basically, you only have the second shift—which I will assume runs from about three in the afternoon until eleven at night—to get busy. I am also assuming that the reason you barely have time alone is because of children who need the most attention from the time they get out of school until the time they go to bed. You are not alone. Many couples are dealing with the same situation. It seems like you can only say hello and good-bye, sometimes with only a wave and not a kiss. You are also probably extremely exhausted, you more so than him. When he gets home and goes to sleep, you are probably rushing to get the kids ready for school, packing lunches, and helping with last-minute homework.

When you do have days off, make the most of them and do not feel guilty about pushing the kids off on relatives. Yes, the two of you should spend quality time with them together, but they have your attention all week. Hubby needs some too. Go to a concert in the park, a museum, or ask the grandparents to watch them overnight so you can take a quick jaunt out of town. You have to do something to reignite the fire in your marriage. Sixteen years is a lot of time to invest. Ironically, I get the most mail asking for advice from people who have been married either seven years or sixteen years. I already knew about the seven-year itch, but apparently the sixteenth year is a benchmark as well.

Last but not least, when thinking about ways to make time for your husband, remember that there are always quickies. They can be exciting because they are spontaneous and release sexual tension. If you have a garage, when he is about to leave for work and the kids are asleep, go out there and jump his bones right there on the hood of the car. Do something totally unexpected. Even one such adventure will put a huge grin on his face and a pep in his step. Once he realizes you are open to quick sex, he will probably make the next move. A lot of men think their women want to be wined and dined first all the time, that foreplay should last for thirty minutes, and that they should be able to stay awake afterward to converse for lengthy periods. Your love is solid, so make him understand that more than wining and dining, you need to be held, even if it is momentary.

Blessings,
Zane

Swinging

$\mathcal{A}$w, the sweet life. Swinging. Having a mate who is so sexually free that he or she has no problem watching you fuck someone else and, in addition, wants to join in. I have an issue with that—a bone to pick, so to speak. I was recently talking to the owner and manager of a BDSM sex onsite club. They have a swingers' night and I was curious how it all worked. They invited me to come and check it out, but I was not available on the scheduled night. However, I was able to discover the basics and was surprised to find out that double standards exist, even when it comes to swinging.

What I mean is that the only people allowed to come to most swingers' events are couples and single women—no single men. I see that as chauvinistic—not allowing men to come so they can hook up with couples looking for a threesome with a man. Where does that leave women who are searching for a second dick in the bedroom? It is like saying that men can fulfill their fantasy of having two women—and we'll even make the selection easy for you—but women are on their own. I realize that it is a rule mostly for security reasons, but since when did crazy women become less dangerous than crazy men? A nut is a nut. There are probably just as many psychotic women as men. I have not done any fact-finding, but most women naturally equate sex with love more so than men. I was talking to someone recently and she said, "It's funny. I will not be feeling a guy at all, but once I sleep with him, I am suddenly in love." That happens a lot. Women can have bad sex, but the fact that they lay down with the man will make them assume it is a relationship in the works.

What I am saying is that if a couple mutually decides to bring someone else into the bedroom, that is their business. However, they need to be prepared for the possible repercussions. From the emails below, you will see a couple of them. Some of the possible outcomes:

- The woman or man will think the third person fucks better than his or her mate and will crave that person more than once.

- The third party will develop feelings for one or both members of the committed couple and set out to destroy the relationship.

- The woman or man will leave his or her mate for the third party if the sex is fantastic.

- One or both parties might view the agreement to bring a third party into the bedroom as a sign of noncommitment and leave the relationship.

Now I am not saying swinging is a bad thing. To each his or her own. It's a huge business. Yes, I said business. They have worldwide conventions for swinging, people take over entire hotels and resorts, and they even have swinger summer camps. Sounds crazy, but I actually know of a camp that is used for schoolkids the majority of the time but for one week a year it is taken over by swingers.

If you are thinking about swinging with your mate, make sure you discuss it openly and make an informed decision. Most men will go for it with little or no hesitation. They will jump at the chance to bed two women at the same time. Women get skeptical when their men want to bring another man in the bedroom, though. They wonder if the man is bisexual or if he does not care. In some cases where the men want to share their women with close friends, this can be a real problem for the women. That really does speak volumes, in my opinion. If your man is willing to bring his beer buddies into your bedroom, he has no respect for you because these are people who hang out with you already and that's not cool. A threesome should not involve someone who is part of your daily routine. That certainly has the potential to create problems. If a man suggests that his woman ask her best girlfriend to join in, that is a no-no because he will be trying to get in her panties day and night after that. Also, what kind of friend does that? I have seen that same scenario turn into disasters; that is a talk show segment waiting to happen.

Consenting adults are entitled to do whatever, and I know a bunch of people who swing and enjoy it. It keeps their marriages fresh, and both man and wife love being able to have a free-for-all with others—sometimes orgy-style—and then go home to raise the kids and bring home the cheddar. All I can say is, be careful what you wish for.

Dear G-Spot,

I have a dilemma. One of my closest friends is into swinging and had mentioned it to my loving husband. So after much prodding by my husband, we threw a swing party in which we invited the friends we trusted enough to do that with. The thing is that one of the guys just made me fly to the moon, whereas my husband doesn't seem to have that touch. How do I tactfully go about letting him know what is going wrong there? I love my husband to death but sometimes can't seem to forget about that wonderful experience and worry about hurting his feelings and ego.

Lost and Confused

Dear Lost and Confused:

That is the danger when it comes to swinging. There's the chance we might find something better than what we have at home. While I am sure the other man made you fly to the moon, you must remember why you married your husband and weigh the sex issue against everything else he does for you. What seems good to us isn't always good for us. That is not to say that you should not try to improve your husband sexually. Whatever you do, don't mention that the other man turned you out. That will mess him up for life and could possibly lead to a divorce. Instead, become creative in the bedroom with him, make suggestions, and take the initiative. The techniques the other man used on you should be brought up casually, such as, "Hey, honey, why don't we try something different tonight and . . ."

I am being kind of vague because you really didn't say how the other man sent you to the moon. It could have been he was better at oral sex. It could have been he was better at digging your back out. It could be numerous things, but remember that everyone has potential. Make yourself a better lover and hope your husband reciprocates.

Blessings,
Zane

Dear G-Spot:

I have been in a monogamous relationship for the past five years with a man whom I adore. He is a sex fiend—okay, both of us are sex fiends. He has been pondering the idea of a threesome; a guy for me and a woman for him. I'm totally for the idea, but one issue bothers me: JEALOUSY. He's an extremely jealous man and won't admit it. I am afraid that I might enjoy having sex with another man and woman. Seeing me with another girl will definitely turn him on, but I am not sure he can handle another man enjoying his "sweetness"—my pussy. I won't front. I have jealous tendencies also. I will not be able to deal with another woman enjoying what I've had between my legs for many years. I will be honest and admit to being selfish. I want to enjoy another man, another woman, and him. While I can confess to my issues, he can't. Do you think that a threesome is healthy for our relationship? How can I comfort his insecurities? I will appreciate any advice you have to offer for you are the QUEEN OF EROTICA.

Looking Forward to Da Dick
and Da Clit

Dear Looking Forward to Da Dick and Da Clit:

Sister, you have already answered all of your questions. You need to forget the threesome because both of you have jealous tendencies. Watching each other fucking and sucking all over someone else will surely kill your relationship faster than anything else. You cannot deal with him fucking another woman and he will have a fit if he sees another man touching you. My suggestion is that the two of you do some role-playing and become those other people. It is safer—both emotionally and physically (because of diseases)—and it will not throw a wrench in your relationship. A lot of people are comfortable with swinging; the two of you are something different altogether.

Blessings,
Zane

Dear G-Spot:

I need some advice. I have been with my boyfriend for a year, and sexually we try any and everything. Now he wants to have a threesome, and while I am down for it, I am afraid he might like her sex better than mine. That or want to continue doing threesomes all the time. When we discussed it at length, he claimed he simply wants to live out that particular fantasy. I love him enough to go through with it, but do not want it to backfire on me. Zane, what should I do? Can you also give me some pointers on sucking dick? I am tired of doing the same boring things, even though my boyfriend loves them. I want to do something different.

Miss Not Too Sure

Dear Miss Not Too Sure:

You need to do several things: mainly evaluate the strength of your relationship and, more important, the basis of your relationship. I realize you are in love, but are you positive he feels the same way? Men are good at masking their true feelings and saying what they think women want to hear. I am by no means saying genuine men do not exist. I am only encouraging you to make sure you have one before you sacrifice and take the leap of faith he is asking of you.

You are definitely taking a risk on it backfiring on you. If I had a dime for every person who thought having a threesome was cool only to end up losing his or her mate to the other person, I would be mad rich. There is no question that she might be able to throw down better than you sexually. After all, this would have to be a woman uninhibited enough to engage in a threesome with a couple in the first place. This leads me to believe she would be a woman of experience with a lot of kinky behavior. On the other hand, if your man truly loves you, then no other woman, great pussy or not, should be able to come between you.

It is a judgment call only you can make. Whatever you decide, make sure you engage in safe sex including condoms, dental dams, etc. Again, this woman would have to be wide open in the sex department to join you, and that means she could have a disease from being out there.

Sucking dick can be an art form. First you should read "How to Really Fuck a Man: The Bottom Line." I give several techniques there, but invest time in doing some research. The internet is a wealth of information when it comes to every sex act on the planet. I encourage you to experiment and

try to come up with something unique and special on your own. That
would really blow his mind.

Blessings,

Zane

Dear G-Spot:

  I have been dating this guy out of state for about three years and our sex
is off the chain. We have tried everything from sex toys to anal sex. I really
love him and I know he has feelings for me but why would he ask me to
have a threesome with him? And then—like a dummy—I told him I would
like to but it would have to be with another man and he agreed. I have wondered what it would be like to have a threesome with him and his friend. So
what is wrong with me? I truly care about my boyfriend and do not want
him to lose respect for me if I went for the threesome. I keep asking myself
how can I really love him and agree to be with someone else? He has not
brought it up to me anymore because I told him how I felt. But now I find
myself really wanting to tell him let's do this.

What Is Up?

Dear What Is Up:

  Your situation could be viewed in numerous ways. While 99 percent of
men want to have threesomes, the majority want to have one with two
women and not with a woman and another man. There is this serious double standard in relationships. My first inclination when you say that your
man agreed to another man is that he is not that serious about you and
simply wants to do something different. It is hard to imagine that he would
regard you with a high level of respect if you do it. Then again, your man
may be open-minded and a freak who wants to see the woman he adores
pleasured by someone else. Generally, men want to see their woman pleasured by another woman because they don't view the female as competi-
tion, and they get something out of the deal as well.

  If I were you, I would tread carefully. I am not saying don't do it, but
you should be prepared if it backfires on you and he drops you like a hot
potato afterward. If you have never seen the Spike Lee movie *School Daze*,
that is a perfect example. One of the females in the movie agrees to sleep
with a frat brother of her supposed man, and the second she does it, he
kicks her to the curb. It was a powerful lesson women have learned over

and over again. I have no idea how old you are, but if you are young, eighteen to twenty-five, I would be careful because it may be a game. Most men that age are still maturing and have no regard for a woman's feelings.

I hope this helps, but whomever you sleep with, make sure you use protection at all times.

> Blessings,
> Zane

Selfish Lovers

$\mathcal{I}$ am going to make this chapter quick. I am disgusted even to think about selfishness because it is one of my greatest pet peeves. Selfishness *period* irritates me, but selfish lovers have reached a special level of trifling behavior. How dare someone expect a person to cater to all of his sexual needs and then want to play possum when it is her turn? Like his or her dick or pussy is made of gold and others should be sweating them like that. If you have a selfish lover, get rid of him or her. I know that sounds mean, but I am serious. If he is selfish in the bedroom, then he is going to be that way in every area and you do not need to be bothered. Life is too short to deal with ignorant people. You can masturbate until you find a lover willing to reciprocate, but do not play the fool and give up your goodies without getting satisfied in return.

Dear G-Spot:

My male friend and I have been talking for about a year now and are ready to take it to the next level. The only problem is that he refuses to perform oral sex on me. He has never tried it and does not plan on trying it anytime in the near future. Now, I love to perform oral sex on my male friends, but not without getting anything in return. I care about this guy a lot, but he is just too boring in the bedroom department. I like to try new and exciting things. He is more concerned with getting his nut and going to sleep. I am a very sexual person in nature, and sex is a big issue to me. Please tell me how I can get my man to try some new things. And how I can get him to perform oral sex on me?

Will He or Won't He

Dear Will He or Won't He:

I wish I could tell you there is some secret mojo you can put on him to get him under your spell. Unfortunately, if he is as stubborn as you say, there may not be a chance in hell of him performing oral sex on you. If I were you, I wouldn't perform oral sex on him either. He seems very selfish and self-centered. What makes him think you get any joy from watching him bust a nut and fall asleep? That's asinine.

My personal philosophy is that if a man doesn't perform oral sex on me and make sure I have an orgasm first, there is no point in him even whipping his dick out. I would tell you just to move on and dump him, but you have a year invested in him so the feelings obviously are strong. At this point, you need to decide which is of greater importance: being with him period or being sexually satisfied. I hate to say it, but I don't think you are going to get both.

Blessings,
Zane

Dear G-Spot:

I'm a twenty-six-year-old female who has a potentially excellent lover but it seems as if he is scared to let himself go sexually. I try to tell him what I need to be fulfilled. Currently, I feel it is all about pleasing him. When we have sex, I want him to hurry up and bust a nut so I can go about other tasks. My sex drive is in overdrive. I'm freaky and want to share myself completely with him through role playing, a little S & M, and whatever else there is to experience. Every time I bring up the subject, he states that I don't love him and that I'm rejecting him by suggesting that the sex is whack. When we first started dating, he was willing to experiment. Now all he wants is head and sex. I try to tell him that his approach to our sexual encounters is boring and not a turn-on but a turn-off. I like foreplay; I like oral sex performed on me as well; and I want a little romance and creativity. Yet I get the same old routine: he gets off and I'm left disappointed. Please suggest how can I reclaim my wild and hesitant lover!

Hopelessly Unsatisfied

Dear Hopelessly Unsatisfied:

I hate to throw it out here like this, but brotherman is being selfish and that is the bottom line. There used to be a saying on birth control/STD posters that went something like, "If he doesn't care enough about you to wear a condom, then he doesn't care at all." Well, it comes to follow that if he doesn't care enough about you to make sure that you are satisfied sexually, then he doesn't care at all. I am sure he says that he cares, that he loves you, and in his mind, he probably does. But you need to make it perfectly clear to him that if he can't make a sincere effort to give you more foreplay and experimentation, then there is no point in your continuing to please him. Why should you be playing a game of musical chairs and be the only one left standing when the music stops?

His ego is probably bruised, because you have mentioned it. However, mentioning it and giving an ultimatum are two different things. If you don't want to take the blunt/harsh route, then the only other solution is to take the initiative and plan some of the things you mentioned and dare his ass to tell you no after you have gone through all the trouble. At twenty-six, he should be old enough to understand that women have needs that must be met. Let me know what happens.

Blessings,
Zane

Dear G-Spot:

I have this boyfriend who gives out slobbery kisses. Why? He acts like he doesn't know how to caress when we are being intimate. He doesn't make any sounds when we fuck each other. He seems to believe I should do all the work. Does this mean he doesn't really care about me, or does he simply not know how to fuck a woman right? When I tease and touch him in the right spots, it arouses him, but he has a hard time reciprocating when it comes to turning me on. Please tell me how I could get him to do me the same way that I do him.

Turnabout Is Fair Play

Dear Turnabout Is Fair Play:

I don't think you have a man who doesn't know how to fuck; I think you have a lazy fuck period. Any man who is selfish enough not to return the sexual favors you extend to him needs to jack off and leave the good sisters alone. I don't mean to sound harsh, but you need to do one of two things: sit him down and nicely state that you need him to be more engaging when it comes to your intimate acts, or put his ass on probation until he starts blowing your back out like the men in my books.

Blessings,
Zane

Dear G-Spot:

I must first congratulate you on a job well done. You are an inspiration to me. I love your books. Keep up the good work. May God bless, guide, and keep you always.

I am a twenty-four-year-old who has been seeing this guy for nine months now. We started out merely talking; then one thing led to another. Trust me, the first time we did it, I was ashamed. I felt like we did it too quickly but, after that, I could not get enough of him. His dick is damn good; I love it. I do everything to satisfy him, from the tongue bath to sucking his dick to licking his ass. You name it, I have done it. The sex is off the chain, but my problem is that he refuses to eat my pussy. He did inform me in the beginning that he did not perform oral sex on women. Is that bad? The fact that I am doing him and not getting it back in return? I don't regret doing it, because I love to satisfy my man in any way possible.

Lost in Love

Dear Lost in Love:

What you have in your life is a lazy, selfish lover. You have gone beyond what most women will do in bed by licking his ass and he still acts like he is too special to taste you. That is a serious red flag. Unless you love this man more than your next breath, I would start exploring other options. It is unfair for you to be such an open and giving lover and have that man hold out on you. Who does he think he is?

See, this kind of thing irritates me. Men, some of them at least, have been brainwashed into thinking that women are on this earth to cater to them (yes, suck their dicks) and expect to get their thrills and not give a damn about the female feeling the same way.

You need to tell the man you are seeing that he either needs to eat you like a buffet or forgo the head you have been giving him. Do not let him get away with that nonsense. You can do better, especially since you are willing to satisfy your lover in every way. You are a hot commodity; just make sure you practice safe sex at all times. Frankly, for all you know, with a man that selfish, chances are you might not be the only sister sucking his dick and licking his ass clean.

Blessings,
Zane

Dear G-Spot:

I have a problem with my boyfriend. I am a very sexually open-minded person. I am down to try damn near everything, but my boyfriend, on the other hand, is very closed off when it comes to sex. He does not like it when I masturbate or have toys. He thinks that he should be my only source of pleasure. When I tell him that they simply add on to it, he assumes that I do not need him if I can do it to myself. He will not even change positions, and when I try to tell him what to do or how to do it, he gets defensive. I love him, but, at the same time, I have needs that he is not handling. I would hate to get it elsewhere, but he will not hear of sexual experimentation. What can I do to get him to see where I am coming from?

The Experiment

Dear Experiment:

Your problem is more common than you think. You have a man who (a) feels insecure in his manhood and cannot handle that you want to use toys for added stimulation, (b) believes that the man should be the aggressor and is uncomfortable with a woman expressing her needs, or (c) both. A lot of people are set in their ways, unable to understand that love is about reciprocity and making sure that your partner is not only as happy as you are, but happier. Your solution is either (a) continue to try to beat a dead horse and compromise your own satisfaction to make him feel good about himself, (b) cheat on him and eventually dump him for the new man or get dumped after being caught in the act, or (c) give him an ultimatum either to start catering to your needs or all bets are off. There is not an easy solution and only you can weigh the importance of the sex against the values of the rest of the relationship.

Blessings,
Zane

Dear G-Spot:

I've been fortunate to fall in love with a wonderful guy. I love him dearly and I know he loves me. He's affectionate, romantic, and my best friend. The problem is he is HORRIBLE in bed. He's very passive in bed and doesn't take the initiative (not to mention he isn't hung or working with a lot). Every time we have sex, I am on top and, frankly, I'm bored. At first it felt good on top, but I think when he noticed that I could do all the work, he stopped trying. I've tried to tell him to be more aggressive in bed and do SOMETHING. And when he got on top of me it was like watching a baby learn how to walk. Every time the baby fell, you just wanted to go pick it up. He got so frustrated that we ended up doing it the way we always do it, with me on top. Recently, I told him if he wanted sex then he would have to initiate it and take charge. His response is that we haven't had sex for the last three weeks and I'm starting to feel the effects more than he is. I don't know how to approach the matter without hurting his feelings. What should I do? How do I tell him he sucks in bed and I want him to know what he's doing? How do I tell him that he needs to learn how to make love to a woman? Please help.

I'm Suffering from PID

Dear I'm Suffering from PID:

Your man is selfish, plain and simple. Any man who would refrain from sex because he does not want to break out some orange cones, put on a hard hat, and go to work is not worth your time. I can tell you care about him, but you have to ask yourself what the hell your relationship is all about if he is going to play childish games—like dick withholding—to teach you a lesson. Normally, I would never suggest that a woman tell a man that he sucks in bed, but I am about to make an exception. Why? Because even though he might leave, he has already done what they call a "constructive eviction" from the relationship. Give that fool an ultimatum, and if he still wants to keep his dick to himself, accept that and move on.

Blessings,
Zane

Relationship Confusion

I wonder if anyone has ever done a study on how many years of his or her lifetime a person spends in complete confusion over relationships. If not, they should. They should study about a thousand people—maybe a hundred is more realistic—for about twenty years and see what the results are. I have not done a survey, but from my own observations, I am willing to bet that most people—whether married or single—spend a bare minimum of two hours a day thinking about their current or past relationships. Even if they are happy ones, there is still that questioning, that foreboding, that wondering what else is out there or if they are doing the right thing. People often question themselves about their choices in mates, their choices in life period.

Are we meant to love one person and one person only during our lifetime? Is there only one ideal soul mate rationed out per person? I don't think so, because if that were the case, how come some people go through as many as six marriages? I know of several people who were on their third marriages by the time they turned forty. Ironically, the ones I know in that situation are mostly males. That's surprising, since men are often thought of as commitment shy. There are indeed men who shun commitment and then there are those men who get married but are still looking. The same goes for women, but women tend to get caught up and confuse sex with love. Sex is not love and love is not sex. Sexual attraction is not the only thing that makes the world go round. It takes a lot more than physical attraction and sexual compatibility to make a relationship flourish and last.

Some people—like one of the women who emailed me below—find themselves suddenly cast back out into the dating world after a long-term relationship. They have no clue how to get back out there and find someone new to date. Some of them are so afraid of being hurt again that they only want to be "friends with benefits," also known as "fuck buddies." To each his or her own, but after a while, even that has to grow old when you find yourself searching for someone to spend quality time with. It's cool until you end up going to see all the new movies alone, attending plays with your coworkers or friends of the same sex, and not having a hand to hold during a concert. What then? Is having a fuck buddy enough then?

No one ever proclaimed that love was easy. Like the title of my recent book, love is never painless. What you need to ask yourself is, out of everything you do in life, how much is love worth to you? If you are one of those people who sincerely want to be alone forever, cool. However, if you do crave that love, that romance, that lifelong friend who will be there for you through thick and thin, I hate to be the bearer of bad news, but you are going to have to get back out there and try your luck again.

Another one of the emails below is from a woman who had a horrible marriage. Again, something that I can totally relate to. The thought of having sex with a man makes her cringe because she is afraid it will be like it was with her husband, a man who disrespected and belittled her whenever he got a chance. It is going to take a lot for her to get over that, but she can. The one good thing about going through a relationship like that is that she can more than likely recognize a good mate when she runs across him. There are good men and bad men, just as there are good women and bad women. The emotional baggage from previous relationships weighs heavily on our ability to move on. We have to allow each person to start out with a clean slate, as difficult as that sounds. Without the ability to do that, people will be so on guard with their emotions that everyone will be out to hurt everyone else first. That is the sad reality of a lot of what is going on in today's dating society. Men not trusting women because of what another woman did, and vice versa.

Ultimately, there is only one way to clear up relationship confusion. Communicate your feelings to the person you are interested in, and if he refuses to listen or does not have the wherewithal to, then you need to leave him alone. There is someone out there for everyone. People who have low self-esteem tend to think that they will be alone forever. The only thing preventing them from finding true love is themselves. Also, do not look for it too hard, because that is a surefire way not to find it. I will give you a prime example. For those of you who have kids, when it comes time every year for them to do a science fair project, you can't find a damn project board anywhere. If they need a red bandanna for the school play, there will not be a single one in the ten stores where you look. The week after the play, you will see the stupid things everywhere. If they need a pair of swim shoes for camp, all the stores will be sold out. As soon as camp is over, they will be fully stocked. The same goes for love. When you are looking for it too hard, you will never find it. When you are merely open to the possibilities, people will come out of the woodwork and you will have your pick of the litter.

In the meantime, while you are waiting for your first love or your next love, love yourself. Take care of you first and realize that not everyone is meant to be in our life forever. All that happens—good or bad—happens because it is supposed to. They are all life lessons. Make sure that you are an attentive student.

Dear G-Spot:

I have been seeing this guy for about eleven months. I love being with him; we can discuss anything; the sex is wonderful; and he helps me out a lot. My problem is that I don't know anything about him of great significance. He has shared some things with me, like where he is from originally, when he moved here, that he has a house and a dog, and what he does for a living. All of that is hearsay, though, because I have no proof of any of it. I have never been to his place and he won't give me his phone number or even call me. We talk on the computer every night for hours at a time, but that's it. On the weekends, he spends the entire day with me, claiming that he has to work late during the week. We have never spent the entire night together. He says that it is because he can't leave his dog at home alone overnight. Deep down inside I feel like he's hiding something or is ashamed to be seen with me. He has met a few of my friends but that's only because they were over at my place when he was there. We never go anyplace or do anything together. He says that he doesn't like meeting new people and has anxiety about it. He seems to have an excuse for everything, but I do love him and he says he loves me. I don't know how to confront him about anything. When I do attempt to talk with him, he gets mad and asks which one of my friends has started talking junk again. My friends do think it's strange that I have never been to his place and that we have never spent the night together. What should I do?

Dazed and Confused

Dear Dazed and Confused:

In a nutshell, you need to leave him alone. He is obviously either in a serious, committed relationship or married. That is the only reasonable explanation for his actions. The mere fact that you do not have a phone number for him speaks volumes, and that is complete bullshit about him not wanting to leave his dog home alone overnight. He cannot spend the night with you because that would be his ass when he got home the next day.

You are a beautiful woman with a beautiful spirit, and this man is taking complete advantage of you. You need to practice self-love and forget about him; cut him off immediately. As long as he is occupying your time and your emotions, you cannot be free to discover a new and real love. You have lost eleven months of valuable time, time that can never be regained. Do not feel bad about this, because it is not your fault. The man is a bastard, a lowdown, dirty bastard at that. He is not worth the oxygen that he is utilizing on this earth.

Do not worry about it, but do cut off all communication with him. Chalk this up to a valuable lesson learned and you will recognize and appreciate a real man when he comes your way. I am sorry for what you have gone through but glad that you reached out to me. In the bottom of your soul, I am sure that you already realized what was up with him. You only needed me to confirm it.

Blessings,
Zane

Dear G-Spot:

I have been dating my man for a year now. I am thirty-seven and he is fifty-one. In the beginning of our relationship, he started reading your books because he is always curious about my interests. Your books opened up an entire new level of freakiness in him and he never had a partner to explore that side with . . . until now. I am a freak, all the way, and he loves it. He is a pleaser and I have never had that before. He lasts, without Viagra, like no man I have ever had. Usually, I make a man buckle at the knees from flexing my pussy muscles on his dick alone. This man craves everything we do to each other like a thirst that has finally been quenched. He says that I am his lady in the street and his freak in the bedroom, which leads me to one of my dilemmas. During our sessions, he calls me vulgar names like hoe, slut, and bitch. He wants me to chant these names back at him during the sessions. In the beginning, the shit was a turn-on, but now I feel like, "What have I created?" I wonder if I am just good for the freaky shit that we do. We have many things in common and enjoy each other's company outside of sex.

My second dilemma is how we can be in a relationship and not have our parents be aware of it. Our families have been *extremely close* for more than thirty years; our deceased fathers were best friends. Only a select few in each of our families knows that we are dating. Our friends know and were surprised, but they highly approve. He believes that it is none of our parents' concern, but I still feel like I am his private freaky treasure. The name-calling during sex does not help. I feel like our parents deserve to know. His kids and my child also approve. Am I reading too much into this parents thing? He says they know but are minding their own business. What do you think and how can I break it to him that those names in the bedroom are degrading without hurting him? I have shared that the names are uncomfortable before but to no avail.

Freaky Treasure

Dear Freaky Treasure:

I can honestly say that I have never heard of a single, fifty-one-year-old man trying to hide a relationship from his parents. Hell, he is more than half a century old. That is crazy and suspect, for lack of a better word. Add to that the fact that your families have been close for decades and it becomes even more alarming. He needs to "claim it," meaning that unless he can be open about his feelings for you with everyone, then he is perpetrating for some reason. Your children and friends know, yet he does not want to discuss it with your parents. Quite frankly, I would come straight out with the shit and see what happens. If he is real in his intentions, he will step up to the plate and profess his undying love for you. If he is full of shit, he will show his ass and, trust me, it is better to see those butt cheeks now than four or five years down the road. As for the degrading names, send his ass a cease and desist letter if you have to, but do not allow it, even if that means splitting altogether. While I do believe lovers should concede to do certain things to please their mates, I draw the line at being demeaned and belittled. I am at a loss, but I hope this helps in some way. This is one of the strangest things that I have ever heard and sounds more like a teenage drama than grown folks' business.

Blessings,
Zane

Dear G-Spot:

I was dating this guy for two years and then we broke up. We are still "friends" if you know what I mean. Sometimes, I feel like we are still together. Recently, he has been acting funny. He has a pet name for me that he used to call me on a regular basis. Now he has begun to call me by my real name instead. When he comes over, he acts like I am not here. I am too young for this. Do you think I should move on, even though I love him?

Confused but Hanging in There

Dear Confused but Hanging in There:

Move on and move on quickly. He is giving you all of the obvious signs. First of all, you broke up but are still fucking, so that is all he has been using you for. I recently did a blog about people still sleeping with their ex-mates and asked why people do it. The majority do it because of convenience and knowing what they will be getting instead of going into a new situation blind. Your friend has gotten to the point where he is ready to move on, but he plans to string you along until he finds the object of his affection. Beat him to the punch and lose his number. You are young and you will bounce back from this. Just make sure you learn from it as well.

Blessings,
Zane

Dear G-Spot:

I'm a twenty-eight-year-old woman who has been single for two years after breaking up with my kids' father. I feel like I have a target on my back, like there is something wrong with me since we didn't work out. I was with him for twelve years and I don't remember how to get back out there. I don't really want a relationship; I just want to find someone to fuck me good when I need it. It's been so long I forgot how to get back in the game. Help!

Completely Undersexed

Dear Completely Undersexed:

After twelve years, it is hard to get back out there, and I have many friends who have been through the same thing. The good part is that you are not looking for a serious relationship, because men willing to dick you down are in no short supply. The only thing missing is you not letting them know you want a dick down. Trust me when I say that the majority of men out there are not going to turn down sex. Do you flirt with men at all, or do you wait for them to approach you? You need to get aggressive. If a man appeals to you, let him know it. Men are egotistical and love to be told they are desired, even more so than women. If you were in a relationship for twelve years, that means you are a seasoned sister. Do not be apprehensive about coming on to men. The only caution I have for you is to make sure you practice safe sex because any man willing to fuck "anyone" on the drop of a dime will fuck "everyone." I wish you well in your endeavors.

Blessings,

Zane

Dear G-Spot:

I grew up in a Christian/Muslim home in South Carolina. Sex was never discussed in our house, and when I was twenty-two and a virgin, I got married. Needless to say, I was terrified of sex and I think I still am. I am divorced now and I believe sex had something to do with it. My ex-husband always downed me and he would get physical. But he would expect me to have sex with him whenever. He did not get what he wanted and of course he found it elsewhere. Now I am curious about sex but, then again, I am not. I am entirely confused about it because I have never experienced it in this "GREAT" way a lot of women talk about. If I think about sex with my ex-husband, I will get sick to my stomach. I do not understand why I feel the way I do. Do you have any ideas? Thanks!

Faith-Hope-Love-Peace

Dear Faith-Hope-Love-Peace:

Your dilemma is one of the main reasons why I do what I do. You are not alone. There are tons of females in the world who have the same negative thoughts about sex because of the actions of one or a few men. Having disappointing sexual experiences at a young age can create a lifetime of yearning for more. I encourage you to believe that there are good men out there, because they truly do exist. I am in the middle of a nasty divorce, but dealing with "evil" has made me appreciate real men when they come into my life. Because of the lack of discussion about sex as you were growing up, you are keeping most of your feelings within. Let me say this: you not only deserve but you are entitled to enjoy making love. Please do not let that one man destroy your life to the point where you regret it in the end. Open your heart, love again, but take your time and choose a man who respects you, adores you, and understands your significance. Feel free to email me anytime.

Blessings,
Zane

Dear G-Spot:

In the beginning of relationships, sex is totally different (some good/some bad) than it is after a couple of years or even months. Why do you think this is?

Changing Faces

Dear Changing Faces:

Simply put, people tend to get lazy once they are settled into a relationship, especially if they have received the commitment they were searching for in the first place. In a sense, once they claim the golden ring (or engagement ring in some cases), they are no longer willing to jump over fences and through hoops to please their mate. This applies to both men and women. It is the responsibility of both parties in a relationship to continue to find creative and innovative ways to please one another. I realize that most people are exhausted by the time they come home from work, but you must put aside some quality time for your mate. If not, what is the point of the relationship?

Do something completely out of character, like meeting him in the parking garage of his office building after work with nothing on but a trench coat and giving him something he can feel before the tedious drive home in work traffic. Go to an adult store together and purchase a sex toy both of you can utilize. Better yet, buy two or three different things while you are there. Pull the shades, bolt the doors, unplug the phones, and hide out in the house for an entire weekend and stay completely undressed the entire time. Or go to a hotel for the weekend and toss on a robe just long enough to answer the door for room service. Give each other a candlelight bubble bath and then lick each other dry. The list goes on and on.

The bottom line is this. You know the old adage, "If you don't make time for exercise, you'll have to make time for illness." Well, if you don't make time for intimacy, you'll have to make time for stress, frustration, disappointment, and possibly loneliness if your partner decides to satisfy his needs elsewhere. Whatever you and your partner do to enhance your sex life, you need to do it together, because you are only as good as the lover lying beside you, and reciprocity is everything.

Blessings,

Zane

Dear G-Spot:

I am the single mother of two, going to law school, and working. I have been writing letters to this man at work for about a week. I realize that I should not get involved with anyone at work, but I cannot help it. My letters are from my dreams that I constantly have about him. I have been dreaming about sex for a long time, but I had never pictured a man's face until his. It has been about two years since I have had sex . . . and I want to have it with him. He tells me that he likes the letters and that I practically gave him a heart attack. He did read one at work and could not get his bearings. My question is: Should I keep up with the letters and invite him over or tell him that he owes me a letter? I am forty-three and ready to roll with him. Should I stop?

Horny at Work

Dear Horny at Work:

I sincerely hope that your coworker is single. Even if he is, that is the tip of the iceberg as far as issues with this situation are concerned. Dating a coworker is always risky, but I will not pretend that people are not fucking in offices throughout the world, sometimes while they are on the clock. However, I believe that you have latched onto this man because he is "convenient dick." He is someone attractive whom you are around a lot, and with your hectic schedule of dealing with the kids, school, and work, I am sure that socializing is practically nonexistent. That does not mean that you should continue to pursue him. I would stop, go back to normal, and see if he makes a move. It may be that he is simply being friendly and trying not to hurt your feelings by stating that your letter almost gave him a heart attack. Of course he will say he liked it. That does not guarantee that he likes

you. While I cannot tell you definitively what to do, I would suggest holding off and seeing what develops on his end. Don't be surprised or disappointed if he never brings it up again.

Blessings,
Zane

Dear G-Spot:

First, let me tell you a little about me. I am a very attractive woman in my
forties but look like I am in my thirties. I have a fair complexion and green
eyes. I am 5'7" tall and 150 pounds. I get a ton of compliments about my
beauty . . . but no dates. I am tired of being lonely, and I want to get married
and settle down with a man I can call my own. Here is the problem. Only
younger men, married men, or attached men approach me. Been there,
done all of that, and not trying to do any of it again.

I want to get with a man my own age—who is truly single—but they run
the other way when I step to them. I am put into the "pretty, yellow, good
hair, light eyes, all the men want her" category, which I hate. I have tried to
develop a relationship with available men my age, but they are intimidated
by me. I am romantic, loving, and sexual, in the prime of my life. I know how
to work it out in the bedroom when I do have a man in my life, but it has
been a good while. I like large, dark-skinned men with bald heads and pretty
smiles. I find them extremely sexy. However, they look at me and assume
that they do not stand a chance. That is simply not true. Meanwhile, I stand
alone, just me and my fantasies of what I would do if I had a man. I am a
good black woman with much to offer, but how do I overcome this "syndrome"? It upsets me a great deal. How can I get what I want and deserve?

Good Black Woman

Dear Good Black Woman:

It's ironic that you should pose this question to me now. I just attended
a book club meeting yesterday where we were discussing a book that had a
chapter on not taking things personally, especially the way others view you,
because it is simply the way they were trained and raised to view people.
One older woman spoke about the fact that she was always confident
around men, even though she is getting up in age and is large. She talked
about how she flirted with a man at a fight last weekend and how he said
he would never forget her because her personality was so outgoing.

The point is that you keep saying that the men you want are afraid to approach you. The solution is simple. You have to approach them and let them know you think they have it going on. It might shock them. Some of them might even pass the hell out, but I am sure any man will enjoy being told a woman finds him attractive and interesting.

I too have been plagued by the younger man syndrome lately. Once I turned thirty, I had trouble finding men my own age to date. The bottom line is to be aggressive and go for what you know. You are undoubtedly attractive. Make it work to your benefit and remember not to let a moment go by if you see a man who interests you. Chances are, he will never come your way again.

Blessings,
Zane

Dear G-Spot:

I was wondering what should I do to get the attention of a brother I want to have sex with? I am a beautiful, sensual sister with a nice figure and all, but I do not know how to exude sexuality in my behavior. As a black woman, yes, I should know this. I flirt a little here and there, and I can turn brothers on mentally. I do turn heads, but how do I maintain that attention?

Female friends say it is my mannerisms. Men look at me all the time, but I pay them no mind because I am afraid of getting rejected . . . I guess. I just don't know. Male friends say brothers are crazy not to go for me, because I have it all. But they also suggest that my mentality frightens weak brothers. I know it is not all on the brothers, and there are things I need to work on myself as well. Please respond.

Exuding Confidence

Dear Exuding Confidence:

A lot of it depends on your situation. Is this someone you work with or someone you know on a casual basis? You say you want to have sex with him, but do you want a serious relationship as well? I will assume that you know him casually and that you do want a relationship. Therefore, my suggestion would be for you to invite him out on a date. I would not have him come over to your home, because some men feel like they are put on the line either to perform or get kicked to the curb. Invite him out for drinks and dinner. Someplace quiet, but not overkill. Do not go to a movie, because that leaves two hours of time where you can't really talk at all. Save that for later. Tell the brother that you admire him, that you think he has it going on, and ask him about his life goals. Where does he see himself in five years? What is he searching for in life? In a woman? Be open and honest and discuss your own needs, because there can be no progress without discussion. If all of his answers seem satisfactory—and by this time, he should definitely know you are interested in him—make a move on him after dinner. You do not have to sleep with him the first night, but leave him with something to think about. Actually, it would probably be better if you made him wait a while, because he will want you even more.

I can relate to how you feel because I was like that for years. I looked straight through men while they were looking at me because I was not interested in yet another disappointing relationship and a bunch of Jerry Springer drama. Then I read a quote that summed it all up for me: "The past is a guiding post and not a hitching post." It is important that we learn from the past, but we must not dwell in it. While the men who rejected or hurt you are somewhere getting it on with their new women, you are hindering your own happiness by letting the maggots remain in your thoughts. Learn to judge each man individually, because there are a lot of sincere, romantic brothers out there who are just as apprehensive about approaching women they are interested in. Guess why? Fear of rejection. Please go for it, because life is short. Let me know what happens.

Blessings,
Zane

Dear G-Spot:

I was in this relationship with a guy for over five years. Sex was off the hook with him. I had the pleasure of growing with him sexually. He and I experienced everything together. The problem is that I was so in love with this guy. He was a wonderful provider and took great care of me financially, but the little things like him saying thank you, you look nice today, or even asking how I was feeling were missing from our relationship. He would never talk to me about us and I began to feel stagnated. The relationship wasn't going anywhere emotionally.

I ended the relationship and then felt like crap. I love this guy but miss "the Dick." It took us over a year to start creeping. Every time he sees me, mostly on a weekly basis, he has at least one of his friends or frat brothers— or whoever else he decides to pimp me out to—join us. Don't get me wrong.

Sometimes I long for it to be the two of us alone. I'm afraid to speak on it because I don't want him to turn around and stop fucking me altogether. What do you think I should do? I am seeking your advice and thanking you in advance for your time.

Confused in Brooklyn

Dear Confused in Brooklyn:

There is no nice way for me to say this so I am just going to say it. The brother is using you. He has no respect for you and you said it best when you chose the word "pimp." While I understand that you love this man, the feelings are not reciprocated and, as hard as it will be to break it off, you need to do that immediately. I hope that you are practicing safe sex with all of these men, but even if you are, we are living in the world of AIDS now and you must be very careful and treat your body like the temple that it is.

Trust me when I say that there is someone out there who can and will love you with the respect and admiration that you deserve. Someone who will tell you that you look beautiful, someone who will ask about your day and thank you for merely being you. This man realizes that you love him to the brink of desperation, and you must get away from him. Do you honestly think that he can take you seriously enough to ever marry you? Girlfriend, email me back when you get rid of him. Nothing good can come from this.

Blessings,
Zane

Dear G-Spot:

My so-called stepbrother—the son of my mother's boyfriend of eight years—recently told me that he has liked me for a long time. He has been trying to deny the feelings for years but now realizes that he cannot go on wondering what if. I am in a relationship and while I do care about my stepbrother, I know a little bit too much about him. He has dated my friends, I have dated his, and I do not think this can work. I do not want to hurt him or pass up something that might be meant to be. Many people have commented that we seemed to like each other, but I have never thought of it like that. We have known each other for more than fifteen years. He swears that I am the one for him. What should I do? Do I run from these feelings and just remain friends? Or do I go with the flow and let things happen naturally?

Lost and Confused in Memphis

Dear Lost and Confused in Memphis:

I am sorry it took me so long to respond, but I really wanted to give your dilemma some serious thought. My first inclination was to tell you to go for it if, and only if, you have true feelings for him. However, you said something to the effect that you had never really thought about it. That leads me to think that you are considering this only because he brought it up and has probably laid it on you pretty thick. Don't enter into a relationship with your stepbrother unless you have romantic feelings for him.

Will it work if you do? Good question, and you are probably the best judge of that. On top of the normal problems of any relationship, you will both have your parents and friends (you did say you have dated each other's friends) to contend with. Most parents would have a problem with this budding situation, but your parents might be cool. You need to know that for sure, so I suggest making a fleeting, teasing remark in front of them, alluding to hooking up with him, and see what they say. The next thing you need to think about is whether or not your friends will try to sabotage the relationship because of romantic interest they might have in one of you.

To me, there just seems to be a whole lot that could go wrong. Add to that the fact that you are already in a relationship. What becomes of him? Is this a serious relationship? Is it one that holds a possible commitment in the future? Do you really want to give it up?

Last, but definitely not least, what would be the backlash if you got together with him, fell head over heels in love, made plans, and then ended up breaking up? You could never go back to the way things are now. As long as you realize that and you are willing to take that risk, as long as you examine everything before you act, then follow your heart. Just make sure you are following your heart and not his.

Blessings,
Zane

Marriages in Jeopardy

*M*arriage is meant to be a very sacred union between two people who have no intention of ever becoming emotionally or physically tied to another person for the rest of eternity. Most people mean their marriage vows when they take them, but oftentimes—these days more often than not, according to statistics—the initial commitment begins to wane and ultimately dissipates altogether. We live in a time when most people who get married before they turn thirty are merely doing a practice run. By their early to midthirties, they might be on their second, third, or possibly even fourth marriage. A lot of this is because of lack of communication, which is covered in another section. Then there is the sexual incompatibility.

When people first hook up, especially during their younger years, they are usually DINK—double income no kids—relationships. That means you can wine and dine whenever, hang out together whenever, fuck all over the house or apartment, sleep late, and scream out each other's names in different languages without a care in the world. Once the kids arrive, the pounds start packing on, financial worries are raised, and our bodies respond to aging, things can change. They have to change. Like that song says, "Everything must change! Nothing stays the same!"

Here is the thing, though. Couples have to learn to endure those changes together, without allowing stress and other factors to come between them. When it comes to sexuality, they have to grow together, remain passionate, be committed to making sure their mate is satisfied, etc. It is too easy to place the blame of a failing relationship on each other and it is even easier

to turn to someone else for comfort. Making things work out is the difficult part. Now, I am not saying that all marriages are meant to be, since
mine was a complete nightmare. However, if you feel like yours is worth
saving and if you truly love your mate, do not give up so quickly. Try to
figure out what you can do to make things improve and encourage your
mate to do his or her part. Having an affair is certainly not going to solve
anything. If you have one, be prepared for what might happen if your
spouse finds out. Evaluate whether the affair is worth losing everything.
Chances are that a roll in the hay is not.

Even if you are not thinking about cheating, do not let your marriage
dissipate into nothing. Fight for it. Read some books, go to counseling,
plan romantic vacations, or do something you have never done before.

Dear G-Spot:

I'm thirty years old and my husband is forty-two. My problem is I can't
connect with him on the sex thing. Once I discovered your site I suggested
he check it out and then I started suggesting little things I learned while
reading your site. He still doesn't get it. Most of the time he brings me right
to the edge, but I can't come. Oral sex is great but I need the big "D" to
back it up. I recently started masturbating and I love it, but I want more. I've
even considered having an affair with an old homey-lover-friend, but I want
great sex with my husband. He's a one-timer and I want that one time to
count. We tried lots of different things and we talk about how we want it
and what we want, but it's not working. Any other tips?

Reaching for Straws

Dear Reaching for Straws:

I'm a bit confused. You've already talked about what each of you wants, so
that isn't the problem. Are you saying that his performance during actual
penetration is lacking? I did notice that there is an age difference, but he is
still young. Are either one of you under a great deal of stress? That can really
affect your sex drive and ability to have orgasms. You say that you can't connect to him on the sex thing. Are the two of you connecting on all other
things, or are there other circumstances that might possibly be carrying over
into your bedroom? Having an affair is definitely not the solution, unless
you are willing to risk the possibility of losing your husband altogether.

My suggestion is for the two of you to continue to try additional things:
role playing, sex in unusual places, romantic getaways, etc. That brings me

to my last question. Is sex taken for granted, or do the two of you still engage in romantic things? If not, that is the place to start. If all else fails, I would suggest counseling before allowing the marriage to dissolve.

Blessings,

Zane

Dear G-Spot:

Zane, I need some serious advice. I am a twenty-seven-year-old woman. I have been with my husband for nine years, married for seven. We have children together and he is a *wonderful man* in every way, no joke. I am happily married, but I want to have sex with someone else, just once. I have not sought advice from anyone I know personally, because no one could understand. I have not been with anyone else as an adult. No, he was not my first. I had three other partners before him, but they were all when I was extremely young. At first, I brushed this off as a phase, but it is on my mind daily. My husband is very attractive and I have no legitimate complaints. What is wrong with me? I have everything a woman can ask for, but this hunger for new dick is almost uncontrollable. I want to go to the other side of the fence, have a quick picnic, and then come back to my life. What do I do? Please help!

Need New Dick

Dear Need New Dick:

You need to forget about hopping the fence for a picnic and chow down in your own bedroom. As you said yourself, you have everything a woman could ask for. Your husband is attractive and he has loved you for nine long years. In today's world, that is like being with a man for fifty years back in the day. Sisters have a hard time finding someone to stay committed to them for nine months, rather less nine years. You do not need new dick; you need to reinvent the dick you already have. Seven years of marriage means you have the proverbial "seven-year itch" and you need to work it out. I can understand your curiosity since your experience with other men was a long time ago and limited, but trust me, when you turn grass over, it is pure dirt, not greener. Put on something sexy, dim the lights, put on some old school slow jams, reminisce, and make love to that *wonderful* husband of yours until his toes curl up.

Blessings,

Zane

Dear G-Spot:

I am a married woman and have been with my man for nearly seventeen years. Our lovemaking sucks the majority of the time. Mind you, we both can reach an orgasm in record time—five minutes or less. It's not my ability to orgasm that is the issue. I can pretty much have them at will, with or without him. I am tired of this rat race, this get yours, I'll get mine, and we can go to sleep. I am also worried because our foreplay and kissing have waned. I really enjoy kissing and it has long been the basis for causing me to get hot and bothered. Whenever I bring it up, he says we do kiss, but I am not referring to bird pecks in the morning. He thinks I am being silly, reading way too many romance novels, and not spending enough time in reality.

Let me back up a little. I am thirty-two and my husband is forty. Again, we have been together nearly seventeen years. You do the math. He was my first lover and, for some reason, I feel cheated now. I think he takes me for granted and feels that as long as he supplies me with sex, I should not be complaining. My question is: Does foreplay mean a lot in lovemaking or am I a hopeless romantic for wanting flowers, candles, slow music, sweet kisses on the neck, back rubs, and tongue kissing until my lips feel bruised? Or is it a rat race to orgasm?

                                                                Hopeless in Denver

Dear Hopeless in Denver:

No, you are not a hopeless romantic. Foreplay and kissing are extremely important for lovemaking, especially for women. The reason being that women—in general—take longer than men to become stimulated. A lot of times, women fake headaches because they know that by the time they get sufficiently aroused, the act is usually over and, therefore, what is the point? Just because you have been together for seventeen years is no excuse for laziness when it comes to sex. You can tell your husband I said that, if you want. Orgasms should never be in the same sentence as rat race. Insist on the romance or withhold the sex. That will bring him around.

                                                                Blessings,
                                                                Zane

Communication Problems

$\mathcal{T}$he word "communication" can send shudders through some people. "Oh, no, they expect me to *communicate!*" Yes, we do and you should. I feel that public speaking or speech should be a required course for high school graduation. I have never seen so many tongue-tied people in my life. So many people who are afraid to express their emotions or tell people what is wrong with their behavior.

The perfect example is talk shows. Our ancestors are probably turning over in their graves wondering, "What the fuck are they doing?" People go across the country to tell the person they sleep next to every single night a "secret." First of all, there should be no secrets—or a need to keep secrets—in a healthy relationship. Second, people should not have to be in front of a studio audience, knowing that millions of people will see them reveal their shame, in order to get it out. A lot of people assume that talk shows are a hoax. I could not disagree more. Just like the people who try out for *American Idol* who should know they sound like sick hyenas but really think they can blow, people go on these talk shows because that is their only recourse for speaking openly and honestly to their loved ones.

Fear constitutes the biggest part of it, fear of how someone will react. Or there is the lashing-out effect—people who want to hurt someone else in public, like the prostitute daughter who comes on *The Jerry Springer Show* to tell her mother that she slept with her man to pay off her cell phone bill. Husband and wife, parent and child, boss and employee, lover and lover— it is all the same. People do not feel like they can be themselves around those they love. I will readily admit that I felt the same way at times when I was much younger, but at a certain point I decided that I was going to live my life for me, and as long as I was not intentionally harming another person, I was and am entitled to do that. How about you? Do you honestly communicate your feelings to everyone? Or do you put their feelings above your own? Do you seek emotional or physical comfort outside of your relationships because of fear that you will be wrongly judged?

Communicating is not about lashing out in anger and pushing someone's hot spots on purpose. That is pure meanness. However, you should express yourself in a calm and reassuring way. Instead of an all-out attack, speak your mind without giving him a way to come back at you. Here is an example:

A young woman is waiting for her husband to come home from work so that she can get to her aqua kickboxing class at the pool. He was supposed to be home an hour earlier but did not call. The kids have been fed, bathed, and all the homework is completed, but she cannot leave until he gets there. When he walks into the door she can say:

A: "Why are you so damn late? I'm about to miss my class!"

B: "I'm so glad to see you. If I hurry, I might still be able to make part of the class!"

Now, if she says A, she leaves herself open to be cursed out with a typical answer like, "Who the fuck are you talking to like that?" But if she says B, what can he say?

I hope you get my drift. Think before you speak and remember that the way you go at a person is the way you can expect him to come back at you.

Dear G-Spot:

First, I would like to say that I think your manuals, stories, and books are tight. I am writing to get your advice on where to find a good man. It seems like the guys who get all up in my face ain't nothing, ain't trying to be nothing, and ain't trying to go nowhere in life. I am twenty-two, a senior in college, and I just want to know what a good girl has got to do to find a good man.

Searching

Dear Searching:

Wow, first let me say that you seem to have a very bleak outlook on life when it comes to men. Not to say that I blame you, because it is what it is and if you have been running into only shitty-ass men, then you have every right to be concerned. Now, since you are a senior in college, I am assuming that there are males who are seniors at the same college who have some goals and aspirations in life. If all the ones who interest you are taken, then start hanging out at meetings and events held by professional organizations, beginning with the particular profession you plan to enter. There is nothing better than common interests, and you will certainly have a bond with someone who decided on the same career as you.

Definitely do not settle for a man who has nothing going on for him. You don't need an idiot laid up on your sofa playing Xbox while you go to work every day. Fuck that. You need someone who will at least carry his own weight. I will not harp on that since you have already apparently figured out that much, and good for you. Some sisters never figure out their actual worth.

Once you graduate, or even if you can before, go on a vacation. If none of your female friends can make it, go alone; explore a new city and the type of men the city offers. Don't go someplace and fuck a bunch of men, but leave yourself open to the possibilities. Maybe have dinner or go to a movie with a man, but keep the situation public. If the man or men you meet are worth anything, they will not be pressuring you into sex while you are there over the space of a weekend. They will be willing to spend some time and effort to get to know you better. If not, fuck them too.

Concentrate on finishing school, because the man for you will emerge sooner or later, when you are not even looking. Meanwhile, if you have sex with a less than desirable man, realize that it is for mere physical release and nothing more. Do not get caught up in feelings for someone who cannot contribute to his own welfare, rather less yours.

Blessings,
Zanc

Dear G-Spot:

My boyfriend is extremely sweet to me and we love each other tremendously. He makes me happy in every way—except in the bedroom. I do not know how to tell him that he needs to improve without hurting his feelings. Please reply and tell me how I can approach the subject with him.

Protector of Feelings

Dear Protector of Feelings:

If you do not open up and communicate with your man, your sexual dissatisfaction will fester inside you like a disease until one day you either blurt it out nastily or you cheat. If you are not satisfied, chances are that he might not be either. For all you know he might have another chick on the side already. I always like to keep it real, so sorry if this sounds harsh. What do you do to blow his mind in the bedroom? To motivate him to pleasure you more? Do you just lie there, or do you lick him all over, suck his dick, and ride him like the pony express? Chances are that you do not. The two of you need to learn how to pleasure each other better. The only way that can happen is to talk about it. Instead of telling him that he needs improvement, ask him how you can improve. He will be pleasantly surprised that you care enough to ask, because most women never do. Here is the key, though. Whatever he says—within reason—you should be prepared at least to try. If there is the slightest apprehension that you may not want to make his desires come to fruition, then do not ask. For sure then, your relationship will be in trouble. Part of growing up is learning to talk openly—with anyone. Start in your own bed.

> Blessings,
> Zane

Dear G-Spot:

My boyfriend and I have been having sex for over a year. We've done it just about anywhere and everywhere, but the last time we had sex, he said that I was really open. He stared at my pussy and said it looked like he could fit his whole hand inside. I noticed that I was kind of loose, but I can't stop fucking him. It's too good. How can I tighten up? He said every time we have sex, it's tight at first but after a few strokes I'm wide open. I haven't been with anyone else, so is there another explanation? Thanks a lot. I love your books. You are a very talented writer.

> Too Open

Dear Too Open:

First off, your boyfriend is extremely rude and insensitive. I hope that youth and immaturity are his excuses. Then again, there really are no excuses for that. To say that a woman's pussy is too big is the equivalent of a woman saying that a man's dick is too small. Unless he is hung like a mule, maybe he is the problem. I say that sarcastically, but men like him really piss me off.

More than likely, you get extremely wet during sexual arousal and that is the reason his dick eases in and out so easily. Some women are naturally heavily lubricated, and the more pleasure they experience, the wetter they get. The problem is when a woman is bone-dry, because something is seriously wrong. I realize that you want to stay with him, so I suggest that you learn how to do Kegel exercises: simply squeeze your vaginal muscles and hold them for several seconds before releasing them. It's sort of like holding it in when you have to pee. In fact, you can practice it when you go to the bathroom. Start to urinate and then squeeze to hold the rest in before releasing it in small streams. This will get you used to squeezing his dick during sex. Another good tool, even though it is not advertised as a sex aid, is the Thighmaster. If you place it up between your thighs instead of between your knees, it will work wonders.

I hope this helps, but on the real tip, any man who would come out of his mouth and say something like that to you is probably not worth your time, especially a man you have been involved with long-term. I wish you well.

Blessings,

Zane

Dear G-Spot:

I have this situation. I am twenty-nine and married for the first time with two children. We are going through some hard times right now and can't seem to agree on our financial situation. I have been a dental assistant for the past year and a half. I make pretty good money. My husband is thirty-eight and this is his second marriage. He drives a truck for a local beer company. He makes decent money, but he has an outside child whom his checks are garnished to support. He also provides all of us with health insurance. Every month I add up the urgent bills and split them between the two of us, but he never has his half. I end up making up the difference as well as buying the groceries, children's clothing, etc. I'm not saying he doesn't pay anything at all, but he will cover one or two bills and nothing else.

Even when we go out on outings, he expects me to pay for everything because I make more money. I work extremely hard for my money and deserve an occasional treat. Sometimes I will splurge for an outfit or get my hair done and will purchase a pair of shoes when I have extra money. He gets angry and declares that I could've bought him something or given him the money. This has become a huge issue since I became a dental assistant and it is making me want out of the marriage. It bothers him that I make more money but he refuses to admit it.

I am having crazy sexual thoughts and dreams about other men. When I got married, his dick wasn't all that—very short and little, but the situation can work when he uses his tongue right. I liked him a lot and I wasn't trying to make sex a big enough thing to prevent him from marrying me. Plus I was scared because I became pregnant less than a year after we started dating so I got married but now feel the entire marriage is a lie. I loved him but was never in love with him, and now that love is quickly dissolving. Please offer me some advice, and keep the books coming, girl.

Sticky Situation

Dear Sticky Situation:

From the onset of your email I already knew your marriage was in trouble. How? Because you said you were on your first marriage. That statement alone indicates that you believe it will not be your last. Many women find themselves—especially as they grow older—dealing with the mixed family situation, myself included. This means we have to deal with men with prior obligations and it is mandatory that they fulfill them, because no child asks to be born and they all have needs. However, that does not mean that his obligations to you and the family you have together are any less.

Being that you pay the majority of the bills, he is being greedy and selfish even to suggest that you should not treat yourself to something special every now and then. After all, when was the last time he bought you an outfit, a pair of shoes, or paid to get your hair done? There are many men who are so old-fashioned that they have issues when their woman makes more money than they do. Ironically, they have no problems helping them spend it or asking for some of it.

Your fantasizing about other men is common. But you need to separate the two issues. One issue is the selfish nature of your husband when it comes to money. The other is the lack of sexual satisfaction you receive. I understand wanting to get married because of the pregnancy, but do not stay in a situation and ultimately waste your life away. So many stay for the sake of the children, but most of the time the children are negatively affected by growing up in a dysfunctional household where there is constant bickering and lack of affection.

You need to search your soul; you need to pray; you need to have a decisive plan of action in case your marriage does end—by the doing of either party—and you need to reevaluate your priorities in life. I don't want to become known as an advocate for divorce, but I am an advocate for being happy. Life is too short to suffer through it.

Blessings,
Zane

Dear G-Spot:

What would be the best way to express my feeling toward this boy whom I really like? I do not know how to express what I feel. Could you give me a little advice?

In Need of Words

Dear In Need of Words:

What do you feel about him? Do you even know? That might be why you cannot express it. If you are infatuated with him, that is normal, but make sure you feel him out first before you throw it all out there. You need to open up some form of communication with him, even if it is about his favorite sport. He might not be what you imagine he is. You might not want him after you get to know him. Like most women, I have thought someone was something different before I got to know him. One such experience almost cost me everything because I really fell for the okey-doke. He was not at all what I thought. Become his friend first, and if that cannot happen, it will not go any farther anyway. Friends sometimes become lovers and sometimes they figure out that they are better off as friends.

Blessings,
Zane

Dear G-Spot:

You have helped me and so many thousands of people, I'm sure, not only to have a healthier and more pleasurable sex life but also to communicate effectively. I try to keep it real, without intentionally offending people. I might catch hell for this one, but I know this girl. Although she is a lame screw and just lies there like a bump on a log, that is not the pressing issue.

How do I tell her that she smells downtown? I generally shower before sex and I attempt to follow the rule of heating up the skillet before you put the meat in. I love giving and receiving oral sex. But, even after showering, the smell is downright nauseous. Please help. I do want to be both sensitive and considerate here.

Needing to Speak on It

Dear Needing to Speak on It:

I have heard this often, from both men and women who want their lovers to be more conscientious about their hygiene. The fact of the matter is that a lot of people are "immune" to their scents and may not even realize that it is a problem. Think of all the people you run across with bad breath or underarm odor who have it every single time you see them. Most have grown so accustomed to their odors that they do not smell them, while they might practically knock other people the fuck out. My suggestion is that you shower with her and scrub her pussy yourself. Hell, make douching sound erotic and tell her that you want to give her one. If the smell continues, she might have a urinary tract infection or something even more serious. Make sure she gets her yearly Pap smear and also encourage her to eat more fruits and vegetables. We truly are what we eat; that goes for both men and women.

Blessings,
Zane

Dissatisfied Lovers/
Lack of Sex Drive

*A*fter careful consideration, I decided to combine dissatisfied lovers and lack of sex drive into the same chapter. When you break it down, they are pretty much the same thing, or—at the very least—a direct reflection of each other. If you are dissatisfied, you will not want to have sex at all. If you are not that sexual or have a low sex drive, then your lover will be dissatisfied. Let's examine why this happens and what can be done about it.

Sexual incompatibility leads to most disappointment in the bedroom. That is a catch-22, though. You should get to know a person emotionally before you jump into bed with him, especially in today's world with deadly STDs. Yet you might fall in love with him emotionally, and once you sleep together, the chemistry is nonexistent. What do you do then? Do you choose love over sex or sex over love? They are not the same thing by far. Anyone can fuck you, but not everyone can love you. If people needed love in order to engage in sex, prostitution would not be the world's oldest profession.

Why is it that prostitution exists? What can a stranger give a person that he cannot get from home or from his current lover? I'll tell you—the freaky shit that his lover won't engage in with him. What is really crazy is that two people might both be out cheating and doing the same exact things in the bed with their other lovers when they could be doing it with each other. They do this because of the fact that they do not want to open up.

Here is an example:

Harry married Sally after falling head over heels in love with her during college. She was the most beautiful woman who had ever walked the face of the earth, in Harry's opinion. She could do no wrong. She was everything he had ever desired and he had to make her his for life.

Sally thought the same about Harry. When she was a little girl, he was the prince she imagined coming along on a horse and rescuing her. She wanted to marry him, have two or three kids, a poodle named Peaches, and a house with a white picket fence.

Harry and Sally decided that they did not need to have sex before marriage. Their families were both devout Christians and it was not acceptable. They planned this elaborate wedding with white doves being released as they were driven away in a horse-drawn carriage to begin their new life together.

They cashed in their savings and purchased a lovely 3,500-square-foot home in the hills with a white picket fence, a playground for the kids they planned to have, and a two-car garage. Everything was perfect and they could not wait to be together forever and a day.

Their parents chipped in and sent them on a honeymoon to Hawaii, to an all-inclusive resort where they could bask on the sunny beaches all day and make sweet love all night. They arrived, checked into the hotel, and Sally went to draw a bath so she could "prepare" for her husband. She put on the flowing white negligee that one of her bridesmaids had given her at her bridal shower, where more than fifty women were in attendance.

Harry showered right quick before Sally soaked in the tub and then anxiously awaited her in the comfortable, king-size bed. He ordered champagne with strawberries and a dozen roses to greet her when she came out of the bathroom. When Sally finally did emerge, she was drop-dead gorgeous and Harry's dick automatically sprouted to attention.

He beckoned for her to join him in the bed. She waltzed over to him and climbed in, covering herself up to her neck with the down comforter. Harry offered her a flute of champagne and they toasted. Then he cut off the lights and got ready to blow her back out. Sally started complaining immediately. It hurt when he sucked her breasts. It hurt when he tried to finger her pussy. She had her legs damn near clamped shut because she dreaded him actually sticking his dick in her because the fingers already made her feel the pain. She barely rubbed his dick up and down when he asked her to. When he asked if she would put her mouth on his dick, she broke down in tears. Harry told her it was okay and then he asked her to please relax so he could enter her. Reluctantly she spread her legs and he struggled to get inside her. She lay there, holding back a scream, as he pummeled in and out of her for what seemed like an eternity while in reality it was less than ten minutes. When it was over, Sally covered herself, turned on her side, and stared at her beautiful negligee now sprawled on the floor beside the bed. She fell asleep wondering if she would ever feel comfortable giving herself to her husband. Harry fell asleep with a smile on his face, convinced that Sally would get used to the dick and would soon be a freak who slobbered on his dick when he returned home from work every night. Guess what? Ten years later, Harry still hadn't had a blow job.

Now let's back it up to the point where Sally gets in the bed and flip the script. Sally's ready to do all the freaky shit she had seen in pornos and read about in books. She really didn't even want to wear the negligee. She preferred to come out butt-naked but decided to follow the predetermined script. However, she was banking on Harry blowing her back out like she had seen Mr. Marcus do a few times in pornos. She couldn't wait to suck his juicy dick until he busted a load in her eager mouth. She had been practicing on a dildo at home, one that she hid underneath her bed.

She got into bed, and instead of Harry reaching for her, he just lay there, like he was nervous. She finally reached under the covers to feel him up and his dick was limp, no erection in sight. That's okay, she tells him. She is excited at the prospect of working him with her mouth until his dick is so hard that it can cut diamonds. She goes down on him with a vengeance, sucking like a newborn baby at her mother's breast. Five minutes later, no erection. Sally remembers some different techniques and starts working him over with her hand and her mouth; still no erection.

After thirty minutes, Sally and Harry decide to call it a night. Harry says that he's just exhausted after the wedding and the long flight. Sally says that she understands and that they will wake up in the morning and consummate their marriage. They do that, but Harry gets only semi-erect and the entire act lasts no longer than four minutes. Sally is calm and knows that Harry needs some time to get adjusted to married life. She figures that he is stressed out and will come around with a quickness once they move into their lovely home. Ten years later, Harry still can barely get it up. He has never eaten Sally's pussy and refuses to let her go down on him because it is futile. He cannot get hard that way.

Maybe the story I made up is a little extreme, but it serves its point. Life is funny; it throws us curveballs. Love is not sex and sex is not love. Which one is more important to you?

Dear G-Spot:

I am a young, ambitious woman in my early twenties. My boyfriend, whom I am madly in love with, and I recently moved in together. Although he is three years my senior, he seems quite immature when it comes to sex. Our sex life is slowly progressing, but he still sucks at oral sex. I cannot make him climax from oral stimulation either, which bothers me. After faking orgasms for two years, I finally had an orgasm from penetration for the first time a couple of months ago. The problem is that I now want sex nearly every night, but since we moved in together and things have grown more serious, he does not want it as often. He also has a hard time giving me compliments. When he does, he is so shy about it that it is like we are little kids on the playground. He is not very appreciative of the things I do for him. I am starting to feel like I need more, both mentally and physically. Do you think there is something I can do to change him, or is it time to move on?

Unsatisfied Lover

Dear Unsatisfied Lover:

There is nothing like young love. It is exciting, it is stimulating, and it is often the most complicated. Why? Because the two of you are still on a path of self-discovery, defining yourselves and trying to define a combined relationship at the same time. It sounds like your boyfriend has had a touch of reality by living with a woman. There are probably surprises for both of you, things and habits that were unexpected. In addition, because he has problems expressing his feelings, that is adding fuel to the fire.

Can you change him? No, no one can change anyone else. That is one of the greatest myths of all time and countless people have fallen for the okey-doke, believing they can change a person after they attach themselves to him or her. We are all creatures of habit. What he is now is what he will be unless he decides to make a change. I would not move on just yet, because the other side of the spectrum may not hold anything better for you. Since you have made a commitment to live together, try to work things out. Plan romantic evenings at your place to make him feel more comfortable, to help him open up about his feelings. If he is really all that shy, ask him to write things down that he would like to tell you. That way you can read it several times, analyze it, and then form a well-thought-out response. He obviously cares about you or he would not be there. The same goes for you. Give it a chance for a while longer, but realize that if things do not improve by the time that lease is up, you should reevaluate the situation and govern yourself accordingly.

Blessings,
Zane

Dear G-Spot:

I recently read your web page and I have a question. I am in a relationship with a girl whom I have been dating for a little over a year, and we have been having sex for a bit less than a year. In the beginning, we had sex often, but more recently, she isn't interested. Surprisingly, though, she has attained orgasms more recently. We were both virgins in the beginning and were inexperienced. I want to know how I can get her excited about sex again. I'm not the typical lazy, do-nothing male: I do the cooking, some of the cleaning, and she gets massages just about every day. We are both college students, so I realize that sometimes our schedules won't always be perfect to find time, but we are living together and I have tried almost everything. I have tried oral sex, but she is uncomfortable with it. Please help and thank you for your time.

College Student Full of Desire

Dear College Student Full of Desire:

Nearly a third of all females have a low sex drive. Part of it can be stress-related. You are both in school, so she is probably worried about grades and possibly holding down a job at the same time, if she is working. It is great that you take a load off of her shoulders by cooking and helping with the cleaning, and giving her massages puts you way ahead of the game. It could be that she does not have the same desire for constant sex as you do. The way sex is portrayed in the media makes it seems like the majority of people are fucking day in and day out. It is probably more like once, twice, or no more than three times a week. Everything is good in moderation, but too much of a good thing can kill the mood. Since she is uncomfortable with oral sex, it might be that she has feelings of guilt associated with having sex outside of marriage. Did she grow up in an extremely religious household? My thought is that you should give her time, if she has not cut off the sex altogether. Maybe, if you can afford it, take her on a weekend getaway. A change of environment can work wonders. I wish you the best because you sound like a good man.

Blessings,
Zane

Dear G-Spot:

After reading "How to Really Fuck a Man," I find myself wondering whether my man is worthy of me teaching him how to fuck. He is a wonderful man. We have been going out for over two years, but I have yet to experience an orgasm with him. He is not very experienced. As a matter of fact, he gave up his virginity to me. I realized that it would be tough for him to catch on, but I did not imagine it taking this long. The fact that he is not that well-endowed does not help much either. It is not that I have been out there doing every guy with a big dick, but the few I have been with all had nice, long penises and also made me cum. Help me, Zane. What can I do to make this work?

Hanging in There

Dear Hanging in There:

In a nutshell, you might either have to grin and bear it or dump him. Two years should be more than long enough for him to catch a rhythm when it comes to your sexual desires and needs. You may be at fault, because how much instruction have you been giving him? Or do you expect him to figure it out? In all fairness, the first thing you should do is seriously break it down to him. Tell him like you told me—that he is a wonderful man. Then tell him that after two years together, you want to take it to the next level. Here is the important thing: you have to be able to clearly define that level. If not, how is he supposed to please you?

Blessings,
Zane

Dear G-Spot:

I have been in a relationship for a year and a half and I am so frustrated. I sent my boyfriend off with your how to satisfy a woman article. I freaked out when I read it; it was like you had written it expressly for me. I especially was feeling the part when you stressed spending little to no time on your woman's breasts yet expecting her to suck your dick until you cum. I high-lighted that section for him. Also the part about eating pussy when you talked about men window-shopping only and them wanting women to do all sorts of things to them and their reluctance to reciprocate. I have told him numerous times that my breasts are the keys to my soul. He gives them a tiny bit of attention and that is all. He never does it good, or for enough time.

I really care for him, but I am not sure it is love. Hard to say you love a man who does not please you. I do not know if I could fall in love with a man who is a lousy lover. I have never had one, ever. I did have one or two I had to train, but eventually they got up to par.

The irony of it all is that this man has more toys than anyone I have ever met. Early on in the relationship, he took me into the bedroom, put some Ben Wa balls inside me, and then said we were going out. He plays doctor with me, too. I have to wait in the lobby. He sends a nurse out to get me. He portrays the nurse and the doctor. He has purchased vibrating panties for me to wear when we go out. I have used them only once because he vi-brated them too much and too often. I am willing to try them again, though. They were kind of hot.

Okay, here comes the big one. He likes to wear sexy women's lingerie. It freaked me out at first and I had major concerns about his sexuality. He also adores anal anything—for him or for me. He claims that he has never been with a man or anyone else—except for myself and his ex-wife, whom he married twenty-four years ago. They have been divorced for two years and I have occupied at least eighteen months of that time. In all honesty, he has indicated that he would like to experience a man at some time during his life.

As far as the female dressing, I have adjusted to it. Sometimes it is a turn-on because I have been with women before, although I prefer men. I can enjoy a woman, especially if a man is present and involved in the act. So when my man dresses in lingerie, it kind of seems like I am getting the best of both worlds.

The bottom line is that he is the worst lover I have ever had when it comes to satisfaction. I have tried to tell him what to do. He does not ever seduce me. Often he wants to satisfy me with one hand under the sheet masturbating me in a way that does not do a damn thing for me. I have reached my limit. My ultimate desire is to live together, or possibly even get married. However, if we do not resolve this, I am leaving, and like yesterday. If he would only do what you indicated in your article, I am convinced that I would be easily satisfied, since I have never experienced these issues in the past. Thank you.

In Lust with a Cross-Dresser

Dear In Lust with a Cross-Dresser:

Your man is a freak and he has been with men before, regardless of the bullshit that he is feeding you. He might have been switch-hitting the entire time he was married. It sounds like it. The cross-dressing and anal play are two sure signs, not to mention his telling you that he has thought about trying men out. Do not be surprised if you run up on him one day with a dick rammed down his throat or up his ass. Since you are bisexual yourself, that may or may not be an issue for you, but you do need to wake up and smell the coffee, because the aroma from his cup is unmistakable.

Being into toys, role-playing, and all the rest is cool but not if it is not satisfying your needs. He has to masturbate you? Does that mean he does not have a healthy-size dick? Or that he cannot work his dick?

You are asking me for advice, but you are old enough to see the truth. This man is not the one for you to be settling down with and marrying. You are not even happy with his ass now. Are you still messing with him because he is "unique," or because you have nothing better to do? You are a grown woman and I cannot tell you what to do, but weigh your options and do the right thing for you.

Blessings,
Zane

Dear G-Spot:

I hope you can help me. This sounds like a dumb question, but they say the dumb questions are the ones that aren't asked. So here goes. My boyfriend and I have great, passionate sex, but for some reason, I cum only when he is on top of me doing his thing or when I am on top of him doing my thing. I never climax when we do it from the back or several other positions. It's not that he isn't doing a good job or hitting the right spots; it feels *really good*. Other girls talk about how they cum when their men hit it from the back. That makes me wonder if something is wrong with me. Zane, please help me. Any advice would be greatly appreciated. Also, if you have any tips on the proper way to *ride,* that would be great as well. Thank you, Zane, for giving me a little of your time. I know you are a busy person.

In Need of Help

Dear In Need of Help:

There is absolutely nothing wrong with you. Different people are satisfied by different things. You say that it feels good in all the different positions, and that is the most important thing. If it were boring you or causing you physical discomfort, that would be an entirely different story. The mere fact that you can obtain orgasms at all puts you way ahead in the game, because there are still hundreds of thousands of women who never achieve a single orgasm in their lifetime. Sad but true.

As for riding a dick, I would recommend sitting facing the man on a chair so that you can keep your feet on the floor for better movement control. Straddle him and take your time moving back and forth. Ask him if it feels good; ask him what way you can move to make it feel better. Experiment with movement patterns until you catch a rhythm that you both enjoy immensely. Communication is key.

Do not worry about lack of orgasms in certain positions. You have a man who satisfies you, so be grateful for that.

Blessings,
Zane

Dear G-Spot:

I'm lucky that I have a mate who has the same sexual appetite that I do. We're both full of creativity, adventure, and spontaneity—it's awesome! The only problem is, just when I'm ready to pull an all-nighter, he's ready to take a nap. At what age do men get like this and are there ways to help them with it? In other words, can you suggest something other than Viagra to keep him awake and aroused . . . after we've already been through a couple of rounds? Or should I be grateful for that and just go to sleep?

Too Much Stamina

Dear Too Much Stamina:

I wish I had an easy answer for you, but some men just can't hang more than one or two times a night. Granted, it is a little bit easier for us women to hang since we don't have to worry about "getting it up." But still, it can be very disappointing to a woman when she is ready to rock a man's world and he is more concerned with getting some sleep. From your initial description of him, he sounded like the ultimate lover, but then your very next sentence made him seem like a two-minute brother. Is he both?

I don't think there is any particular age that a man tends to fall asleep immediately after sex. In fact, I think men are like a day. In the morning (teens to midtwenties), they get theirs, doze off, and then wonder why the young women are smacking their lips and rolling their eyes when they wake up in the morning with a hard-on wanting some more before school or work. In the afternoon (midtwenties to midforties), they realize that it is just as important to please their lover as it is for their lover to please them and, hence, they make a sincere effort to do so. In the evening (midforties and up), they begin to feel like they came, they saw, they conquered, and now they just want to watch the news, maybe even a game, and then hit the sack and break you off a piece or two as the mood comes and goes.

That time line is just a guesstimate on my part, but I think you get my drift. The reality is, no matter what age, a man needs some motivation to "get it up." Therefore, if you want some more, put on a hard hat, lay out some orange cones, hang up a Woman at Work sign, and do just that. Get to work and motivate that man with some whipped cream and some sexy lingerie, and finish him off with the hoover (and I don't mean the vacuum cleaner).

Blessings,
Zane

Dear G-Spot:

The guy I am fucking is not a freak like my baby's daddy. He is not into eating me out after he cums inside of me or licking my asshole, etc. How can I get my current man to get into all of that? More important, how can I get my baby's daddy to stray again—in my direction? He is married and scared to take a chance on fucking me again. Yet he is always telling me how good my pussy tastes and smells. Can you think of any tricks to make him fuck me again? I am just curious. Thanks.

Just Curious

Dear Just Curious:

Why would you want a man—hellified sex or not—who is married, got you pregnant, and is still with his wife? He might think your pussy is the bomb diggity, but it is obviously not banging enough for him to make a commitment to you. Most men would not eat a woman out after they cum inside her pussy. They would turn up their noses and damn near throw up at the thought. Licking assholes is another matter, but here is the deal. You cannot make your current man do a damn thing he does not want to do. If sex is that important to you—more important than everything else he brings to the table—go into a freaky chat room and send instant messages to some of those dudes who have pussy-eating suggestive screen names. Granted, most of them are full of it and probably do not know if the slit in a pussy is horizontal or vertical, but you might luck out. Do not try to trick your baby's daddy into fucking you again. The only thing that might come from that is another baby and him still laying up in bed with his wife every night.

Blessings,
Zane

Dear G-Spot:

I cannot believe that I am writing you this email, but I have read all of your novels and value your advice. I am not sure if this is cause for concern, but I believe something may be wrong with me. Both my man and I are in our forties. I began masturbating years ago and have had some awesome solo experiences. I have a "Big Country Man" who is attentive, passionate, and loving. He does not enjoy tongue kissing, but he will go downtown in a heartbeat, enjoying my pussy for breakfast, lunch, and dinner.

I can have an awesome orgasm—because I make myself have them—but I cannot seem to have them with him. I love him very much and I realize that he is a good man. I can honestly say that he not only loves me, but he is *in love* with me. Our lovemaking is beautiful. I will be on the brink of climaxing and then it suddenly goes away. Even though I get wet, I do not have those out-of-body experiences. To top it off, after an hour or so of going at it, I dry completely out.

My man does not mind diving in face-first to lube me up, but sometimes the effect is only momentary. Now here comes the truly disappointing part. He has not been satisfied totally either, so he masturbates until he cums, which makes me feel like I have not accomplished my job. How can I have an out-of-body experience with him? Hell, I would settle for simply climaxing. I would like to please him and stay wet long enough for him to cum inside of me.

How Do I Have an Earth-
Shattering Orgasm

Dear How Do I Have an Earth-Shattering Orgasm:

Your situation is not totally bad. You have a man who loves to eat your pussy, and some women would cut off their right leg for his clone. I do understand your dilemma, though, and something needs to give. He should not have to masturbate to cum and neither should you. Obviously the two of you need to have a serious discussion and try to figure out what both of you can do to improve. Like you said, both of you are in your forties. That means you have plenty of experience, and if you cannot discuss sex openly now, then you need counseling. As far as your dryness, you may have to use a lubricant from time to time. I would also talk to your gynecologist to see if he or she has some suggestions on why you are drying out. Our bodies go through different stages. Do you drink a lot of water during the day—the suggested amount? You might be dehydrated or become dehydrated after an hour of sweaty sex. That is like going to the gym and doing three miles on the treadmill when you are already lacking fluids. It sounds silly, but start drinking a lot of water before sex and see what happens. I once went to have my blood drawn and had to sit there and drink water for thirty minutes because I was so dehydrated they could not find a vein. Meanwhile, you jack your man off and have him jill you off. That in itself will be an exciting improvement.

Blessings,

Zane

Dear G-Spot:

I am a twenty-three-year-old woman in a relationship with a twenty-four-year-old man. When we first got together, one of the things that had me sprung was the sex. He has a nice-size dick and he used to know how to work it, keeping me quite satisfied. About seven months into our relationship, he suddenly stopped being able to perform. Our sex lasts all of two minutes and that is really stretching it. It has gotten to the point where I do not even want to bother getting myself all worked up when I am not about to cum from his quick sex. He noticed the decline in my sex drive and suggested we try different and new things. We did and it was fun while it lasted, but he still cannot last long. I am so frustrated, because I love him dearly. It has been a year and a half now and I cannot see myself leaving him. Yet I am not sexually satisfied. Please help me.

All Worked Up

Dear All Worked Up:

Here is the ugly, cold reality. You and your man are not sexually compatible. The only thing left to determine is what—if anything—you plan to do about it. You must ask yourself how important and vital a healthy sex life is to your relationship with this man and how it affects your feelings and attitude toward him. You say that you cannot see yourself leaving him and that you love him dearly. Does that mean you love him enough to forgo sexual satisfaction for the rest of your life?

There are many women who don't want to be bothered getting worked up for what will surely be another disappointing sex act. I would suggest that you ask your man if he is willing to go to counseling. You really need it, and while I will not go so far as to say that he needs sexual dysfunction therapy, it seems like he is close. I would first go to counseling together to see if he has a mental block in regards to opening up sexually. Some men, like the character Jason from my novel *Addicted*, have something in their past that causes a mental block, similar to some women.

I wish you much luck in rectifying your problem. The one thing that I can guarantee you is that the issue will not resolve itself and it is highly unlikely that the two of you can resolve it alone.

Blessings,

Zane

Dear G-Spot:

I have been with my boyfriend for almost a year. When we first started dating, in our earlier months, the sex was extremely good and I assumed it would only improve. However, he was laid off from his job and was so stressed that we were no longer making love. I communicated my feelings about it to him and he was too distraught to discuss it, so I dropped it momentarily. Once he did get another position and everything seemed to be getting better, we were still not having sex. I began to feel angry and deprived. No passionate kissing, no foreplay, no nothing!

Well, he has been laid off again and he is going through another stressful period so—you guessed it—no sex. I finally spoke up and told him I was ready to break up and move on. I'm forty-two years old and he's forty-four. I enjoy my sexuality and I want more than him simply to hit it and roll over. I want the foreplay; I want the freakiness. I realize we are not on the same page sexually. Our drives are different and he's not putting forth much effort to ensure my pleasure. He has promised to do better, but I have yet to see any results. Any suggestions?

Freaky with a Nonfreaky Man

Dear Freaky with a Nonfreaky Man:

Money is truly the root of all evil. Nothing can kill a person's sex drive more than being stressed out over work or money—basically the same thing. However, when people are in love, they have to make concessions to please their mate because otherwise they are being selfish. You did not say it, but I sense that you have sincere feelings for this man. Most sisters would have walked the first time he decided to withhold sex because of outside influences. Since you are still there and apparently have not cheated, that speaks volumes.

I hesitate to give you advice, because you have already done the main thing I would have suggested: you have communicated your feelings to him, but to no avail. The bottom line is that you have to decide what is important to you, because I do not honestly believe there will be a quick improvement. It might be a long time before your man feels sexually vibrant again, and it may be forever. Some men start to become impotent in their forties, sad but true. You need to remind him on a constant basis of his promises to you, and you also have to do your part to arouse him. I would ask him what fantasy he has always wanted to live out and try to make it come true. It could simply be that he has become bored. After all, if he is forty-four, that means he has been sexually active for decades, and everyone needs a switch up. Do something totally out of character for you. Become a different woman altogether. Take him completely off guard and see if it helps. Act like a teenager and fuck him in the backseat of the car—even if it is in a parking garage. Lie on the dining room table, spread whipped cream on your pussy, and tell him to eat you for dessert. I would not give up yet, because good men of any age are hard to find and they are even harder to find as we get older. Many are lifelong playas or so bitter about past relationships that they would not recognize a good thing if it slapped them in the face.

Blessings,
Zane

Dear G-Spot:

My boyfriend and I have been dating for about two years now. I love him; I do. However, I am not as sexual as him. When we have sex, it is banging, but when we do not have sex, it is cool with me as well. I simply do not see the need to live on his dick, you know? It is not that I do not have sexual desires; I just do not have them to the same extent that he does. My greatest fear is the "If you won't, someone else will" theory. Although he has not given any indication of it, it might someday come into play in our relationship. What are your thoughts? What's a girl to do?

I Wanna Sex You Up . . . Kinda

Dear I Wanna Sex You Up . . . Kinda:

The good news is that you do have sex with him. I sense that you and your man are rather young, and young men live, breathe, and eat sex. That is a fact of life and only means that he has a healthy and normal sex drive for a man his age. As for you, your sex drive is normal as well for your age: take it or leave it. That may or may not change over the years, because some women are just as happy being completely celibate and concentrating on their careers as they are getting laid, especially if they feel the sex is not going to be worth their time. That is another issue altogether. You are not there and I hope you never will be. If you are saying that he constantly asks you for sex and you often deny him, he honestly might cheat and there is nothing you can do to stop it. A man with cheating tendencies who feels it is acceptable to bed numerous women will do it, even if you are letting him inside your sugary walls every damn night. Do not worry about something that has not happened. He may be totally faithful and adore you, be patient with you, and settle for the amount of sex you are giving him. Unless he has said different, I would not make a mountain out of a molehill.

Blessings,
Zane

Males

$\mathscr{M}$any males reach out for advice from me, and that makes them leagues ahead of most men, because a lot of them simply don't give a fuck what women think. I am not male-bashing, just speaking the truth. Men tend to turn to other men for advice regarding women, and that is just plain stupid. The only people who can truly say how women feel are women. So thanks, fellas, for realizing that.

Here is a typical stupid conversation between two men:

Male 1: Hey, Money, what's up? You ever get into that fine girl's drawers?

Male 2: What fine girl?

Male 1: That one who lives over on Rainbow Avenue.

Male 2: Oh, you gotta be clear, boy. I got fine girls from one corner of this city to the other.

Male 1: Damn, Money, I thought a city had four corners.

Male 2: You know what the fuck I meant. Anyway, yeah, I hit that. She was loving every second of it too.

Male 1: How could you tell, son?

Male 2: 'Cause she was laying there, stiff as a mofo board, while I drilled this big pipe in and out that poontang.

Male 1: Stiff as a board? That don't sound too hot. She wasn't grinding on you and shit?

Male 2: Let me educate you, fool. Women don't do all that grinding shit when you slamming them like they've never been slammed before. When they doing all that moving around, that means they think you can't handle yours and they need to help you out.

Male 1: Word?

Male 2: Word up! Shit, I'm 'bout to go hit that again right quick.

Male 1: Aw, she gonna give up some more pussy, huh, Money?

Male 2: Man, she's gonna hook me up out both sides of them drawers. I just gotta catch her first, though. Her cell's been going straight to voice mail for a few days.

Male 1: Maybe she's still recuperating from that dick slaying you gave her.

Male 2: And you know that.

(Meanwhile over on Rainbow Avenue, the girl is fucking, sucking, and riding the hell out of a new man and hoping that fool Male 2 gets the point and stops ringing her damn cell phone.)

I have a lot of male readers, and more and more show up at my book signings—all ages and races—to tell me personally how I have affected their sex lives for the better. I had one police officer stand in line in Detroit for me to sign a book to him, his wife, and their unborn child. He thanked me for the second child, because his wife was now wearing him out in the bedroom.

Below are a few emails from males, but I must say to the ladies to please, please, please talk to your men, because they are not mind readers and neither are we.

Dear G-Spot:

Let me begin this email by saying I'm coming to you because you don't know me from Adam—at least I don't think you do—and I'm hoping anonymity will provide you with the freedom to answer without prejudice.

I don't have a situation, as so often is the case. There isn't one isolated incident where I could give specific details and describe only one lady. But this is the gist of a continuous pattern of behavior. At this point, I take public transportation to work, which in Chicago is a people-intense venture. In other words, lots of women. At the church I attend, I'm in a position of authority, which also places me in view of the congregation. Let me just sum it up: I seem to get lots of stares. I don't want to come across as vain or make it sound like I'm "all that," because that's hardly what I think. I do have to give a little detail about my person to make this clearer: I'm 5'9", 250 lbs. (with a gut), light complexion, thinning hair, a mustache and goatee, and I wear glasses. I try to dress nicely but am fairly conservative. I'm not what I would call a "prize."

I guess my confusion is figuring, what do the stares mean? I could understand if my hair was smooth and wavy, or my skin was clear, but to me, I have one of those faces that fade into the crowd. I'm not tall, I don't have an athlete's body (maybe the body of an ex–football player with a huge gut!)—so why all the stares? On a few occasions, I've caught women staring at me like they wanted to tackle me right then and there, but why? Help me understand what is on your minds. Oh, by the way, I am married and my wife is about as attentive as a wall. I know she has her own "issues," so if she did find me attractive, she wouldn't tell me and she certainly wouldn't be the active aggressor. I'm sure she loves me, but even a guy wants more love than "I cooked dinner for you and gave you children, what more do you want?"

I guess if I sum it up, I'd ask this question: If women—including my wife—find anything worth looking at, is that all there is to it, is it me, or is the world just the most confusing place to live and die in anonymity?

Too Sexy for My Shirt

Dear Too Sexy for My Shirt:

As for the stares, most women today realize by the time they reach a certain age that "pretty boys" are up to no good. Women begin to notice other qualities in men. I get the impression that you must look like a very friendly, approachable man. Women like that.

Because of all the playas out there, black women are gradually becoming the fourth or fifth generation of our race who will never be somebody's wife. If I were you, I would just be flattered like all hell and bask in the attention women are giving you. Most men would kill to get stares like that.

As far as your wife, how much attention are you giving to her? People often think that traits should be present in someone else and not in themselves. You mentioned nothing about how you make her feel special. Maybe the two of you are in a rut. Go back to being romantic, like you were when you first wanted her attention.

Blessings,
Zane

Dear G-Spot:

I have a girlfriend. I love her so much and I believe that she loves me also. Recently, I have been suspecting her of cheating. I have seen her with two different guys on two different occasions. She convinced me that she is not involved with them and that she is faithful. She also finds it difficult to heed my advice and warnings. Zane, I really love her and I do not want to lose her. Please, what can I do?

Lovesick

Dear Lovesick:

Seeing her with two men does not mean that she is cheating. I sense that there are other underlying reasons for your suspicion that you did not mention. However, unless you catch her doing more than just being around someone, I would not be concerned. Ultimately she will either straighten up and fly right or fly away altogether. Whatever the outcome, you cannot control it, because if she wants to be with someone else, you cannot stop it. I would keep doing what you are doing and profess your love, but women will have male friends throughout their life, even when they are married with four or five kids.

Blessings,
Zane

Dear G-Spot:

I have a curved penis and I'm very self-conscious about it. It's not extremely curved or anything, but I notice it. Most women say it does not bother them, but I notice during sex that whenever I thrust hard, women seem to flinch, almost as if I am making things uncomfortable. As a result of this, I get very embarrassed whenever a partner looks directly at my penis. Am I making too much of this?

Embarrassed

Dear Embarrassed:

It is interesting that you should address me with this problem, because I was involved in a discussion several months ago with a group of women who all claimed men with a curved penis turn them on. They said that it conformed more to the shape of their vagina and caused them to reach orgasm quickly.

Not that I have done a personal inspection of every penis in America, but I think most of them are curved to some degree. As far as the women flinching, are you well-endowed? It might be more about that than the curve. Don't feel embarrassed when a woman stares at your penis. Be proud, because it is a unique feature about you. Maybe they are staring because they like the way it looks and, more important, they like the way it feels. To answer your question, I think you are making way too much of this and should just continue to please your partner without any reluctance.

Blessings,
Zane

Dear G-Spot:

The lady I am dating has a problem. Her pussy is not very tight. She had a child about nineteen months ago. I have been reading up on Kegel exercises on your website. The problem I have with her is that when we have sex, it does not feel like I am in there. I cannot even get mine. Do not get me wrong. I like to be in there for a long time but, man, a brother can get tired after an hour or two. This has never happened with another woman. I brought this to her attention and asked if she had ever done Kegels. She had never heard of them. I would like to keep dealing with this woman. She is nice and a delight to be around, but if the sex is not there, then I am ready to pull out. Now I am seeking your advice on what to do. Zane, please help a brother out.

Trying to Stay Afloat

Dear Trying to Stay Afloat:

I am kind of reluctant to think that childbirth itself is causing her vaginal looseness. For some women, sexual arousal causes the vagina to balloon out to a certain extent. Pelvic exercises will certainly help over time, but for an immediate fix, I would suggest experimenting with various positions. The doggy style is especially good for increased tightness, or you could try positioning her up high on a pillow and entering her at a downward angle. Another great position is to have her get her legs as closed as possible instead of spreading them. I love that position myself. Since you really like this woman, I would not be so quick to give up because of a loose vagina. You can also try Ben Wa balls, if she is willing, because they can be very helpful for vaginal muscle control. Last but not least, you can try my own personal method. A thigh exerciser placed up inside the inner thighs as opposed to inside the knees as intended.

> Blessings,
> Zane

Dear G-Spot:

I have this problem meeting women. It is not like I am unattractive or anything. I am a twenty-nine-year-old man who is 5'4½" tall, 230 pounds, with green eyes, a neat haircut, and a nice smile. I made a New Year's resolution to get down to my ideal weight of 165 pounds and so far I have lost fifteen pounds; fifty more to go. I am shooting for October. I am hearing impaired but I can talk and read lips as well as use sign language. I have a J-O-B and I am in the process of going back to school so that I can better my career.

Lately I have been working on my confidence, the way I approach women. I am convinced the "Hi, baby" shit does not work and most women find it a turn-off. I keep getting the married women or the ones who already have a man. What you said about complimenting women is true. I have tried it and am surprised when women smile or blush when I say they are beautiful or have a pleasant smile. There was this one particular lady who worked at Foot Locker. She was cute and short but she was also two months pregnant. I could not tell. I was asking her for some help with FUBU shirts and she was more than willing to assist me. I like a woman who has good taste in clothing and is kind enough to help, even though it is part of her job. She did not mind helping me pick out something nice. I asked if we could exchange numbers and she said, "I'm pregnant and I've got a man, boo." I was like, "Oh, damn! My bad!" I asked how many months she was and told her congratulations. I do not have any kids yet but would like one or two.

I hope you can give me some advice. I am not trying to be a player or a baller or a pimp. I am just a nice guy who would like some female friends to date for a change. I hope to settle down with a lifelong partner, if I can find someone who hits me like Mike Tyson would knock out someone in the first or second round. I am ready. I just need your help. If you cannot help me, it is all good. I do appreciate you letting me vent at you.

In Search of Mrs. Right

Dear In Search of Mrs. Right:

I think you are just caught up in a cycle that a lot of single people find themselves in these days. For some reason, there are a lot of eligible people, but none of them are hooking up. I would just relax, go with the flow, and eventually the right woman will come along when you least suspect it. That is great that you are losing the weight, because anything that helps you feel better about yourself is a definite plus. I have a bachelor page on my site if you would like to add your picture and a brief bio. I am not sure what kind of feedback the men are getting, but you are more than welcome to place yours on there.

You might even know the woman of your dreams already. Oftentimes our soul mates are right in front of our faces and we miss out on them because we are looking in all the wrong places. You are very sweet; I can tell as much from your email. Do not believe the theory that all women want bad men or thugs. You are a treasure.

Blessings,
Zane

Anal Sex

*O*h, I can hear the lips smacking and see the eyes rolling now. "Aw, hell no, Zane is not going there!" "Zane is a nasty-ass hoe!" "See, that's why I don't be reading her shit! Hey, let me hold your copy for a couple days, though!"

Okay, here is my dilemma with those of you completely against anal sex. Why is it okay for a dick—the thing that he uses to urinate—to enter a woman's mouth but not her ass—the thing that she uses to shit? Don't have a logical response, do you? Men want . . . scratch that . . . men *expect* women to slobber all over their dicks, deep-throat them, and swallow their seminal fluids. Most women feel compelled to oblige them. They call it "handling their business." To me, having to taste a dick and balls—especially if they are kind of rank—is less appealing than taking one up the ass. After all, your shit already stinks!

Sure, it might hurt at first. In fact, I would be surprised if it didn't hurt initially. But who first had vaginal penetration and/or sucked a dick like a pro straight out of the gate? I can answer that. None of you. Now, I am not saying that you should engage in anal sex. I am only trying to convince you not to be so judgmental. To each his own and all that jazz. Some want to try it; some have done it and wish to improve upon it; and some have the shit down pat—no pun intended. Either way, I could not possibly write this book without covering the topic of anal sex.

There is another thing that mystifies me. Why do most heterosexual males make a big show out of homosexual men having anal sex, yet think it's cool to ram their dick up a woman's ass? A nasty, socially unacceptable act, no matter who engages in it, is still a nasty, socially unacceptable act, right? I must be fair and point out similar nonsense about the female point of view. Why do most heterosexual women make a big show out of homosexual women eating each other's pussy, yet are ready to "spread 'em" at a second's notice as soon as a man licks his lips? Same thing with their titties. They are appalled when a woman sucks another woman's breasts, even if they themselves were breast-fed as a baby. Let a man say he wants to be breast-fed and watch her lose her bra like a quick-change artist. Same thing with a man whipping out his dick to get head. I think my point has been made. Stop demeaning others unless you are prepared to hold a mirror up to your own face!

There are no specific, detailed instructions on how to have anal sex. The initial experience is different for everyone. Similar to preparing for childbirth, you can never truly be prepared. Lamaze classes are cute; they can be a fun, bonding experience for parents, and the breathing exercises might be a good talent for a future yoga regimen to lose the after-baby weight. When your ass goes into labor and those contractions kick in, most women say, "Fuck Lamaze! Who the hell is Lamaze anyway? Whoever they are, they don't have a big-ass baby trying to split their pussy wide open!"

I bring up childbirth for a couple of reasons. For one thing, just like trying to heed advice from a man who cannot and a childless woman who has not experienced labor, please do not listen to someone trying to tell you how to have anal sex or, worse yet, educate you on the consequences, when he or she has never done it. There is a surefire way to shut them up, especially a sister who thinks she's Miss Know-It-All. Once she starts making typical statements, be ready with quick comeback lines to catch her off guard.

And it goes a little something like this. Hit it!

Miss Know-It-All: Humph, anal sex hurts like a mofo!

Comeback: Really? What does the pain feel like? Describe it in detail for me.

Miss Know-It-All: If a man has a really huge dick and goes all up in you, you won't be able to ever hold your shit.

Comeback: That's wild! When's the last time you shit on yourself? Did it trickle out or kind of just flow like lava?

Miss Know-It-All: Men are always trying to take their dick right out your ass and put it in your pussy!

Comeback: Wow! Is your urine ever brown afterward?

Miss Know-It-All: Some dudes are so nasty. They might take you off guard one night, take their dick out your ass, and slam it clear down your throat!

Comeback: Oh, yeah? I'm sure a man has fucked you in the pussy and then slammed it in your mouth. Which one tastes better to you? Your pussy or your ass?

Get my drift? If you know for a fact that Miss Know-It-All is making statements based solely on things she has heard and not done, you need to zone her the fuck out. On the flip side, there is Mr. Know-It-All, a brother talking out the side of his neck who has not experienced it either.

And it goes a little something like this. Hit it!

Mr. Know-It-All: Fucking a chick in the ass will make your dick fall clear off.

Comeback: How long did it take the doctors to stitch yours back on?

Mr. Know-It-All: You can catch all kinds of STDs from ass fucking!

Comeback: That's fascinating! Are the fluids running through her ass coming from a different bloodstream than the fluids running through her pussy and her mouth?

Mr. Know-It-All: Once you fuck a woman up the ass, she'll get sprung and won't give up the pussy ever again. They love the tighter feeling.

Comeback: Damn, we need to add that to *The Playa's Handbook* right after the "Once you go black, you'll never go back" quote.

Mr. Know-It-All: Fucking a chick up the ass means you're gay. Straight up. Only homos engage in that shit.

Comeback: So that means you don't get head then, right? Only homos
engage in that shit, too, right?

Get my drift again?

The second reason I brought up childbirth is that those of us who have
endured labor know the ugly truth. People try to sweep it under the rug,
either because they are too ashamed to talk about it or don't want to warn
people and want them to suffer like they did out of pure meanness. Brace
yourself, because here it comes. When the baby is finally coming out, it
feels like you are taking a mastodonic, elephantine dump! Yes, it is true. I
don't know why pregnancy manuals dance around the issue. In the throes
of agonizing contractions, women feel so much like they need to shit that
some of them actually do, right there on the birthing table. Thus the practice of some hospitals giving women enemas to clean their pipes when they
first come in. You can take this at face value or not, but many an asshole
has been stitched up in birthing chambers worldwide. I have had four live
births, two by vaginal delivery and two by cesarean, and I would rather
have my stomach cut open again any day of the week.

If they really want to help women give birth easier, somewhere among
all the breathing techniques and propping up pillows, they need to teach
women how to relax their ass muscles. That's the bottom fucking line!

It is also the starting point in preparing for engaging in anal sex. Just
like women are encouraged to do Kegel exercises and wear Ben Wa balls to
learn how to control their pussy muscles better, that is the key to better,
more comfortable anal sex as well. Beyond that, the only wisdom that I can
give you is to take it slow, find a comfortable position for you and your
partner, and read the following few emails. Whether or not you choose to
participate in anal sex, whatever you do, don't have an anal personality
when it comes to people doing what they want in the privacy of their own
homes.

Dear G-Spot:

I am seeing a man who gives me great sexual pleasure. We are sexually
compatible except for one thing. He wants to have anal sex and I do not feel
comfortable with it. However, I would like to try it but I do not know how to
get over that uneasy feeling. He has not pressured me. As a matter of fact,
he asked once and I said no and he never asked again. During foreplay, he

will rub my anus with his finger, but he goes no farther than that. We have been together for a year. Sexually, we have gone to great heights and I would like to go to the next level with him. How can I get over this feeling and try to enjoy it?

Eager to Please My Prince

Dear Eager to Please My Prince:

Since you are really uneasy about this, I would first suggest that you do some soul-searching and decide if you really want to engage in anal sex. Are you considering doing it because he asked you, albeit once, or are you considering doing it because you think it will feel good?

If you truly desire to experience anal sex, this is my suggestion. Lie on your side, facing away from him, and tell him to lie behind you. Have him PUT ON A CONDOM and then use some type of lubricant. Make sure it is not a lubricant that will weaken a condom, such as Vaseline. Take your time, engage in conversation, while you slowly ease back on his dick. Take it a little at a time, less than half an inch if necessary, and do not move back farther until your anus is adjusted and relaxed with him inside of you.

The first time, he doesn't have to put it all in. Just tell him not to make any moves and allow you to do it until you have taken all that you can bear. Then tell him to slowly start moving in and out. This is a good way to do it the first time because you are in total control. After that, if you liked it, try it again, and eventually he will be able to please your anus the same way he pleases your pussy. However, if you don't enjoy it, tell him thanks for the experience but it is simply not for you.

Blessings,
Zane

Dear G-Spot:

I like your manual on how to fuck a man. I was pleased with myself after reading it and realizing that I've done most of the stuff without a teacher —just my men and my imagination. While reading, I had some thoughts about anal sex. I have done it before and was extremely uncomfortable afterward and with having semen in my ass. I was also in a dwindling relationship at the time. Does anal sex screw up your shit, your regularity, and stuff like that?

Shit Disturber

Dear Shit Disturber:

Anything can cause damage if not done correctly. However, as a rule, no, anal sex does not screw up your shit and regularity. If it was really uncomfortable for you, either it was not done right or it is simply not for you. If you are considering having anal sex, there should be no cum in your ass because you should be practicing safe sex, whether vaginal or anal. That is, unless you are in a monogamous relationship, you are confident that your partner is faithful, and you have both been tested. I am glad you enjoyed the manual and please take care.

Blessings,
Zane

Dear G-Spot:

I loved your site. I learned and was amused about the sexual experience. I have some questions about anal sex. My boyfriend wants to do it and we have tried it once, but it was so painful that I am afraid to do it again. Please help. Another thing is, how do I please my man by sucking his dick? How do I do that?

Backdoor Action

Dear Backdoor Action:

As far as sucking dick, please read "How to Really Fuck a Man: The Bottom Line." I think you will find it very helpful because I go into sucking dick in detail.

As for anal sex, it is not for everybody. If you are totally comfortable about trying it again and not just to please him, then try this. Lie in the bed with your back to him and relax by holding conversation. Let the head of his dick press up against your ass and take total control. Gently, and at your own pace, ease back onto his dick, even if it is only for a centimeter at a time. This might take quite a while, but take it in stages, making sure that your anal muscles are completely relaxed before you take any more of his dick in. If it becomes too painful, stop and tell him you can try it again later. Once you do get enough of it in (it doesn't have to be all of it), then you stay in control and start moving around on his dick. If he is not down with this plan, then tell him all bets are off. You are the one intaking something into your rectum, not him. Please let me know what happens.

Blessings,
Zane

Dear G-Spot:

Hey, Zane, I absolutely adore your books and your ways of writing erotica. I have to admit that I am a sex fiend . . . kind of . . . maybe just a little . . . well, dammit, I am a sex fiend. I am not a sleazy whore or anything, because I have been with only a handful of men. My issue is that we have always had anal sex and I do mean *always*. Is there something wrong with my pussy? Is it too hairy? Not hairy enough? I need to know how men like to have their woman's pussy look, smell, and taste. I realize this sounds absurd, but I am a woman full of curiosity and I need to know the deal. Could you write me back and tell me how to have my pussy looking good, smelling good, and tasting good 24/7?

One more thing. When these men have fucked me in the ass and cum inside the condom, I have always wondered how I will know that they have not left cum inside of my pussy when I do have vaginal sex. Again, I have only had anal. Will the condom leak? When they switch condoms, will some of the cum end up getting on the new condom he places on his dick? I have finally made some progress in my career and I do not want to get pregnant. I could not possibly attend to a baby. Thank you dearly.

Unsatisfied and Lightly Confused

Dear Unsatisfied and Lightly Confused:

I am damn near as confused as you. Why would you allow men to fuck you only in your ass in the first place? Where did that philosophy come from? I wish I knew where you lived so I could study the demographics and figure out what the hell they have in the water around there. While some men—and I do mean just some—enjoy anal sex, all of them love pussy, or at least that is the general consensus. I hate to get graphic, but I cannot imagine your pussy being less appealing than your asshole, which carries many more germs. If they will fuck you in your ass, they should have no hesitation to fuck you in your vagina.

As far as hair or no hair, that is a personal preference either of the woman, man, or both. It is generally easier for a man to eat you when there is no hair, but you are just trying to get fucked at this point, not eaten. Some men shave as well to make themselves smoother when a woman is sucking a dick. What you eat has a direct effect on how your pussy smells and tastes. Of course, cleanliness/good hygiene is essential. Again, I do not see how that could be a major issue with you if men are performing anal sex on you. If you had said all men wanted you to give them blow jobs but not fuck, then I might question your pussy but not under these circumstances.

Condoms can always leak. It is best to use two forms of birth control at all times, but condoms should definitely be one of them to prevent the exchange of bodily fluids as much as possible. Sperm is collected mostly at the well at the tip of the condom, and if a man removes it correctly, none should get on a fresh condom.

Sweetie, my advice to you is to concentrate on that career that is taking off and leave these deadbeats alone that you have been dealing with. A man who cares about you would not be trying to fuck you in the ass only; he would want to make love to you the old-fashioned way and make you feel special. None of these men are worth your time.

Blessings,
Zane

Orgasms

*O*rgasms are more sought after than tax shelters and winning lottery tickets. Everyone over a certain age wants them. We tend to blame our lack of climaxing on others, but victory begins within ourselves. I have received countless emails from women who are in search of "the big O," and most of them have never tried to please themselves. That is the very first thing that both men and women should do. Once they meet that challenge, they can begin to instruct others on what pleases them.

There are various reasons why someone may not achieve an orgasm, the biggest reason being a mental block. Truthfully, the inability to have an orgasm can be caused by stress, depression, and anxiety, or it can be caused by anything from alcoholism and drug abuse to digestive problems and yeast infections. I do have the feeling that a lot of the people who have issues probably have something wrong with them physically.

Other than seeing a doctor, my only true advice about orgasms is to try every possible scenario and see what works for you. Some women cum when their breasts are sucked, some when their pussies are eaten. Then there are other women who flat-out hate for men to go down on them and it is a complete turn-off. Some men cum when their balls are licked and others cum from the heat of being deep inside a woman's pussy. Some other men don't like blow jobs or can cum only during anal sex or in a certain position.

One thing is for sure: if anyone can ever find a surefire way for people to achieve a guaranteed orgasm, these multibillion-dollar technology corporations won't have a thing on them.

Dear G-Spot:

I am twenty-five and I cannot cum. I have tried masturbation and my man really pleases me to the point where I have no energy. Yet I still cannot cum. Please help me. Thank you.

Cumless

Dear Cumless:

There could be various reasons why you cannot attain an orgasm, both physical and psychological. If you are under a great deal of stress or have feelings of anxiety or guilt about being sexually active outside of marriage, that can cause it. Certain medications, specifically antidepressants, can cause it. Also, some physical conditions and diseases can cause it. I would suggest seeking medical help. There is certainly something wrong with this picture.

Blessings,
Zane

Dear G-Spot:

Zane, I am a twenty-nine-year-old male who has problems keeping an erection for long periods of time. I do not crave sex as much as before, and I am becoming what most women would call "a minute man." I have an open mind and I like to try new things sexually, but lately I have experienced "short cummings." Besides Viagra, what can I do to fix my problem?

Short Cummings

Dear Short Cummings:

Your lack of sex drive can be caused by various things. You may just be under a lot of stress, or you might have some sort of infection. Particularly because it is a new condition, I would look into it. A thorough physical should be scheduled with your physician, and one of the things he should be sure to check is your thyroid function. As far as premature ejaculation, you can try two things. When you feel yourself about to cum, pull out for about thirty seconds and wait, then enter the woman again. This stop-and-start method works for a lot of men, and once you learn to control it, you might be going at it all night. Similar to women learning how to control their vaginal muscles, men can also learn to control the sensitivity of their dicks. The other option is to take your dick out when you are about to cum and squeeze the head for about thirty seconds. That has the same effect. Last, you can use some numbing creams purchased over the counter—such as those used for toothaches—to somewhat make you lose sensation so that you can go longer. I would not be too concerned; most men deal with this at some point in their lives, but rarely is it permanent. Most important, try to relax and cut some stressful factors out of your life.

Blessings,
Zane

Dear G-Spot:

I am a young woman who just started having sex with my boyfriend. We have a wonderful relationship—loving, caring, and everything is great. But when it comes to sex, I do not know what I am supposed to feel. I have never had an orgasm and this whole situation is just so new to me. Help. What can we do for better stimulation?

In Search of the Big O

Dear In Search of the Big O:

You say that you are young, and that is a good thing. You are asking for help and suggestions now instead of going ten more years without ever experiencing an orgasm. First off, you can't expect your boyfriend to know how to stimulate you until you know how to stimulate yourself. Yes, I am telling you to masturbate. In fact, I want you to masturbate until you have an orgasm, even if you have to do it every day for the next month. That is the only way you will truly know what turns you on.

I am not saying go out and buy a vibrator or dildo. I am not even saying you actually have to finger yourself. Just lie in bed, dim the lights, put a sheet or towel between your legs, rub your nipples, and fantasize about something you have always wanted to do or experience. Dream about your boyfriend, dream about two strangers, dream about anything as long as it makes you wet.

How much do you really know about your sexual desires? Is kissing a vital part of intimacy for you? Do you like a man to fondle your breasts slowly or palm them roughly? Do you want extensive amounts of foreplay or do you prefer quickies? Do you like to be on top and in control or do you prefer for him to take total control in the bedroom? Does it turn you on to have sex in unusual places? Does the possibility of being caught by someone make sex even more enticing?

I suggest that you talk to your man. If the relationship is wonderful like you say, that should be fairly easy. You should be able to discuss anything and everything. However, if you don't feel comfortable doing that, do the next best thing. Have him write down his top ten sexual fantasies and you do the same. Email them to each other. More than likely, things will come out that would never come out in words. Once you have traded lists, seriously consider doing all of them within reason and only if you are totally comfortable doing them.

Sexual compatibility takes time and it doesn't happen overnight. I know it looks like that in the movies, but this is the real thing. Invest time, show patience, and eventually it will pay off. Please keep me posted.

Blessings,

Zane

Dear G-Spot:

I have a problem. No matter what we try, I cannot cum. I have tried everything with him and by myself. Can you give me some pointers? I need major help.

Extremely Backed Up

Dear Extremely Backed Up:

Are you sure you have tried EVERYTHING? Vibrators? Dildos? Telling your man what you need from him? Does he perform oral sex on you? If so, then that really leaves only one thing. You have some sort of mental block that is keeping you from attaining an orgasm. Nothing kills an orgasm faster than stress. When you have sex, is your mind on something else? Try to clear your mind and just concentrate on the moment. If you need more foreplay, tell him so. If you want him to bang you up against the wall, tell him. If you want to go have sex in an unusual place, go for it. There is nothing worse than having sex and not getting any satisfaction out of it. Unfortunately, there are a lot of women in your same predicament. Are you in a serious relationship, or are you seeing various men? Is there something in your past that affects the way you deal with them? I still believe that masturbation is the key. If you are masturbating and not getting satisfaction from it, then you are doing something wrong. When you have the space and opportunity, start masturbating and do not stop until you have an orgasm, even if it takes all night. Remember that out of all the sex toys, all the men, and all the foreplay, the mind is the most sexual body part of all. Until you can free it, you will probably continue to be backed up.

Blessings,
Zane

Miscellaneous Questions

I get a lot of questions from readers about a broad variety of subjects. I wanted to put a few of those not covered elsewhere out there so that everyone can realize that the only bad question is truly the one never asked.

I believe that most of the confusion or lack of knowledge is due to the fact that people have to find out about sex from peers and not experts. I am glad that school systems nationwide have started to implement sexual education courses at a younger age. Some parents are livid, but they must realize that our youth are not dummies and their hormones will begin to rage whether we want them to or not.

I put a couple of questions about pregnancy in the mix because a lot of women—and men—get nervous in the bedroom when a woman is pregnant. They are either uncomfortable with the extra weight, the fact that "a third party" is present while they are getting their freak on, or they fear harming the baby. Unless it is a high-risk pregnancy or someone has a venereal disease, it is okay to engage in sex during pregnancy.

With that said, let's jump right into the questions.

Dear G-Spot:

My husband is out of town but will be back in a few days. I am three months pregnant but do not want this to stop me. I want to blow his mind, outfuck him, and make it unforgettable. Please help me. I look up to all your books but I want to hear it from Zane.

Pregnant but Not Dead

Dear Pregnant but Not Dead:

Not only are you not dead, you are barely pregnant. This is way too early to be worrying about the difference in sex during your pregnancy. At three months, you should be as active as ever, both in and out of the bedroom. Outfuck him, huh? You go, girl. You have read all of my books but I would suggest trying my "Sex Games from A to Z" that can be found later in this book. I guarantee that there is something on that list you have not done.

As your pregnancy progresses, start having sex on your side or, if you need to, ride him. Hey, that might be something right there for you to blow his mind with. Do you usually ride him like a buckaroo, or does he do all the work? Honestly, my sister, without knowing what you are already doing to work him over, I can't tell you how to improve. But I can say this: every day is an opportunity for a new adventure.

Blessings,
Zane

Dear G-Spot:

I have a boyfriend who I suspect is cheating. Sometimes, when we don't have sex for a couple of days, his balls tighten up. Then, sometimes they are sort of loose. I am confused, because some people say that a man with tight balls means he has not had sex in a while and loose balls mean that he has been fucking. Is that true or not?

Truth Seeker

Dear Truth Seeker:

In my humble opinion, that is a myth. While men do get buildup after not having sex for a while, there is not a clear rule of thumb in determining whether or not they are cheating. He could be jacking off. He may produce more sperm at certain times of the month than other times. Quite frankly, the fact that you are worrying about his balls tells me that you probably suspect him of cheating for other, more profound reasons. If you have to question his fidelity because of his testicles, you need to reevaluate the relationship altogether.

Blessings,
Zane

Dear G-Spot:

I am almost thirty-six weeks pregnant and I wonder if there is anything that I can do to keep my baby's daddy's attention. When we have sex, it is all fine, but when we are not around each other, both of our minds wander. What can I do to keep our attention on each other?

Keeping It Real

Dear Keeping It Real:

Some men find pregnant women to be incredibly sexy. Apparently you think that your man's mind is wandering because you have gained baby weight. The bigger question is why is *your* mind wandering. Sex during pregnancy can be great, if it is done safely. A lot of society tends to disassociate pregnant women from sexuality. That is not true. Often our hormones are most vibrant during that time. The men tend to be scared that they will hurt the baby. Thus they shy away from it as your term gets closer to delivery. That is perfectly normal behavior and you should not be concerned.

Now, you might feel uncomfortable because you are working with a bigger booty than before and a bigger stomach, but that is where talking to your man about your concerns comes in. As you near baby time, you may be so concerned with a new one entering your life that sex could end up the last thing on your mind. Again, that is normal as well and everyone is different. I have heard of some women who literally try to fuck the baby out so they can go ahead and deliver.

Sex during pregnancy is perfectly safe, but you should lie on your side while doing it or get on top to protect the baby. If your man is going to eat your pussy during your pregnancy, do not allow him to blow air into your pussy. It could cause an embolism and block a blood vessel.

Since you are in a committed relationship, you should not have to worry about contracting diseases. Otherwise, I would tell you to be careful on that end. However, barring any complications during your pregnancy, you should be fine.

Let your mind wander right back to your man and you encourage him to feel free to be open with you about what he is feeling during this time. You are very lucky, and your child will be raised in a loving, compassionate home.

Blessings,
Zane

Dear G-Spot:
How do I make my girl squirt?

Cum Seeker

Dear Cum Seeker:

Believe it or not, a woman can ejaculate up to two cups of fluid, mostly from stimulation of her G-spot. A lot of women do not recognize the signs of when they are about to cum and many think they are about to urinate, which is impossible during an orgasm. Yet they tend to hold back because of fear of embarrassment if they did pee on a man's dick. You have to marinate your girl's pussy; make it good and wet. In my personal experience, orgasms are stronger with a full bladder than an empty one. Also, you should try out the yoni massage on your girl. You can find it on the internet.

Blessings,
Zane

Dear G-Spot:

I was wondering if you could give me and my girlfriend some tips on creating a better sex life. If things do not improve, one or both of us will end up stepping out on the relationship. Please help.

Seeking Improvement

Dear Seeking Improvement:

That is an extremely vague question. I have to know where you are before I can tell you where to go. However, the mere fact that you assume that one or both of you will start cheating any second now speaks volumes. Have you ever sat down with your girlfriend and discussed this issue? While I appreciate your reaching out to me, the solution begins at home with opening up about how you feel. Tell her that you want to be more experimental and more daring when it comes to sex. Ask her what she has always fantasized about or how she feels you can satisfy her better. Tell her how she can please you more. Again, I wish that I had more details, but for all I know the two of you might be way ahead of the game from other people and I cannot help without more knowledge.

Blessings,
Zane

Dear G-Spot:

Can you get pregnant if you have sex while you are on your menstrual cycle?

Clueless

Dear Clueless:

You can get pregnant 365 days a year, menstrual bleeding or not. That you can't get pregnant during that time is a commonly held myth that should be "put to bed" once and for all.

Blessings,
Zane

Dear G-Spot:

Does a girl have to shave her pussy in order to fuck, or should she leave it the way it is naturally?

Au Naturel

Dear Au Naturel:

A shaved pussy is not a prerequisite for fucking. Some women have a forest between their legs and their men find it arousing. Others get a regular bikini wax so that there is not a hair in sight. I have not done a poll, but I would guess that most women use a regular shaver from time to time to make sure that things don't get out of hand down there. A shaved pussy carries fewer germs, is easier to keep clean, and cuts down on the humidity down there. To shave or not to shave is a personal preference.

Blessings,
Zane

Dear G-Spot:

If I watch a porno flick, should I be embarrassed if my woman walks in while I am jerking off? Or should I continue and see what she does?

Porno King

Dear Porno King:

That depends on your woman. Do you get the impression that she frowns upon such things? Some women still have negative thoughts about their men self-pleasuring themselves, not to mention watching porno flicks. However, if she is secure in the relationship and her sexuality, she might find it arousing to see you do it. In fact, she might even join you. There is only one way to find out. Do it and see. If she completely loses it, maybe the two of you need to sit down and have a serious discussion to see if you are sexually compatible.

> Blessings,
> Zane

Dear G-Spot:

Last year, a man who is not my ex brought out the real freak in me. Every time we had sex, we did 69s. We both enjoyed porno films, played sex games, did various positions, and he even ate me out in the bathtub. Since we broke up, I want to do that with every guy I am with, but I am afraid that I will scare them off. What can I do?

> Freaky Deaky

Dear Freaky Deaky:

There is nothing wrong with being sexually uninhibited. As for the men who cannot handle it, that is their problem. Do not sacrifice yourself or your needs to try to appease others. If certain men are intimidated by you, then they will probably bore you to death in bed anyway. Be yourself and another freaky man will be coming around to sniff your drawers any day now.

> Blessings,
> Zane

Masturbation

$\mathcal{I}$ probably get the fewest questions about masturbation, because most people either get it or don't. I do tell a hell of a lot of people that they need to masturbate because it is healthy and sometimes vital for a person to understand her own sexuality. What makes me giggle are all the myths surrounding masturbation. Here are some of my favorites:

If you masturbate, you will go insane.

If you masturbate, you will grow hair on your palms.

If you masturbate, you will go blind.

If you masturbate, you will never be able to climax with a real partner.

If you masturbate, other people will be able to tell by the look on your face.

If a man masturbates, he will not be able to produce sperm.

If you masturbate, that means you cannot find a regular partner.

Listen up, all of that is *bullshit*.

Masturbation is healthy, and according to the study conducted by Albert Kinsey during the 1940s and 1950s, over a fifteen-year period, approximately 95 percent of men and 60 percent of women masturbate. I would venture to guess that the number for women is even higher now, since there is a lack of eligible men in a lot of cities and because of diseases like HIV.

Masturbation is a great stress reliever for both sexes. For men, it can be a great tool to learn to control premature ejaculation. A lot of men jerk off before they go out on a date because they realize it will take them longer to bust a second nut. A lot of women jill off because it helps them alleviate premenstrual cramps. It can be a great sleep inducer for everyone, just like the actual act.

Most important, and the reason that I have told women to masturbate countless times, is that it is one of the only ways that a woman can determine what turns her on sexually, without having to go through frustration with a man who cannot utilize psychic powers that he does not possess. Women are very mental when it comes to sex, and by allowing their minds to roam free, alone in their own beds, bathtubs, or wherever, they can work through their emotions and feel themselves up until they know what they need a man to do to them.

If you cannot climax on your own, introduce sex toys into the process. Vibrators never fail, and those new "bullets" are off the chain. They make it so easy to wear them right inside of you while you go to work, take the kids to dance class, or walk down the aisle in the grocery store. By using the little control on a string, attached to the bullet inside your pussy, stress should be a nonissue in the lives of women today. Point-blank.

Again, I do not get a ton of emails about masturbation, but everyone should be doing it. I have included *one* email question, to show how there is much confusion. For complete details on how to masturbate, please read "The Art of Masturbation."

Dear G-Spot:

I was wondering if masturbation is what caused my penis to curve. Do you think masturbation causes this? It goes to the left. Or am I uniquely blessed? Thanks!

Natural Curve

Dear Natural Curve:

While it has often been speculated that masturbation causes a curved penis, there is no evidence to that effect. I would put it right along with the other masturbation myths about becoming blind or sterile. You are simply blessed, darling. Just enjoy it. I am sure your female lovers do.

Blessings,
Zane

The Size Factor

*O*oh, yes, I am about to talk about dick size. This is such a sensitive topic to men that most women would never bring it up, unless the man is hung like a mule and they want to give him accolades. I chose only two emails for this topic because when it comes down to it, there are only two possible scenarios. Either a man's dick is going to be too small for the woman he is fucking or too big for the woman he is fucking, plain and simple.

There is no exact science about what size is too little and what size is too big. The average dick is about seven inches long when erect. That is more than enough to fuck a woman right, if the man knows what he is doing. On the other hand, it takes two to make sex a pleasurable experience. When it comes down to it, your lover is only as good as you are in bed. If you are boring, he will be boring. If you are experimental, freaky, and willing to go all out to please him, if he has any sense, he will do the same.

The *last thing* a woman should do is say something degrading about a man's dick size. What the hell is he supposed to do about it? You meet a guy. You think he is fine. You think he is brilliant. You think he has it going on professionally, has a nice crib, and he is romantic. He sends you flowers, buys you presents, takes you out wherever you want to go. You feel like you might be in love. Yes, you could definitely love this man because he is everything you have ever dreamed of or conceptualized in your mind. Then you decide to go all the way and give up the drawers. You plan this awesome, romantic evening where you plan to seduce him and rock his world. Your kissing is amazing, you damn near cum in your panties when he starts sucking on your tits. He fingers your pussy like a master and even eats you like eating pussy is going out of style. You are ready, so damn ready that you cannot wait to fuck him six ways from Sunday. You want him to take you in your bed, in the bathtub, on the kitchen counter, on the living room floor, everywhere. The moment of truth. He whips out his dick or you whip it out for him. Instead of the big juicy dick that you imagine spit-shining, you have to practically squint to get a visual. Oh shit, what are you going to do now?

Will everything you felt about the man before he whipped out his dick change? Will he suddenly become an idiot that you want to get the fuck out of your crib? Do you start wondering if it is too late to catch *Jerry Springer* or wash your hair for work the next morning? Do you place so much value on the size of a dick that you cannot see the forest for the trees? Some women are shallow like that, blaming a man for something that he has no control over. Other women still feel the same way and decide to find a way to be satisfied, even if that means being satisfied in different ways.

Say the opposite happens: he whips out his dick and the entire room goes dark. His dick is so big that you do not think you can fit even the tip of it in your mouth and the mere thought of it entering your pussy makes your legs clamp shut. Will you fake a leg cramp? Will you ask for a rain check? Will you cower in the corner in fear and tell him to leave like he is suddenly a stalker?

Life is strange. Women with big breasts want smaller ones. Women with small breasts want bigger ones. Women with big asses want smaller ones. Women with small asses want bigger ones. Women with big lips want smaller ones. Women with small lips want bigger ones. No one is happy and most men are not totally happy with their dicks. As many men as there are out there who wish they had bigger dicks so that they can wreak havoc through pussies all over the country and become legendary, there are those men with dicks so big that they are embarrassed to bring them out because they think women will never see them again.

If you look at most porn movies, the men do not have elephantine dicks. They are mostly normal size, but when they get to slamming them into women, they work it like they are getting paid. Oops, they are getting paid, but you get my drift.

All of this is my opinion, but I feel that if a man is good to you, respects you, loves you, and caters to all your needs, then a smaller dick can be worked around. Would you rather have a man with a juicy dick who is fucking all your friends, calling you a bitch, and slapping you around? No, didn't think so. If men's dicks were on their forehead, that might be more helpful in choosing a lover, but they are not. We can judge them only by other matters and wish for the best. Just like food, though, everything that looks and tastes good is not good for us.

For the men out there worried about not being big enough, if a woman cannot appreciate you for your other values, then she is not worth your time anyway. Love should be unconditional; beauty will not last forever. Good hearts are eternal.

Dear G-Spot:

My man and I have been together on and off for about five years. We did not have sex during the first two years of our relationship. Like a lot of males, he bragged about his dick size. When we had sex for the first time, I realized his "big dick" was nowhere to be found. Don't get me wrong. He pleases me, but it is not enough. I do not want to tell him that his dick is too small because I love him. I do not want to hurt him, but I cannot keep going on like this. I have asked friends and they say that there are pills that can be helpful. That is fine, but I do not know how I am going to get him to take them without telling him what they are for. Do you know of any other methods that can help? Thank you for taking time out of your busy schedule to read and respond to my message.

Desperate Times Call for
Desperate Measures

Dear Desperate Times Call for Desperate Measures:

Are you talking about dick growth pills? If so, forget about it and don't believe the hype. Being able to grow a bigger dick is like being able to change your skin color; it is what it is. Some men have mastodonic dicks and others have pencil dicks. They cannot help that part of their physicality. I am glad that you are happy with your man, outside of his dick size. I am also glad that you did not dump him because of it, once you found out.

Now, because of his size that does not mean that he cannot please you. I have seen men with smaller dicks have women begging for mercy before because they had mastered working with what they have. Then I have seen men with big dicks fucking women who looked downright bored. Do not listen to your friends unless they plan to hook you up with someone better once your man dumps you. That is exactly what he will do—in order to save face—once you bring up his lack of girth. Men are very sensitive about that. That is worse than criticizing a woman's weight; she might be able to do something about her weight through the right diet and exercise.

My suggestion is that you experiment with positions that are better for deeper penetration, such as doggy-style or with you on top of him. Those two positions are great for getting him as far up in you as possible.

Blessings,
Zane

Dear G-Spot:

Can a sister get some words of wisdom . . . please? I met this guy. A great guy who is gorgeous, with the physique of a bodybuilder, a good sense of humor, and he is really sweet. He is financially secure with no drama and no romantic ties. Did I already say that he is gorgeous? The only thing is that he is so messed up in the head when it comes to getting physical. He is afraid of rejection. He is very large and has not had any in a year because women will not let him near them after they see what he has in his pants. He is really thick and 11½ inches long. I explained to him that it is the gift that God gave him, trying to give him a pep talk. I assured him that there is a method to everything and that I am sure we could work something out. I am a trouper and not scared of a big dick. I will not reject him. What can I do to soothe this situation? What can I do to make sure that I am ready for this and will not rip myself open? He is so big that condoms cannot fit him well. At least, we have not found one that can accommodate him. Any suggestions?

Dick Trouper

Dear Dick Trouper:

First off, let me say this: You lucky, lucky girl! Seriously, though, I have been in this same predicament before. I was dating a guy from London who was the sweetest person and he and I really hit it off until . . . I saw his dick and almost fell out. He told me it was an early Christmas present. I started shaking like a leaf. Looking back on it, I wish I had had the nerve to go for it. One of life's biggest regrets. I was young then. I definitely wouldn't hesitate now.

With that said, the best advice I can give you is to make him feel comfortable by telling him how much you desire to be with him, how you can take it slow at first and engage in some heavy foreplay and then move into the actual sex act. He does not have to push it all in you at first, maybe not ever. It's comparable to anal sex. The best way to do that the first time is for the woman to ease back on the man's dick a little at a time. I would suggest you do the same with vaginal sex. Stick the head in and once you feel relaxed, move down on it a little farther, relax, and then move even farther.

If he is still hesitant, you might just have to plan the ultimate seduction. Plan a romantic evening and entice him into bed. As for condoms, have you tried Magnums? If those do not fit, you might have to get specialty condoms.

If you really like the man, do not give up. Life is short and, you never know, he just might be the one.

Blessings,
Zane

Dear G-Spot:
I met this guy who is too fine for words. We decided to be "fuck buddies." We would talk on the phone for hours about what we wanted to do to each other. The first time we had sex . . . My God, the brother tore my ass up. I was screaming at the top of my lungs for him to stop. He was so deep that I felt him in my gut. It hurt like hell but it was so damn good at the same time. Here is the bad part. During the entire thing, I did not move. I could not move. I was in too much pain. The brother did not tell me that he was packing like that. Now every time that I see him, I want him right there. I want to suck his dick and give him the pussy. But I do not want to disappoint him again. What do I do?

OTB

Dear OTB:
First let me say that a big dick does not guarantee hellified lovemaking, but it seems like you lucked out. I wish there was an easy answer to your dilemma, but it is going to have to be like riding a bike: practice will make perfect. You will have to grow used to his size over time and, trust me, you will. Been there, done that. Since you are feeling him the way that you are,

do not be deterred by his size. Do everything that you were doing before, just on a "larger scale." If you like this young man, you must conform but do not fear him, for that will lead to nothing but unnecessary confusion.

Blessings,
Zane

The following email does not fit into any of the chapters I outlined for this book, but I had to include it because it is one of the saddest emails that I have ever received in the ten years that I have been giving advice. This young lady reconfirms that I must continue to do what I do, despite all of the naysayers who want to live my life for me. She is a prime example of why the cruelty of this world must stop. The men who used and manipulated her are probably laying up somewhere with their wives, but she is damaged for life, thanks to them.

Dear G-Spot:

Thanks so much for such a wonderful website, as well as your entertaining books. They are such a wonderful escape from what can often be a depressing world. My question may be a bit complex, but here it goes.

First, some background. I have not had any enjoyable or even "healthy" sexual experiences. In fact, I have not really had any except one with a man whose ultimate goal was to find out what it would be like to have sex with a "fat girl." He spewed that at me when I called him the following day. That was not only unmemorable but seemingly criminal to me. It was over in less than three minutes and the experience was all about getting what he wanted. He never touched any part of me other than what he had to touch in order to get what he wanted. Outside of that experience, I have only the horrible experience of being molested from the ages of five to twelve. I was forced to perform every conceivable sex act and the terrible situation robbed me of ever feeling like a "full woman." Instead of a woman, I feel like a damaged piece of meat. My past has been difficult, but I'm trying to be proactive in changing my future.

I had my first orgasm two months ago during a session of self-pleasuring, the only sex that I am having right now. I am thirty-eight. Yes, I am pretty late to get my first "big O," but I really want to take my sense of sexuality back after such a horrid past. I have concentrated on releasing myself from the negative feelings, my low self-esteem, and my hesitation even to engage in masturbation to please myself. Reading your books started me on that road.

I have gotten a lot of books that deal with sex, self-pleasuring, and some educational DVDs. Although I will probably never have sex with a man since I am not what society would consider a "beautiful" or "desirable" woman, I still want to have an active, enjoyable sex life with myself. I am 5'9", 300 lbs., dark-skinned with short hair, not the "stats" that men yearn for in a woman. Even though finding me undesirable is unfair, it is a fact. I am a realist so I am not merely "ragging" on myself when I state that men do not want me because of my looks.

The sexual experience I mentioned earlier left me believing that my body will be considered simply horrid to a man. I have large breasts—size 48I—that droop almost to my waist because they are heavy and dense. That man made sure he told me how "sick" my breasts and my body were to him. That did not stop him from ejaculating with me, but then men do not need to find you appealing to have sex with you. However, since men are very visual, I would not be considered pleasing to a man's vision by any stretch of the imagination.

I realize that was a lot of "history" on me, but I wanted to give you some indication of the experiences that have led me to where I am now. Finally, here is my question. What is the best way to go about building a healthy sex life in the absence of having sex with a man? I have purchased a few sex toys that have been fun to play with, but sometimes they do not seem to be enough. Maybe I do not have the right toys. I have tried porno movies, but I do not like them because they take me back to the sexual molestation of my youth. They are focused purely on men and their desires. They have nothing to do with making love to a woman. They make me feel the same nastiness I felt every single time that I was raped.

I am looking for some other form of pleasure that can leave me feeling satisfied. Could purchasing the services of an escort help me in experiencing more sexual fulfillment? At this point, I am at a loss concerning what I should do. You are quite the sexuality "guru" and any suggestions would be quite appreciated.

Manless Sex

Dear Manless Sex:

I am speechless and so full of emotion right now after reading your email that I am in tears. You do not have to conclude that you will have a

life full of sex alone. While I know that it is hard to overcome what has
been done to you, every day is a chance for a new beginning. Despite how
you feel about your appearance—mainly because of assholes who have
chipped away at your self-esteem throughout the years—you are a beautiful woman both on the inside and out. Paying for an escort might serve an
initial purpose, but at the end of the day you will probably regret it and feel
even worse than you do now. You were abused and that abuse has damaged
you, but you can be repaired.

I would like to personally help you, if you will allow it. What can I do? I
am not sure, but I am willing to try. You are special and I want to make you
feel special. You are not alone and I do not want you to feel that way. I am
not even going to make suggestions about you preparing for a life of sex by
yourself. I will not settle for that and I will make sure that you will not
either.

Blessings,
Zane

Sexually Transmitted
Diseases—STDs

$\mathcal{I}$ could not possibly do this book without a discussion of sexually transmitted diseases—STDs—because at the very least they can disrupt your health and, at the worst, they can take your life. There are many types of diseases, so I am just going to give a brief listing of them here. For more information on these diseases, please visit the Centers for Disease Control and Prevention at www.cdc.gov. You can also call them toll-free at 1-800-CDC-INFO (1-888-232-6348 TTY).

The most common sexually transmitted diseases are:

- Chlamydia ("the silent disease")

- Human papilloma virus

- Gonorrhea

- Herpes

- Hepatitis A

- Hepatitis B

- HIV/AIDS

- Syphilis

- Trichomoniasis

- Crabs

- Chancroid

- Nongonococcal urethritis

- Granuloma inguinale

- Lymphogranuloma venereum

- Molluscum contagiosum

For a complete listing of symptoms and cures, you can also visit www
.epigee.org/guide/stds.html.

It is essential that you practice safe sex if you intend to be sexually active. Do not rely on someone else to protect you because, ultimately, everyone is out for himself or herself. If a person is infected with a disease, he is
not going to be excited about revealing it to you, nor will he feel like he
should forgo self-gratification to shelter you. Some people intentionally
spread disease and you have to be sure—doubly sure—that you ask a lot of
questions about a person's sexual history and practices, as well as use protection.

Once you are sexually active:

- Use only latex condoms.

- Use some type of spermicidal liquid with the condom.

- Use a condom or dental dam for oral sex.

- Make sure that the condom is used correctly.

- Don't sleep with someone whom you suspect or know has multiple
  sex partners.

- Realize that birth control pills, diaphragms, and IUDs do not
  protect you from sexually transmitted diseases.

- Be honest with your partner the second you notice something
  might be wrong with you; the two of you should get examined at
  once.

- Get a Pap smear at least twice a year.

- Take an HIV test at least twice a year.

- Don't allow alcohol or drugs to cloud your judgment when it comes to making sexual decisions.

Oftentimes I have been accused of encouraging people to engage in unsafe sex or to be promiscuous. That is not true. I write erotica, fantasy, and I do it as a way to help people discover their sexuality, embrace their sensuality, and get their minds to explore the possibilities. The best relationships are monogamous, loving relationships where two open-minded individuals constantly find new and innovative ways to pleasure one another. With the way things are going, there may come a time when "imaginary sex" is the only safe sex, so there is nothing wrong with getting a head start on that one.

Do not keep condoms in a hot place and do not use them past the expiration date. The proper way to use a condom is to take the condom from the package and hold it by the tip to get rid of any air, then put it on the top of the dick and roll it down until it covers the shaft. If the condom breaks, stop having sex immediately. If it remains intact, once you are done, hold it by the bottom as you pull out slowly. Throw the condoms in the trash and never reuse one because it will not be effective.

As for the new female condoms, the closed end goes inside your pussy and the open end stays out. Grasp the flexible inner ring of the closed end and squeeze it with the thumb and middle finger until it is elongated. Squat or lie down and insert it into your pussy. Put your index finger inside and push it as far up as it will go, making sure that it does not get twisted. The outer ring should be visible at all times and you should gently place the man's dick inside of you. Make sure that the man's dick is inside the condom and not on the side, between the condom and your pussy walls. Once you are done, twist the outer ring and pull it out. That way, you are trapping the fluid inside the condom. Discard it in the trash.

Dental dams are pretty self-explanatory. You simply make sure that you keep the dam between your mouth and your partner's dick, pussy, or anus while you are doing what you do. Never reuse them and make sure you throw them away immediately.

While abstinence is the only true safe sex, I am not even going there in this book. If you were not interested in fucking, or already fucking, you would not be reading it. However, if you find yourself in a situation where the only sex available to you is obviously risky and sending chills up your spine, I highly recommend masturbation until a suitable partner comes your way.

Sex Toys

*T*hey say that kids have a shitload of toys these days. Well, they are certainly not the only ones, because as freaky as I am, I am amazed at how many new sex gadgets they come up with on a weekly basis. The adult toy industry is a multibillion-dollar business. When I inquired about getting them directly from the manufacturer for my own line, the minimum yearly order had to be at least three million. I was like, "What the fuck? Is it like that?" Apparently, it is.

A complete guide to sex toys would be an entire book of its own, but I do want to mention a few personal favorites and the top choices of some of my dear friends—my "Zaniacs."

The most popular new toy is the bullet. I have a few and they are good to have handy. The bullet—sometimes referred to as an egg—is a small vibrator that the woman places inside of her pussy or ass (or both if she has a double-headed one). It is controlled by a remote control on a string and can be worn as she goes about her day-to-day life. This is preferable over a dildo because it would be kind of hard to drive or walk down the street with a nine-inch dildo hanging out of your pussy. You can adjust the speed of it and let's just say, if you don't already own one, get one ASAP.

Now, I am not saying that dildos are not valuable, but they are best kept in the bedroom. I know some women who do not leave home on a trip without their dildos. If they don't have their toothbrush, they have their damn dildos. These are good if you want to do a lot of moving in and out as the bullet (or egg) stays in place and kind of moves on its own. Dildos can be an incredible turn-on if you masturbate in front of your mate or want him to help a sister out by using it on you, in order to hit your G-spot. They have these new glass ones that add to the suspense. I always wonder, What if that shit breaks? The danger of having a cut-up coochie actually makes some women cum from the mere thought of it.

The rabbit is cute and it is actually a bullet or egg with a piece of rubber shaped like a rabbit that is placed on top of it. The rabbit gets inside of you and tickles you into a climactic and shuddering orgasm. This is a really useful tool. But my favorite is the butterfly. Now, that is truly the shit. It is shaped like a butterfly—obviously—and it stays outside of you but it vibrates the hell out of your clit. The great thing is that most of them come with leg straps so that you can put it on, wear it under your sweat suit or business suit, and get your jollies off all damn day. Both the rabbit and butterfly are controlled by remotes on strings. Want to try something really different? Put on a butterfly and go work out at the gym, do some kickboxing with that bad boy on. You will never view life the same way again.

Penis pumps are good for getting a man hard and so he can maintain an erection longer. A lot of men shy away from using them because it means admitting that they have an issue. All I can say is that a hard dick is better than a soft dick, and if it does not work on its own, there is nothing wrong with using a gadget to get the action going. Cock rings are an easier solution, provided that he can at least get it up. Cock rings are placed at the base of a man's dick and can help him stay erect so he can possibly blow out a sister's back.

Anal beads and plugs are for those who want to have something in their booty while they have something else in their cootie. They give the same sensation as having a person's fingers going in and out of your ass during sex. It is not for all, but it is for many, and you should never knock something before you try it. Also, these can be good toys for those who are unsure if they want to take the plunge and have anal sex. They can "test the waters" and see how much pain might have to be endured with the actual act. They can also let a person know if she might gain some pleasure from anal fucking.

Here's the bottom line. They have a ton of freaky shit these days. There are vibrators that lick and suck on your pussy; sex swings that give an entire new spin on Tarzan and Jane; exercise balls on which you can put interchangeable dildos to get an ass and thigh workout while you get a pussy workout at the same time; a type of riding harness for a woman who is on top. All kinds of shit. They have pogo sticks with dildos attached and even an actual "fucking machine."

If you want to know more about sex toys and/or want to purchase them or become a sales representative, please visit my website at www.eroticanoir.com.

A Personal Note from Zane

I want to close out this book with a brief commentary, something that I have started doing with my novels as well. I want to explain my purpose behind writing it. *Dear G-Spot* represents what I have been doing for the past ten years, listening to others communicate their needs, wants, and desires as well as express their disappointments when it comes to love and lovemaking. In this life, most of us will have sex, and it is unfair not to enjoy it to the utmost.

For my critics, I hope you now realize that my readers do appreciate me and I am doing something good instead of promoting promiscuity and unsafe sex. Quite the contrary, I am a huge advocate for safe sex practices because while sex can be great, it is never worth dying for. This has been a wonderful experience and a journey down memory lane as I sifted through tens of thousands of emails to compile this book. Remember that passion and sensuality are universal and so is love.

Zane

How to Really Fuck a Man: The Bottom Line

irst, let me say that I am not professing to be the world's greatest lover, but this little manual comes by special request. Mostly from men who have read one or more of my erotic stories and told me, in response, that they wish more women were as comfortable about their own sexuality as I am. And even a couple of women who said they wish they could express themselves more openly but are too shy or apprehensive ever to do it. So, anyway, here goes my version of getting the most out of fucking/making love/doing the nasty, whatever you want to call it. Men can share it with their mates and women can either take my advice or throw it away, but here goes.

Some of the most confusing, disappointing, and lonely experiences in life are sexual, and some of the most beautiful and earthshaking ones are sexual also. Having had some of both, I prefer the good sexual experiences.

Everything you have ever done in your life you have learned to do. Sex is no different. You learned how to balance your checkbook and you must learn how to fuck a man.

There are four major aspects to fucking:

1. Heightened sensitivity
2. Appetite

3. The desire to give

4. Sexual skill (yes, I said skill)

To heighten your sensitivity, take off all your clothes and sit down at a table with several different items on it from around the house, such as lace, a silk scarf, a powder puff, whatever. Turn off all the lights or put on a blindfold and then rub these items gently against your skin all over your body and savor the different sensations they give to your body and the way they stimulate you.

Take a bath and then lie naked on a bed with clean sheets and dim the lights or turn them off. Take your favorite lotion and rub it all over your breasts and stomach. Then your thighs and ass. Then go to sleep and wake up more relaxed.

Do tongue exercises on a regular basis. Stick your tongue straight out as far as you can and then slide it back in your mouth as far as you can. Try to touch your nose with your tongue. Try to touch your chin with your tongue. Encircle your lips in a clockwise motion with your tongue and then reverse the motion to counterclockwise. Repeat these exercises whenever you get a few moments.

Get a double-scoop ice cream cone and lick all around it slowly. Then put the whole mound of ice cream in your mouth and savor it. When it starts to drip down the side of the cone, catch the drops on the tip of your tongue.

Close your eyes and run your tongue over the tips of your fingers, down around the palm, your wrist, and up your arm to your elbow and explore the different sensations you feel.

Do Kegel exercises and don't procrastinate. You are going to need those strong muscles when you get right down to it.

Dance closely with your man and close your eyes, tuning out all other distractions. It is good preparation for fucking, 'cause when you fuck, the woman must be able to follow the man's lead and tune into his body rhythms and style as well as him tuning into yours.

Go out and buy some sexy-ass underwear, not the cheap stuff but the things that will make you feel sexy all day long, even when you have a business suit on top. The feel of satin or silk against your skin is very sexually arousing.

But the best way to heighten your sensitivity is to MASTURBATE. Yeah, I said it, and now I am going to tell your ass how to do it too.

Masturbation will strengthen and increase the flexibility of your sex muscles, teach you which parts of your body are most aroused when caressed, what type of clitoral manipulation turns you on most, how to achieve multiple orgasms, or how to have an orgasm at all, for those women who never have them.

The vibrator can be mad cool and don't be ashamed to buy one. They sell them at every drugstore under the mask of a facial massager. Lie down quietly with your eyes closed and tune into the feel of your body. Then let your mind float to something that excites you sexually, such as making love to your man, the man who was in line in front of you at the grocery store yesterday, being gangbanged, whatever turns you on. No one knows what you are thinking but you.

Let your vibrator be his hands and dick, and caress the inside of your thighs, your breasts, and your clit with it. If one fantasy doesn't work for you, move on to another. You have all the time in the world. If not, make the time. You must have patience.

With your hands, teach yourself to reach an even higher level of sexual stimulation and you will discover even more areas of arousement you can never find with a vibrator. Most women don't directly stimulate the clit with their fingers but all around it because the clit is often too sensitive.

You must masturbate on a regular basis in order to truly learn what satisfies you. You can't learn to play the piano by only going near it three or four times a year. When you have educated your body to the point where you are multiorgasmic, you can direct your man on how to please you better. If you don't know what sets your body off sexually, how the hell should he?

You can masturbate in the bathtub or shower. The water can be a major turn-on, or you can insert a number of different objects into your vagina— but nothing that will fuck your shit up like a Coke bottle or something that will leave splinters, so be careful.

The two best things, other than a vibrator, are a dildo and Chinese silver balls. You take three little balls and put them in your pussy. Then you take the vibrator and move it around on the outside of your pussy and it makes the balls jump around inside. THAT IS THE BOMB.

Masturbation can even reduce the severity of menstrual cramps, so give the shit a try. No one ever has to know unless you tell him or share it with your man who, trust me, would love to watch.

Now on to your sexual appetite. Sexual appetite is extremely important to good fucking. Without it, you don't really want to do it and your man can sense it, and that is a major turn-off.

Learn to understand your many sexual moods. What time of the day are you most sexually aroused? What turns you on and off? Do you prefer getting a few hours' sleep first and then waking him up in the middle of the night to fuck? Etc.

If you don't understand what I am saying, begin keeping a diary of what time of day you become sexually aroused, what time of day you have sex, what type of fucking gets the best sexual response from you, etc. After a few weeks, you will learn a lot about yourself.

To keep his ass from wandering off to the hoochie next door or at the job, you must have three things: imagination, sensitivity to his moods and desires, and courage to experiment with different sexual techniques.

When you make love to him and he doesn't give back, either he is selfish and you need to dump his ass, or he is inexperienced and, if he is worth it to you outside the bedroom, you must take the time and have the patience to teach him. Don't waste yourself on a sorry-ass man, but don't hold back with a worthwhile man either.

How can you tell if a man is worth fucking? Easy. Pay attention to the way he kisses. If he is rough and attacks your mouth, he will be a rough lover and probably put your ass in traction. If he slobbers, he isn't sensual. If he uses his tongue badly or not at all, he will be just as uncreative in bed. Men who are great lovers use their tongues imaginatively from the first kisses on.

Also pay attention to his body language and the way he touches you. If his caresses turn you on, more than likely so will his dick. If he treats your breasts like grapefruits, tell him to get the fuck. There are many signs of whether or not a man is a great fuck. You just have to learn to recognize them. But once you have that desire to give, here is how you do it.

Let's get down to the nitty-gritty and talk about skills. I could draw this out for pages and pages, but let me just skim through right quick. If you want more details, email me or something.

First of all, there is much more to stimulating a man than his dick. His whole body is a minefield of sexually arousing spots—like his nipples, the inside of his ear, and his belly button. However, the most important one is his mind, not unlike your own. Telling him what you plan to do to him can be just as much a turn-on as actually doing it, you follow?

In order to be a good kisser, let your lips go almost limp, ease the tension from your chin, and then slip your relaxed tongue gently into his mouth. Kiss him everywhere with the improved and relaxed tongue muscles achieved from doing the exercises I described earlier. Everywhere from his eyelids to his nipples and, when you come up for air from a long kiss, suck his bottom lip into your mouth for a brief moment; men love that shit.

When he penetrates you, work those pelvic muscles—don't just lie there like an ironing board or a rag doll. Suck in your pussy muscles like you are trying to imprison his dick. Move your ass in slow, circular motions. Relax, constrict your muscles around his dick, and relax again. This is where the before-mentioned Kegel exercises come in handy. And, without even getting into it, all women must master the art of riding a dick, so be sure to work on that.

As for oral sex, kissing a man's dick is a whole lot less unsanitary than kissing him on the mouth because the mouth tends to have more germs. You are exposed to more infections at a PTA meeting than in bed.

There are two reasons at least to try oral sex. First, trying it will probably make all fear dissipate and increase the sexual pleasure you experience. Second, your man loves the shit. :-)

As for how to suck the dick, I will cover that quickly. The most common way is to kneel in front of him, take the dick in your hand, and run your tongue around the head until moistened. Lick your lips and form a ridge on your mouth over your teeth with your lips to avoid biting him. Then, holding the base of his dick in one hand, take it into your mouth slowly until you feel comfortable taking the whole thing in. Only by experimenting will you discover what speed and movements your man prefers. Practice makes perfect.

Then you can move on to more advanced techniques such as the butterfly flick, the silken swirl, the hoover, gnawing, whipped cream wriggle, the hummer, and the tingler. Yeah, all that. LOL.

In the butterfly flick, you locate the most sensitive part on any man's body and flick your tongue lightly over it. On the underside of the dick, about two to three inches below the head, is a ridge called the corona. Work that shit with your tongue like you are strumming a banjo. This is also a good time to go for the balls and the little patch of sensitive skin between his balls and the crack of his ass. Never forget that balls need love too.

For the silken swirl, you continually lick his dick clockwise or counter-clockwise with your tongue while taking the entire dick in and out of your mouth. It is hard to do, but if you continue the tongue exercises I gave you, it will become easier with time.

To hoover, you use your mouth like a vacuum cleaner. Sucking his dick into your mouth until it is halfway in and then, still exerting the vacuum pressure, slowly start to slide his dick out of your mouth. This double pressure is great for making a man's dick hard when he is having trouble obtaining a full erection.

As for gnawing, I will leave that shit alone 'cause it is self-explanatory. Most men don't like it, but some do, so when in doubt, ask his ass.

The whipped cream wriggle is self-explanatory as well. Spread some whipped cream all over his dick and lick it off. If you really have a sweet tooth, sprinkle some coconut or powdered sugar on top.

To do the hummer, take his dick in your mouth and vibrate your throat muscles like you do when you are gargling, which makes humming sounds emit from your mouth. (No need to belt out a rap song.) It can be a thrilling experience.

The tingler is my personal favorite. Take some mouthwash into your mouth before you insert the dick, making sure not to swallow it and letting it trickle out of your mouth while you suck it. It stimulates the man's dick just like mouthwash stimulates his mouth, and it gives you a minty fresh taste when you get up to kiss him after you are done.

As for positions during oral sex, they are too numerous to mention. There is the 69 position, of course, and if you don't know what that is, you shouldn't be reading this, so go watch some TV now, please. You can also lie side to side with you resting your head on a pillow while you take his dick in and out of your mouth, which is good for him because he can handle his pelvic thrust movements better on his side. You can kneel between his legs while he sits on a chair or lies on the bed, or you can tackle it from below while he stands up, you can lie on the bed with your head hanging off the side upside down and suck it that way, or you can do it my favorite way: have a man dick-feed you while you sit on the edge of the bed or on a chair. Ummm, being dick-fed is the bomb diggity. As for swallowing cum, only about a third of women are willing to do that, and even fewer love doing it, like myself. To each her own, but if you don't intend to let him cum in your mouth, have an alternative plan of action.

Let me also mention that your hands play a very powerful role during the entire fucking experience. Caress him all over, rub your fingers down the center of his spine, give his ass sensual massages, whatever's clever.

Now for the really touchy subject, ANAL SEX. Don't be shocked. Plenty of law-abiding, professional people do the shit every day and love it too.

First, let him explore your anal area with his mouth and tongue. Hell, you can lick his ass too. As long as both asses are clean, go for it. When in doubt, shower or bathe together first. Then, let him insert a finger or two into your ass while eating your pussy or while you are riding his dick. Chances are, after that you will be craving his dick all up in your ass.

The best position is lying on your stomach with your ass elevated off the bed by a couple of pillows. Let your man lubricate your ass and his dick with some K-Y Jelly or Vaseline and then slowly enter you fully from behind until it is all in. Then he just simply fucks your ass like he fucks your pussy. Sounds simple, huh? It is. If he is too rough on you, kick his ass, but most men are willing to take their time and be considerate of your needs in order to make it a pleasurable experience for both of you from day one.

Once you have relaxed your sphincter muscle, anal sex is the bomb. Let him play with your clit while he is fucking you in the ass and you will have the ultimate orgasm to boot. Let him cum in your ass and you are likely to convert to anal sex for life.

If your ass hurts after anal sex, you have probably failed to relax tense muscles and may be sore for a bit. But once again, practice makes perfect.

I am gonna touch upon two more things and then I am outtie. First, I would like to encourage you to explore different places to fuck, 'cause having sex in the bedroom or even in the house, for that matter, all the time is mad boring. Be willing to fuck your man anywhere, and he is yours. Also, try new positions for sex. My personal favorites are being banged up against the wall slowly from behind, having a man walk around the house fucking me while bouncing me on his dick, and the flying 69, which is when a man holds you upside down against the wall and you perform oral sex on each other. Hey, don't knock it till you try it.

Last but not least, remember that, not unlike yourself, your man has a whirlwind of fantasies. If you feel uncomfortable talking about it, make a little game out of it and give him a homework assignment and tell him to write them down while you do the same. That can be the biggest turn-on, reading what your man really fantasizes about. Trust me; been there, done that. Once he gives you his list, try to fulfill each and every one of them, if at all possible, and as long as you think they will turn you on too.

On that note, I wish you all a lifetime of hellified sex. Any comments, positive or negative, along with any questions can be emailed to zane@ eroticanoir.com.

Peace and love,
Zane

How to Make Love to a Woman: Mind and Body

*L*et me once again say that I do not profess to be the world's greatest lover or anything like that, but I felt "How to Really Fuck a Man" deserved a counterpart and have had several requests for one, especially from men, which is a good thing because it shows that some of them are really concerned about pleasing their women. For that, I applaud them. Most men feel that being too sensitive is a turn-off to women, but they are so wrong. I would, like most women, give praise to any man who is sensitive and in tune with his true feelings and can express them to his mate.

Now is a good time to say a word about safe sex, because I have gotten quite a few negative comments from people assuming that I am promoting unsafe sex, sex with multiple partners, sex without protection, etc. Let me say this right off the bat. People are gonna fuck whether I write about it or not. I don't believe in casual sex, because meaningless sex is mad boring and frankly, in this day and age, not worth the risk. My stories are my fantasies and, while some of the things in them are indeed true events, I think making love with someone you care about is the SHHH Bomb Baby and the stories are written from the point of view of two people being in a relationship. People are adults and they make their own decisions. All I am saying is that sex can be good or bad. Why not discuss it openly so it can ALL BE GOOD?

While this chapter will talk about actual sex acts, a woman's most sensual organ is her mind; make love to that and her body will follow. Therefore, I am going to cover that first, and most thoroughly, because it is, by far, the most important.

First of all, I have received a lot of email from both men and women asking why some women seem to be so uncomfortable dealing with the sex issue, especially when it comes to talking about or experimenting with new things like masturbation and oral and anal sex. My answer is always the same.

When we are born, we all have a sex, and even babies explore their sex organs. For example, when my daughter was two, she pointed to her chest and said, "My titties!" At first, I was appalled and then I thought to myself that it was really cool. So I told her, "Yes, those are your tits!" My point is, why lie about it?

The problem is that most parents would have tried to repress her sexual discovery by saying that the word is inappropriate, telling her never to point there again, or even spanking her. That is a major part of the problem with women today.

As children, little girls are taught that certain things are taboo, like touching themselves "there" and thinking nasty thoughts. Some parents even still tell their children that if they masturbate, they will go blind. So after years of being brainwashed into thinking that certain things are a no-no and a sin, why shouldn't people have sexual hang-ups? After all, most people respect and listen to their parents' points of view before anyone else's. That is why it is so important that parents do talk about sex, drugs, and all other vital issues with their kids instead of letting someone else do it. However, I feel they should do it the correct way and be honest about it. The sexual urges are going to come about, whether they like it or not, so they should tell their kids the truth and that's that.

All I am trying to tell the men is, it took years for your lady to get certain things instilled in her brain, so have patience, work with her, and realize that it may not change overnight but it will be well worth the effort and the wait. Women are taught, "All men want is your body. When men get what they want, they won't respect you and will only use you."

Most women have not been provided access to the same healthy outlets for excitement seeking as men, nor have they been invited, as men have, to digest all the stimulation they need and at whatever potency they need.

When a man talks vividly about sex, he is a man's man, but when a woman does it, she is considered a freak. Why is that?

Oftentimes, discussing your most intimate desires can be easier with a stranger than the one you love, because you are so afraid he will get the wrong impression of you. And, I have to be honest, I know that some men are guilty of making their woman feel that way. Men have a tendency to think that they should be the first one to experience certain things with a woman and yet they are the first ones to brag about how many times they have done it in the past.

For example, I was dating a guy once and I asked him how many women he had slept with. He was fast to blurt out this ridiculously high number, boasting about it, in fact. However, when I asked him did he want me to answer the same question, he said, "Hell naw!" and he said that any number I could possibly tell him over three would be too high in his mind 'cause it was "different" for women.

Men, let me say this, women have a past too, so get the hell over it and enjoy the fact that she knows what she is doing already. Why do you think so many men are obsessed with being with virgins? Let me school you: virgins don't know shit about pleasing a man, so why the obsession? Tight pussy? All pussy conforms back to normal size. Hell, big-ass babies pop out of them, you follow? I think you all get my point. Make a woman feel comfortable about discussing her sexuality, and nine out of ten times she will. Men tend to make us repress our sexual desires and, ironically, they are the ones who would benefit most from them. Lack of communication is the number one reason relationships fail even when masked with other excuses like money issues and infidelity. There can be no progress without discussion, and that goes for in and out of the bedroom.

Speaking of infidelity, a brief word. I am not going to give a sermon on it 'cause it deserves a chapter all by itself, and in my upcoming book, it will probably get one. However, I would just like to tell the men two things. Number one, if you take the energy you exert going out and chasing other women's asses and put that same effort into the woman you have at home, your wife or girlfriend can be the best sexual affair you ever have because she loves you already. And number two, when you cheat on a woman, you do serious damage because she will never completely trust you again, you make it worse for the men who come into her life after you, and is it any wonder she doesn't want to experiment with sex with you when she knows you are out sticking your dick in other women's asses? Who wants to suck a dick that she knows has been elsewhere the night before? I mean, let's get real.

I do have to say a quick note to the women too, though. No matter how many pies you bake, how much pampering you do, and how neat and cozy a household you keep, men want their sexual needs met, and if you don't do it, someone else will. Have you ever noticed that when a man is single, no one wants his ass, but the second he gets with you, hoochies appear out the clear blue sky wanting your man? It is a dog-eat-dog world out there, which is why my lover shall remain nameless.

So people, don't take the easy way out 'cause it has the fewest rewards. Trickin' and trampin' never pay, so talk to your mate. You would be surprised at how great it could be.

Now, on to what women DO and DO NOT WANT!

Women do want you to:

1. Attend to the nonsexual aspects of your relationship. If a woman is not feeling good and comfortable about you or the relationship, the door to sex will be closed. Whether it is a new or developed relationship, make sure you are indeed relating.

2. Be there for her when you say you will be. Don't make dates and then break them or forget about plans, and never take business into the bedroom while you are being affectionate or sexual; that is a major turn-off 'cause it makes the woman feel like she is not the center of your attention. Which means don't let your eyes keep roaming around the room as if you're searching for someone better either. I hate men who do that shit. :-)

3. Let her know how you feel about her. Pay her compliments, 'cause some women in established relationships can't even remember the last time their man told them what he finds beautiful, striking, attractive, exciting, or sexy about her. Dayum shame, I say.

4. Listen to her and take her words seriously, especially when she says no and when she requests a change in what you are doing. Many women feel they don't get listened to sexually (and generally). It drives them crazy and, sometimes, even out the fucking door.

5. Learn to enjoy nonsexual touching and sensuality. Cuddle, bathe together, give foot and back rubs, wash and brush her hair. Women don't always want touching to lead to sex.

6. Be honest and do not misrepresent yourself. Lying in order to have sex comes from the childish idea of conquest. Don't say you can't have babies when you can, that you will use a condom when you won't, that you love her when you don't, that you are not married when you are, and that you are disease free when you know your ass isn't. If you are not the right person for her, why not just accept that fact and move on?

7. Take responsibility and a woman will appreciate you all the more. It is as much your responsibility as hers to make sure the kids get in bed, to ensure privacy, and to make sure she doesn't get pregnant. I am sick of sorry-ass men saying it is the woman's fault if she gets pregnant. What kind of fucking tree did they fall off of? A coconut tree most probably, 'cause they have heads with nothing but liquid inside. Reality check, men. HELLO!

8. Start slow and gentle and away from her pussy unless it is one of those rare clothes-ripping-off-got-to-have-your-ass-or-I-am-gonna-bust moments. Before you grab a woman's breasts or her pussy, kiss her in other places and arouse her. Men get hard when the wind blows, but women need some stimulation to get their pussy wet. Which is the reason, by the way, that some women fake headaches at sex time. 'Cause they know good and dayum well by the time their man busts a quick nut in them, they will barely be sexually aroused, rather less able to have an orgasm themselves, so why fuck in the first place? So now you know the REAL HEADACHE!

9. Express yourself sexually. Even though men are supposed to be the big sex talkers, oftentimes the only way your woman knows your ass came is 'cause you stopped moving. So talk to us and tell us what turns you on. And I don't mean telling us that by relating how some woman in your past got your juices flowing either, 'cause that is a big no-no.

10. Take rejections gracefully, 'cause even bomb-ass lovers get turned down from time to time. If she doesn't feel like it, so be it. Don't pout and shit. There will be other opportunities.

11. Take sex any way she is willing to give it. If she doesn't want you to bend her into a pretzel that day, do it doggy-style. If she doesn't want to swallow your cum, shoot that shit someplace else. She accepts it when you have those two-minute brother days, so stay flexible and open to the possibilities.

12. Be adventurous and imaginative, suggest new ways and places. Ask her to fuck you in the backyard sometimes, in the shower, on the roof, in the car even if it is parked in the garage. Men are often guilty of the same thing they accuse women of: lack of imagination. Chances are, you make her aware that's what you want and she will reciprocate.

13. Confront problems, especially your own. If some aspect of sex is problematic, don't pretend it doesn't exist.

14. Be romantic every now and then. Most men are romantic only when they are trying to hook your ass, and then, once they get settled into a relationship, they sit on the couch, drink beer, watch sports, and pass gas. Remember to act like this is the first or second date once in a while. Romance has more to do with the way you act than making fancy plans and buying things. Make a woman feel loved.

15. Last but definitely not fucking least—and men, this is vital—keep your ass awake after sex, at least some dayum time. SHEESH! A woman wants to hug, talk, stay connected in some way for at least a moment or two after fucking. Otherwise, she is likely to say, "He got what he wanted, now his ass ain't interested!" and that will surely lead to trouble. I know there is nothing worse than a man fucking me, then cumming and saying some shit like, "I could fall asleep just lying here inside you!" Don't no woman, with a dangling-ass condom inside of her, want a man falling asleep two seconds after sex. Fuck all that!

Hell, I was going to do a women DON'T WANT list, but I think I have covered enough with the DO WANT one. This is much more detailed than "How to Really Fuck a Man" but, guess what? I am a WO-man, so this is more my thang: talking about what a woman wants, 'cause some of you men are straight-up clueless.

Now let's get to the sex. And I will try to narrow this down 'cause I could talk about sex for *dayz*.

Women need emotional stimulation, bottom fucking line, and sometimes (I know you men will hate this), when a woman is making love to you and you are not providing her with what she needs emotionally, she fantasizes that she is fucking someone else. That she is on an island with two men ravishing her, whatever. It is very important that you make a woman feel like she is the complete object of your desire, 'cause some women have low self-esteem anyway.

For example, take the women on the talk shows who come on there ready to kill each other over a man who is fucking them both. I can't see how in the world those women could lie down with the man, rather less get sexual enjoyment out of being with him. But that's my point, most women won't play that shit. You better make her ass feel like she is the one, or you won't be getting none. Ya know?

As for the actual act of making love, women love to kiss because kissing on the mouth is the most intimate sex act of all. Which is why some prostitutes won't do it at all: it is so personal. But when you kiss a woman, don't slobber all over her mouth, don't try to suck both of her lips into your mouth like you're a fucking vacuum, and don't try to shove your tongue down her throat. Move your tongue in slow, circular motions. Men kill me when they move their tongues so fast you think they are running in a race or something. Men can benefit greatly from the tongue exercises I covered in "How to Really Fuck a Man," so do that shit.

Women love their nipples sucked. Hell, when a man sucks my nipples the right way and for a healthy period of time, my ass will cum like all hell, and I am not alone. The problem is that most men are in such a hurry to get to the coochie-coo, they don't pay our nipples enough attention. They suck each tit about thirty seconds and think they are done. Fuck all that! You need to give a woman at least a good ten minutes of nipple concentration.

And don't suck only on her nipples; lick up underneath her breasts and suckle on the whole thing. Take both breasts your hands and suck on both nipples at the same time; drives a woman crazy and makes her feel so desired. A word to the ladies, though: if you are planning on having sex, don't put powder all over your breasts. I understand those with big breasts wear powder at times to keep them bad boys from sweating, especially in summer, but men don't want to have to ingest powder either off the breasts or the pussy when they go down on you.

Now, let's do a brief overview of eating pussy. Yes, eating pussy. For those men who still go downtown only to window-shop, I have a revelation for you. Unless you start making some purchases while you are there, your lady might find a frequent buyer someplace else. While being caressed with the hands and fingers is a great turn-on also, there is nothing like a man eating your pussy good.

But . . . there are a few things I should say to those men who think they belong in the Pussy Eaters Hall of Fame but really belong in the visitors' line to get in and see the pictures of the ones who are really in there. A woman's clit is very sensitive and can't take a great deal of direct stimulation. You should concentrate more on the areas around the clit and never try to shove your tongue all the way in her pussy and, for goodness sake, never bite on the clit. Chances are, if you are doing that, the times you think a woman is trying to pull away from you 'cause the pleasure is too much for her and you grab for her and tell her to give you your pussy back, her ass is pulling away 'cause that shit hurts.

Also, when you are eating a woman's pussy, use your hands to caress her breasts. In fact, use one hand to caress her breasts and finger her ass with the other. You would be surprised how many women experience a feeling of loneliness while a man is eating them out. You have your head buried between her legs and she is staring at the ceiling. Some more sexually open women, those who masturbate—and I can't stress the benefits of that enough :-)—take the initiative and fondle their own breasts, but they shouldn't have to. So use all available hands and get busy with more than just your tongue.

I am gonna make this short 'cause this is making me horny.

As for the actual sex itself, here is the nitty-gritty.

Most men have the misconception that the bigger the dick, the greater the pleasure. Ummm, naw. While I will be the first one to admit that looking at big dicks can be sexually arousing just like big breasts on a woman sexually arouse men, I am not fucking a man with an abnormal-size dick and most women I know would agree. Just like breasts, more than a mouthful is a waste, and there is no way in hell a normal woman can deep-throat a long-ass, thick dick, and riding one or having it inside you can be extremely painful.

I like men with normal-size dicks. What is normal? I would say a good size is anywhere from seven to ten inches. Personally, if I had to choose, I would pick thickness over length and I will tell you why. Only the first few inches of a woman's vagina are extremely sensitive and so that is why many woman can achieve orgasms better when the man hits the walls instead of trying to get his dick all the way up in her stomach. I like a man to slowly grind his dick in me instead of pumping it into me like I am a gas tank. I also prefer to ride a dick slowly instead of riding a dick like it is a pogo stick. I do love it doggy-style but not for the reasons one might suspect. While it does allow the dick to go farther inside of a woman, the biggest benefit to having sex in the doggy-style position is that it allows the woman more freedom of movement. When we are pinned up underneath a man with our ankles over our head, it is mighty hard to participate. While you men are so-called knocking the bottom out, we are feeling like the losing contestant in a wrestling match. It feels so much better to be able to guide some of the movement ourselves.

As for oral sex, I agree that women should at least try sucking dick 'cause the shit is the bomb :-). However, just like anal sex, if a woman is not ready for it emotionally, the shit ain't happening. But when she is ready, let her do her own thing. Don't stand there and shove your dick in and out of her mouth; let her control the rhythm and the pace. Sometimes a woman just wants to savor a dick and lick it all over instead of having it pounded in and out of her mouth. So take heed to my words, 'cause if you persist in doing it your way, her ass may not be so willing next time. I already discussed the swallowing issue, so no need to go there except to say if she doesn't want to, just like everything else, that is her prerogative.

On to anal sex. Not all women are gonna do it, pure and simple. That is still considered a serious taboo and most women think it will hurt so bad they refuse even to try it. Then there are the contradictions. Men talk trash about homosexuals fucking each other in the ass but then they want to turn around and fuck their women in the ass. Confusing, huh? You may be able to solve the problem by doing what I said earlier, COMMUNICATING.

However, if a woman is willing to have anal sex, make sure you let her guide your dick in and make sure you use a good lubricant and a condom. Hell, use a condom period. But don't try to systematically shove your dick in her ass all at once. Remember that you are not the one on the receiving end of that bad boy, so let her control the motions. Some women prefer to be flat on their stomach, some prefer to be in the doggy-style position, and some prefer to lie on the side. But after discussing anal sex with some of my fellow sisters who are anal retentive like myself, the consensus is that anal sex is most pleasurable with the woman's legs on the man's shoulders, in the missionary position so to speak, because it allows for more clitoral and vaginal stimulation.

I am gonna end this now, but I will be writing much more on this some other time, by saying that the worst mistake men make during lovemaking is wanting to receive more than they are willing to give. There are some men who are still concerned only with their own pleasure, and they are the worst lovers on earth, in my view. If I run into a man like that, who wants me to do this and that to him and offers little or nothing in return, his ass doesn't have to worry about seeing my ass again nor many of my fellow sisters in pursuit of the ultimate sexual satisfaction. Men who want to suck a woman's nipples for ten seconds and then expect her to suck his dick till he cums are not high commodities in this world. Nor are two-minute brothers, but sometimes that can't be helped.

For those men having trouble sustaining an erection, I do have a suggestion: Baby Orajel. I am dead serious. The numbing effect allows for decreased levels of sensitivity in the male, thus allowing sustained performance for those who are overly sensitive and easily stimulated. There is also a very expensive root called yohimbe found in Chinese stores that is great for sustaining an erection.

Hmm, other than that all I can say is adventure and variety are the spice of life. Drink some warm tea while eating a woman out and let it trickle down to her ass. Stick a Flintstone Push-Up ice cream bar in her vagina and then let her watch you lick her pussy off of it. Put some Ben Wa balls in the freezer and then insert them in her and fuck her with them inside her. Be experimental with ice, whipped cream, honey, all the usual stuff. And by all means suck her toes and her ass; she will cum from the mere thought of you. :-) As for other ideas, you will just have to wait and read them in my stories. I don't want to give all my secrets away just yet, dayum!

A final note to the brothers: A WOMAN IS ONLY AS GOOD OR BAD IN BED AS THE MAN WHO MOTIVATES HER! SO IF YOUR

WOMAN IS JUST LYING THERE LIKE A RAG DOLL, BUT YOU KNOW SHE REALLY HAS THE BOMB-ASS PUSSY, ASK HER WHAT IS WRONG. C-O-M-M-U-N-I-C-A-T-E!

Peace be to the real and, as usual, any questions or comments, good or bad, email me at zane@eroticanoir.com.

The Art of Masturbation

"When in doubt, stroke it out!"

There are a lot of books trying to tell people how to masturbate, but they sound more like plans to build a model car than telling how to get your freak on, so here is the art of masturbation according to Zane.

Basically, masturbation is sex involving one person, but it doesn't have to mean touching your dick if you are a man "jacking off" or touching your pussy if you are a woman "jilling off." Jack and Jill—get it?

"Manual sex" or "mutual masturbation" is when two partners get each other off without actually kissing, sucking, licking, or fucking. They manually make each other cum.

Some people masturbate in groups. I know what you all are thinking: Zane is going way out there again! Well, I am, because I don't like my shit to be boring, so deal with it or stop reading. When people masturbate in a group, it can be called several things, including a "circle jerk." When it is a bunch of men sitting around the crib getting their shit off, it is called a "Jacks" party. When it is only women, it is called a "Jills" party, and if it is a open freak-for-all, it is called a "Jack and Jill" party. Like duh?

The "parties" can involve everyone getting each other off by feeling each other up, or everyone can do his or her own thing while people watch. It is up to the participants to lay down the law before the shit even goes that far.

Before I go any further, let me resolve all the typical myths and superstitions attached to masturbation.

Will a man's dick get bigger or smaller from masturbation? Hells naw! If that were true, half the men would be lifting dumbbells with their dicks and the other half would be limp-dick leprechaun midgets.

Can you catch a disease from masturbation? That shit is so stupid I am not even going to go there. If you honestly have to sit there and ponder the issue, you need to seek professional help immediately 'cause your ass is stupid.

Can masturbation cause a dick or pussy to become deformed? Hmmm, let me think! Hells naw! Do you have any idea how many people masturbate? That would mean everybody's shit would be fucked da hell up.

Can other people tell if you have been masturbating? Well, there is a possibility there, because most people are in the best mood after they cum, so if you are married and you haven't been getting none, your mate may be able to tell if you start dancing around the house and singing "I Did It My Way" after your ass has been locked up in the bathroom for a half hour.

Is masturbation only for people who can't get some "real" sex? Once again, hells naw! Truth be known, people who masturbate are generally more open sexually than their counterparts. Basically, if you don't masturbate and play around with things, how will you know for sure what gets you off best? Your mate can't tell, 'cause the only psychics are clocking $3.99 a minute from fools who call them up when they don't have shit else to do. By the way, and this doesn't have a damn thing to do with the topic at hand, if psychics know so damn much and can pick winning lottery numbers, why are all their asses still working? Maybe we should all utilize our ten free minutes, blow up the phone lines, and find out.

Here are some more of my favorite myths in no significant order of importance, because they are all bullshit.

- You will make yourself sick if you eat your own cum.

- You will go blind, bald, insane, grow hair on your palms, and your dick will fall off.

- You won't be able to get jiggy with a partner if you masturbate. Chile, please!

- You will become obsessed with masturbation. I cannot tell a lie. I might have that problem, but it's all good. Better than being obsessed with eating chitterlings.

- You will burn in hell for masturbating. Oh, well, I better buy me a thong bikini, 'cause it may get kind of humid down there.

There are several other terms for "jacking off," including "beat your meat like it owes you money," "butter the corn," "choke the sheriff and wait for the posse to come," "educating Peter," "evicting the testicular squatters," "five against one," "getting in touch with your inner self," "givin' Yul Brynner a high five," "hand-to-gland combat," "inoculate the newborn," "launching the tadpoles," "little pinky hit the Slinky," "meet your right-hand man," "one-eye target practice," "pumping gas at the self-service island," "running the whackathon," "sifting through the nest to find mama bird," "spit-shining the boots," "squeezing the cream filling from the Twinkie," "surfing on the milky highway," "take matters into your own hands," "teach your dog to spit," "tug-o'-war with ol' Cyclops," and "wanking the one-eyed wonder worm."

Likewise, there are several other terms for "jilling off," including "brushing the beaver," "doing my nails," "doing the two-finger slot rumba," "finger blasting," "flicking the bean," "going mining," "makin' waves for the man in the boat," "making soup," "nulling the void," "paddling the pink canoe," "parting the Red Sea," "playing the beaver," "playing the silent trombone," "rolling the dough," "strumming the banjo," "surfin' the channel," "the two-fingered tango," "tickling the taco," and "toggling the bit."

Now, for those sexually repressed people turning their noses up at me right about now, let me ask you why the hell you are still reading this. There is nothing wrong with masturbating, because if you don't want to touch your own dick or coochie-coo, why the hell should someone else? I have often wondered why people think it is kosher and acceptable to touch someone else's privates and not their own. At least you know where yours have been. You follow?

Sex Games from A to Z

*W*anna spice up your sex life? Wanna turn your mate the hell out? Then stop doing the same shit in the bed all the time and get creative. I often get requests, from both men and women, wanting to know how they can enhance their sex lives. So here is my rendition of the ABCs.

Assume the Position. This is fairly simple and has different variations. You handcuff or tie your partner's hands to the headboard or, if you prefer, you can tie them behind his or her back. Your partner is at your mercy and you can have your way with them all night long. If you live in a basement apartment with pipes on the ceiling or have something else you can use, you can tie him or her up to the ceiling while standing. This is great with the woman tied up because you can fuck her while she is standing or you can lift her up on your shoulders and eat her pussy.

Belly Button Shots. Pour tequila into your mate's belly button and lick the right side of his or her chest and shake some salt on it. Squeeze some lemon or lime juice on the left side of his or her chest and then lick the salt and make your way down to the belly button with your tongue so you can lap up the tequila. Then trace a trail back up to the lemon or lime juice with your tongue and lick it off. Repeat on each other until you can no longer refrain from jumping each other's bones.

Cum for Me, Boo. Resort to drastic measures and whip out the sex toys to see how many times you can make each other cum in the span of one evening. Whoever makes the other person cum the most wins and gets pampered and waited on for an entire weekend or whatever else you may want to wager. This can be very delightful, especially if both partners have an oral fixation.

Do Not Disturb. Spend an entire weekend in a hotel room with the Do Not Disturb sign on the door. Take snacks and plenty of water for hydration purposes and fuck the hell out each other until both of you can barely walk. It may sound harsh, but you can't knock it until you try it.

Erotic Endeavors. Both you and your partner make a list of your sexual fantasies you want to play out. Trade lists and then set a deadline to make all of each other's fantasies come true.

Feast. Zane's variation of cleaning out the fridge. Instead of throwing away all the half-empty bottles of this or that lurking in your fridge, place a blanket on the floor (so your asses won't get cold) by the open fridge door and get down on the blanket butt-naked. One at a time, take turns selecting items from the fridge to eat off each other. If you are one of those people who eat out every night because of a busy schedule and have an empty fridge, pick up a couple of items such as whipped cream, chocolate syrup, and cake frosting (yes, I said cake frosting) on your way home and satisfy your "sweet" tooth.

The Game. Break out all the old favorites like Monopoly, Scrabble, checkers, Chutes and Ladders if you are a bit slow, or chess if you got it like that. You can even play charades. Whatever game you choose, whoever loses has to become the "sex slave" of the winner and do everything he or she demands.

Happy Birthday. Throw your mate a surprise private birthday party when it is not anywhere near his or her birthday. Order a birthday cake, buy presents that are all sexual in nature such as lingerie, sex toys, and edible underwear, and watch his or her face light up when you take them by surprise.

Indecent Proposal. This is a variation of truth or dare, but truth's ass is out of town. Dare your mate to do something outrageous sexually. Something you know your partner thinks he or she is too prim and proper to do. This game works only if both partners are willing to let go of all sexual inhibitions.

Just Do It. Meet your mate at the door one day and cut the bullshit. Like Nike says, "Just do it!" Oftentimes, people dream about fucking all day and then tense up when the time comes to put up or shut up. They wait for their partner to make the first move. Fuck all that! Go for yours and break the world record for getting naked in the least amount of seconds. Better yet, answer the door butt-naked.

Kinky Game. Sit down together and compile a list of kinky things you both want to try, such as S & M, using Ben Wa balls, butt plugs, anal beads, dildos, whatever, and make out a schedule for the week. If you are not quite there yet, make out a list of unusual positions you want to try. No matter what, stick to the schedule and do a different thing every single night for an entire week.

Life Imitates Art. Very simple! Watch some movies, preferably pornos but some R-rated movies have vivid sex scenes as well. Pick out some of your favorite scenes from movies and act them out with your partner. If you really want to get jiggy with it, break out the camera and make your own version of the original film.

Mother, May I? Enough said. Play Mother, May I? in the bedroom, and you can't do a damn thing without getting permission first. Okay, so I still have a little girl lurking in me.

Naked Twister. It doesn't get any easier to explain than this. Hit up a toy store and buy the old-time favorite kids' game Twister. Take it home, get butt-naked with your mate, pop in *Cooley High* or *Shaft*, make a pitcher of Kool-Aid, and play the game. Of course, being naked gives it an interesting "twist" (no pun intended).

Open House. This can be done in two ways. If you live in an area where kids go to bed at a decent hour, open up all your curtains, shades, and blinds late one night, turn on all the lights, and freak the hell out of each other. I know it sounds silly, but the mere thought that someone might be watching can be a fantastic turn-on. The other way it can be done is to fuck each other in a house full of people while taking the risk that someone might walk in on you. This can be very exhilarating at holiday dinners where some old-fashioned relatives might catch you getting busy.

Public Display. Now, you have to be very sexually open to do this shit, but hey, I am, so I can recommend this shit. Fuck your mate in a public place such as on a subway train, city bus, or even airplane. Go to the movies and buy some nachos. Take the warm cheese spread and pour it on your mate's dick or pussy and perform oral sex in the theater and then fuck him or her. Go to a fancy restaurant and disappear under the linen tablecloth and have oral sex. Fuck in elevators, in public restrooms, on a picnic table, in the laundry room, in the stacks at the library. Let me quit 'cause my ass is getting excited just thinking about it.

Q & A. One of my favorites, 'cause no one likes a dumb-ass person in bed. It is a trivia game. In fact, you can play an actual game if you like, such as Trivial Pursuit. Your mate has to get a certain amount of answers right or he or she can't get none that night. You can even watch *Jeopardy!* or *Wheel of Fortune* and play this, or, if you have been with your mate a considerable amount of time, ask questions about you that he or she should know the answer to. This game can be fun, especially when your mate is feenin for some sex and you make him or her earn it.

Recycled Virgin. Both you and your partner take turns pretending you are virgins. You take one night of the week and he or she can take the next one. Have your partner walk you through it and calm your "imaginary" fears by giving you step-by-step instructions. You can act shy and timid and keep pushing your partner away when he or she gets to certain "bases," and it can be interesting to see how long you can pretend not to know a damn thing. I mean, how many "experienced" people can just lie there when they are getting fucked royally?

Spelling Bee. Umm, another favorite. For the men, spell out the alphabet on your woman's clit and even spell out her name. For the ladies, do the same with his dick and/or balls. You can blindfold your partner or have him or her close their eyes while you spell out something and they have to try to guess the word. You have to have some major tongue skills in order to pull this one off, though, 'cause I don't think they sell Hooked on Phonics for oral sex.

Talk Dirty to Me. Phone sex the hell out of each other, pure and simple. If you have a cell phone, call your mate from the car and have phone sex on the way home so that by the time you get there, it will be time to set it off, and I don't mean robbing banks like in the movie. Unless, of course, you are talking about robbing cum banks.

Under No Circumstances. You gotta love this one, and it is a game of mind over matter. It also requires a hell of a lot of willpower. Without tying your partner's hands or confining him or her in any way, announce that he or she cannot touch you no matter what you do. That means you can't touch a woman if she does a lap dance or even if she sucks your dick. Same goes for the women. No touching whatsoever or you will have to pay the penalty. My suggested penalty is that you must perform oral sex on your mate for twelve hours straight if you fuck up.

Vision Quest. Bet your partner something sexual in nature and then go outside. Pick a certain item such as a red canary or a squirrel or a butterfly. Whoever is the first one to spot the object—and yes, it must be verified by the other party to prevent cheating—wins the game. If you really want to get creative, play that old favorite Cars and pick a certain make or model of vehicle beforehand. Whoever's turn it is when that type of car drives by is declared the winner.

What Flavor Is It? Go to a sex shop and purchase different flavors of body oils. If you happen to live in a small-ass town where the local Wal-Mart is the closest thing to a sex shop, go to the cosmetics section and get some different flavors of lip gloss. This game works better with the woman as the test subject. Place a different flavor on each part of your body—your lips, your neck, each breast, your belly button, the inside of each thigh, and your clit. Your man has to lick each spot in turn and guess the flavor correctly or no nookie. Hmm, I wonder what flavor works best on a clit. Cherry, maybe. Get it?

Xtra Naked. Cover the bed or floor with an old blanket or something you don't mind messing up and then get naked. Cover each other with baby oil from head to toe so that you are both very slippery, and then fuck. It will be hard even to hold on to each other and private parts will be slipping and sliding everywhere, but it is mad funny.

You Do Me. Mutual masturbation. Get each other off. Or, for those who have a dildo hanging around, you can fuck your woman with a dildo until she cums. Whatever's clever!

The Zane. The Zane means taking all of my suggestions for sex games and playing each and every one of them in the span of two months. I wonder how many of you can do it, 'cause that means fucking EVERY NIGHT. If you decide to take the Zane Challenge, email me at zane@eroticanoir.com and let me know the results.

Dear Zane . . .
A Lust Letter from a Fan
William Fredrick Cooper

*T*his letter demonstrates how reading my books can fuel the imagination to such a point that readers can create their own fantasy and live vicariously through the pages of a book or the fantasy created around those pages. This particular fantasy letter was created in the mind of William Fredrick Cooper, whose imagination has also created two great novels, *Six Days in January* and *There's Always a Reason*. Creating fantasies like this with your partner after reading a Zane book aloud to each other might be just the spark needed to rekindle a flagging romance.

Dear Zane,

Can I fuck you? No, not realistically, though the vision of penetrating you to the hilt with something rich and thick makes a certain part of me stand at attention.

A twenty-one-cum . . . I mean twenty-one-gun salute is in order here, for I am *Nervous* writing this. Demure yet devilish thoughts invade me. I am *Addicted* to the *Sisters of APF* as they are *Gettin' Buck Wild* with me in my dreams. Loins ablaze while my body is aflutter in arousal, the thought of adding some *Chocolate Flava* to my vision of creating *Sex Chronicles* with you sure leaves a brotha spent. The *Skyscraper* at my groin wants to find your *Dear G-Spot* so badly when reading your stories. And when it's all done, there'll be no *Afterburn*, honey. This hungry *Heat Seeker* is ready for twelve rounds with the author who has liberated the libido of many a woman.

Zane, can I invade your dreams and awaken your senses with an erotically captivating fantasy? Can I be the fantastic phallus that you crave as much as the air you breathe, if only for a moment in dreamland?

Can I make you cum tonight, the way you have made so many others?

I thought you'd say yes. So sit back, sweetie, and allow me to take your hand, as we travel into my land of make-believe.

I'm a pretty ordinary guy, about five-eleven, athletically built, been married before, and I pay my taxes. There are two things, however, that people tend to notice and remember. First, I'm very bowlegged and muscular, and I get my share of comments about my body. Second, I have a very long . . . um, part of me. About ten inches in length and two in thickness, it seems to draw as much locker-room attention from men as it has from my former spouse and the women I have stroked down. Though dark and lengthy, I think it's the width and hook when erect that make it exceptional.

I get all kinds of nicknames for my hardness. A couple of guys call me "Mighty Man," and my ex-wife's label for my masculinity was "Wonder Dick." In fact, she kept K-Y Jelly in her nightstand the entire time we were together. As she lay back awaiting my movements, I rocked her with the rhythm and stamina from an elongated tool, then made her sigh with pleasure with my sweet embrace.

She loved sucking my veined heat, and was a past master at deep-throat. Watching my member vanish and reemerge in her oral cavity, she carried me to a higher pleasure plateau each and every time she embraced my fullness. With nary a gag, the fluidity of her oral strokes combined with eager, hungry moans always made my toes curl. After swallowing my man-juice, she would give me that pleasure-pain feeling men experience when she nibbled on my sensitive bulb. Damn, that shit felt good. Makes me wonder why I ever divorced her.

But this isn't about her. It's all about you, Boo. Can I call you that? I hope you don't mind.

My life had been in a downhill spiral ever since I walked into my office a year ago and immediately was called into my superior's office. After he gained the position as senior managing partner of our law firm, I never felt as if he wanted to coexist with an intelligent black man in the position of director of litigation support.

Sure enough, my gut feeling proved to be right when the human resource manager told me I was terminated, briefly stating that "the department was going in another direction." Though my first instinct was to grab her and say, "Bitch, my supervisor is the asshole you should be getting rid of," remarkably I remained calm, even as Knucklehead Nuclear had the audacity to invite me into his office to, in his words, "talk about it." What the fuck was there to talk about?

Needless to say, I wasn't a happy camper. Without a job for nearly a year, I meandered my way through agencies, six months of unemployment checks and job interviews for positions that, as told by headhunters after meeting with potential employers, I was either overqualified for, wanted too much money for, or, in one instance, the potential employers thought "I might get bored with." Being unemployed can also stall the dating life. Can you imagine me catching the eye of a potential queen, exchanging numbers, making that first phone call, and when the topic of employment surfaces, summoning the courage to tell her that I'm between jobs? Sadly, lonely nights accompanied the instability. Craving the warmth and affection of a potential goddess, there were many evenings I wanted to feel the inside of something deep, something warm, something that clenches and unclenches around my tool if I made it feel good. The ragged, aroused breaths of a woman are only in fantasy when jobless, and the salty, squirting spurts of satisfaction you'd love to share are reserved for five fingers, a palm, and a cold washcloth afterward. Instead of passionate kisses, feverish foreplay, and tender lovemaking, my nights were spent watching Lexington Steele, Byron Long, Wesley Pipes, and others doing their thing with women they'll never see again after those adult movie scenes.

Soon, watching those films became tedious as well, and I now needed to temper dual melancholies. Not only was I without a steady income, but my sexual cravings had me feeling like Robinson Crusoe on a deserted island. Knowing that Hanna and her five sisters could only take the edge off so much, I wondered what additional methods of self-manipulation he utilized for erotic fulfillment. It seemed that everything I did reminded me of sex.

Even treating myself to a day at Times Square conjured up forbidden desires. Walking along Eighth Avenue made me reminisce about another time in my life when I was forlorn, and how I learned to master my sexual craft by watching peep shows all night long. Mesmerized by all of the pounding on screen, I studied all techniques, as I wanted to make sure my shit was proper when my opportunities presented themselves. *Having a big stick is good only if you know how to use it,* I mumbled, and while in appreciation of the culturally fresh quality-of-life renovations, part of me longed for the sleaziness that was stripped away.

Turning back and strolling onto Broadway, I decided to visit the bookstore in the lower level of the Virgin Music Megastore and peruse the erotica section. Running across *Gettin' Buck Wild: Sex Chronicles II*, I shrugged my shoulders as if to say, "Why not?" and purchased it. After all, I saw so many people, young and old, reading your books on the New York subways and was like, "What's so exciting about a Zane novel?" Being well versed in horny literature, I read too many tales that were supposed to make my nature rise and, upon completion, felt like a woman disappointed when a lover couldn't maintain an erection.

Dimming the lights at home, I turned on my computer's MusicMatch and put on Luther Vandross's "Think About You." As I longed for a job and holding someone special, a familiar place on my couch found me, and I cracked open my entertainment for the evening.

It would be hours before I left that space. My sexual wanting intensified by what I interpreted through your words, so many fantasies ran amok. Feeling fuckstrated, my yearlong "no job–no pussy" drought felt like decades as I devoured story after story and thought of you. Role-playing, I envisioned us in a desolate subway car after a Broadway show, sharing a quickie. My tool was hard as steel as I fondly fingered your canal. Hoping you would straddle me while no one was looking, I wondered if you had motion in your femininity, or in the alternative, would I need to take the lead from below.

I was pleasantly surprised. Now inside of you, our hips were synchronized in mutual pleasure as I enjoyed the aroma from your cherry-scented panties. Playfully pinching those cute nipples, you surpassed every fantasy when your booty bounced at top speed. You tremble now, uncontrollably. Instead of you jacking me off after your orgasm, I demanded that you stay on board as the captain went down with his ship, that is, after Daddy released hot juices inside of you. After my climax, the passengers at the other end of the car took notice of what transpired and applauded raucously. Sharing an impish grin, our thoughts were one. We brought out the freak in each other.

Next transforming into the Rastafarian with D-I-C-K across his T-shirt, I had a deep bass tone to my voice as I seduced you in a movie theater. My name was Orlando, and I wanted to stimulate your clit after I placed Red

Hots in my mouth. I loved the cinnamon flavor of them, yet when mixed with pussy juice, the flavor seemed better, so I had to dine on you.

Majestically munching on you while Al Pacino graced the screen, no, I'm not Tony Montana in *Scarface* but the detective who fell for Ellen Barkin in *Sea of Love*. Courageously captivating your clitoris, I was a magician with my tongue, as the dessert downstairs was indescribably delicious. Hearing your heavenly moans only served as confirmation that my oral skillz were spectacular, and spelled with a capital Z. Capitalized and underlined four times, I might add.

After you came, I entered your warm heaven with my erect hunger. Feeding you more and more of me, you pumped your hips so that I could invade your treasure deeper. Fat and juicy, you swallowed me and, surprisingly, begged for more.

"My God!" you screamed. "You feel amazing!"

Our hips quivered as you matched me stroke for stroke. Both of us were grunting from the sloppy, slurping sounds your cunny made as I stroked and stroked. Praising my thug loving, you talked so much shit in my ear.

"Fuck me! Fuck me good, Stallion! Keep going! So good! So deep!"

Our bodies fused as one flesh in desire; your moans got louder, huskier, and deeper. Soon, you succumbed to my rhythm by shuddering intensely while screaming. Not far behind, I released my gooey appreciation inside of the protective coating. Fantasy fulfilled, I awakened from my lust with a stream of semen to my chest. Wishing you in my presence cleaning up my soup with your tongue, the cold towel used to clean myself served as a sad substitute. But I did find solace in the fact that I would be at the bookstore tomorrow to get another one of your novels.

Returning to the source of my erotic crime the very next afternoon, I made a beeline to the arousal section once more and purchased *The Sisters of APF: The Indoctrination of Soror Ride Dick*. As opposed to waiting until my arrival home, I decided to acquaint myself with the investment club women in an adjacent, in-store bakery. Once seated, the return ticket to dreamland was punched, and the spaceship traveled at light speed to get there.

First introducing myself to Soror Deep Throat, I envisioned us in my garden of love. Her bare knees digging into the soft blades of grass, I wanted to see how good she really was at fellatio.

"Hands behind your back, Honey."

"What for?" my lover in fantasy asked.

My response was not of words, but action. Smirking, I reached behind me and picked up a pair of handcuffs.

"No hands tonight, Honey."

My swagger was met with a look of equal transformation. Her altered intensity matched mine with a tender, trash-talking tone.

"You want me to take all of you? You want me to swallow all of your juices? Is that what you want, Baby?"

Hearing that intimidated and aroused me all at once, but I remained poised as I locked her wrists together and removed my leopard-print G-string. Thinking my length and girth would unnerve her, I was stunned by her aggression. Her mouth watered like a drenched tunnel, and after licking her lips in anticipation, she swallowed hard to keep herself from drooling.

"Mmm, I want to suck Big James and his giant peaches."

Puckering her lips and kissing up and down my length, she caused that special part to throb intensely. Pausing ever so briefly to allow my precum to explore her taste buds, she peered upward from my groin.

"Are you sure you want no hands, Daddy?"

I nodded, and her pipe-draining process continued. Shaping and stretching her jawline, Ms. Deep Throat consumed half to three-quarters of my shaft without choking. Damn, she was good. Bobbing fluidly, each oral stroke had the white lava boiling within. Grunting while my knees sagged, I regrouped slightly as my body stiffened in preparation for a volcanic release. Feeling my purple bulb pulsate, Soror Deep Throat locked those lethal red lips tightly around my steel and applied maximum suction. Within seconds, my breath shortened. Straining, I groaned helplessly as an eruption of fluid left me. That she made gulping sounds only brought more from me, not to mention the intense spasms that accompany sexual heat. As if rendering me weak wasn't enough, she sucked on my tip until I begged her to stop. Before I collapsed to the grass below, we shared a tender kiss as I released her from bondage.

"Next time, let me use my hands," she ordered.

Sister Cum Hard was next, washing ashore on that deserted island I spoke of earlier. I was about to extract juices from what seemed like the umpteenth coconut when I felt a sudden tap on my shoulder.

"Don't you think it's time for a real meal, Sugar?"

Startled by the foreign tone, I turned to see something delightful, delectable, and potentially delicious. To say that seeing a strawberry-and-whipped-cream-adorned honey hole was a little more pleasurable than the volleyball of Tom Hanks's affection in that movie *Cast Away* was a gross understatement. Starving for food and hungry for companionship, the famished fire in my eyes met an equally aroused smile.

"Come and get it, Baby."

She didn't have to say it twice. Pressing her back to the sandy shore, it took all the control I could muster to take my time. I hadn't been with a woman in quite some time, so I inhaled the scent of her fruit-flavored body as our tongues wetly wrestled. Slowly and seductively, my hands traced the outline of her firm, almond-shaped breasts. Following my fingertip compass, my lips perused candy, berry-sweet nipples. I was eager to get to my treat below. However, I remained steadfast in my patience, for school was open for the professor. Soror Cum Hard was being treated to a crash course in dessert dining by an oral connoisseur.

Lovingly lubricating her navel with an animated critter between rescued lips, I bypassed her pleasure zone, but not before partaking of a strawberry, kissing those luscious stems leading to her heaven on earth and sucking on her pretty toes. She had already cum twice. However, Slow Hand Luke wanted to awaken and arouse every sensitive nerve in her body. Her love spot would be drenched and dripping before I got lost in her sauce.

I snapped my fingers, and instantly our mood was enhanced by Usher's "That's What It's Made For." My head bobbing to the tempo of the song, I wondered if she ever had been tongue-lashed to the rhythmic beat. My answer came swiftly as my mouth finally met the middle of her chestnut-colored inner thighs. Scrumptiously slick and glistening, I could tell that her kitty had been neglected. Fluttering and flickering, I set out on a deliberate course to bring as many orgasms as humanly possible from Ms. Cum Hard.

Knowing every trick in the pussy-eating arsenal, I utilized indirect stimulation of her G-spot by rubbing my chin against her entrance, driving her crazy. Next, it was inward bound with my nose while my lively lizard swirled in a circular motion at the space between honey spot and anus. Finally focusing on her large clitoris, I attacked her bead as if it were my last meal. Sucking and nibbling as I slid three long fingers into her drenched forest, I wanted to feel the orgasmic contractions she experienced just as much as she did.

True to her name, Soror Cum Hard came forcefully, repeatedly. As I loved her labia, a river of tasteful juices poured from her as she begged for more.

"Stick your tongue in me, Professor," she wailed as her body shuddered. "Stick it inside of me."

Cream-colored cum juice mixed with the dairy products made for an awfully good beverage. Delightfully drinking from her fountain, I responded to her pleadings by spreading her lovely dancer legs far apart and ramming my entire face inside of her. Locking my lips at her triangle, I tried to drain all the pulp of her paradise. She couldn't take it for long, for the cords of her neck strained with pleasure. Deep groans left her as she moved in circular motions.

Grinding her hips hard and steady against my face while building the tempo and momentum of the moment, Señorita Cum Plenty would experience another set of climactic convulsions. My appetite finally satisfied, our mouths met once more, fully expressing mutual appreciation.

"So, when's the ship coming?" I asked.

Soror Cum Hard chuckled.

"You have one more APF sister to please."

I nodded approvingly.

"Right. How could I have forgotten?"

Assistant District Attorney Ride Dick loomed deep in my mind, for if ever there was a kryptonite to this Superman, it was a woman who can make it bounce like the hydraulics of a MTV lowrider while I'm deep inside of her. Sexually speaking, I have returned many women to the missionary position. Not that I was a control freak or anything like that; but truth be told, they were down with a rhythmless nation.

Simply stated, not a lot of women can ride a man properly. That grinding on top in the cowgirl or reverse cowgirl position simply doesn't work here, the latter being my fault as much as theirs, for when hard as steel, I hook to my stomach. If a woman can straddle me properly and lift her pelvis up off my member, flutter her hips like a butterfly while contracting her muscles around me, then she has me dead to rights. Some men like nice and sloppy blow jobs; others prefer to selfishly pound the kitty until the cops come knockin'. As I climbed the mountains, I prayed that Soror Ride Dick's bronco techniques would be both my sweetness and weakness.

Entering the island's tropical rain forest, the skies opened up as I searched for the last of the sorority sisters. Wanting to please her as much as she would me, my arousal intensified tenfold when I entered a dark, wooded area.

My hunt for the woman in question ended abruptly when I was caught off guard by her, suddenly, swiftly, with animalistic passion. Out of nowhere, my eyes were covered as I was pushed against a tree, and a slithering object between feminine lips forced my brim open. Meeting her ferocity with equal aggression, I removed her hand from my eyes and saw a vision of perfection. Her full breasts saluting me, she had a small waist that dipped seductively, flaring out to firm round hips and strong legs. Loving the sexy skin she was in, I knew that Soror Ride Dick was willing to receive as much as she could give.

Resuming our kiss, we danced from the bark and fell to the ground. Dirt now mixing with limbs, lust, and the torrential downpour, we both smiled, nodded, and melded together in a muddy passion. You would have thought we had known each other forever, for our movements were synchronized. I would gyrate left, she right, and our pelvises met in the middle. She would utilize stomach muscles to make her wide hips tick clockwise, and I followed suit, only counterclockwise. Opening our eyes, we stared deep, and again nodded. No words would be said during this rendezvous; the only sounds would be moans she would yield as I dug her back out and the groans I couldn't shield when she made her honey dance on my erotic life force.

There was no foreplay with the counselor, only unchained barbarianism at its very best. Entering her from the missionary position while spreading her legs wide, I locked her ankles and thighs with my forearms and went to work. A sensation of hot fury consumed her as I unleashed my full repertoire. Utilizing figure-eight motion, V-movements and fisted push-up strokes, flutter pelvic pumps and slow, circular hip gyrations, my mission was to seek and destroy her syrupy sweet spot.

Rotating inside of her, my hooked heat uncoiled completely. With the pride of an everlasting stallion, I continued to thrust and lunge through the core of her. The long, low, lust-laden wails she issued encouraged me to get that glassy-eyed look of rapture from her.

Penetrating deeper, the squishing sounds of something saucy blended perfectly with squeals and squawks, only intensifying my dance. It was incredible, Soror Ride Dick's stamina, that is, for she actually began taking the pouring perspiration from me into her eager mouth. This woman was bad as she wanted to be. And I loved it.

Soon, I broke her down as I increased the tempo. Digging deeper and stirring things around with my reliable fuck fastener, I found that spot that sends women over the edge and concentrated on her orgasm. Wanting to feel it and determined to see it, the signs were slow but revealing. Clawing at the grass as she growled like a tigress, her fingernails sank deep into the soil below. Desperate gasps escaped her as a warm river of juices left her. Shuddering intensely, tears formed in her eyes as she curled her body into a fetal position after I removed myself. Recuperating quickly, she smiled devilishly and nodded in approval. Round One was a TKO.

Repositioning ourselves as the crystal sky drops ceased to fall, Soror Ride Dick positioned herself astride me, and her attitude and self-confidence took over. Lodging me inside her internal firestorm, her mouth met mine with a kiss that encouraged me to enjoy the ride. And I became putty in her hands as she released an amazing array of skills on me. Moving her midsection like a belly dancer, she fluttered her hips like an out-of-control butterfly. Next rolling them while clenching the muscles of her five-alarm blaze, the assistant D.A. varied the pace of her foray. Feeling the rumblings of my erotic explosion swell, Soror Ride Dick must have felt the ascension of my inner fire as well, for she increased the tempo to the speed of a runaway locomotive. Rising and falling on my tool while continuously clamping and clutching, she looked down at me with a wicked smile.

Nirvana came quick as the combination of violent trembles, unrepressed growls, and ragged breaths left me light-headed. Heat and cool waged a wild war with my loins as I felt a sudden, sharp thrill leave me by way of a sticky, salty substance. Screaming as my legs went limp, then numb, I tried to speak. However, Soror Ride Dick covered my lips with her index finger and closed my eyes with her free hand. Rising quickly, I heard the sound of ruffled leaves and restored my vision. The shadow of her moved quickly as it disappeared into the jungle.

Soror came. Soror saw. Soror conquered.

My journey on the planet make-believe was disturbed by the mood of an agitated store cashier ready to close shop.

"Excuse me, sir. It's nine o'clock. The store is closed."

"My bad," I responded while closing my book swiftly.

There was a change in the woman's disposition once she saw the cover.

"I see that you like Zane."

"I sure do. I finished this book in three hours."

"Do you know that she'll be signing at the bookstore tomorrow night?"

Eyebrows arched, my face wore a mixture of excitement and intrigue. She recognized the look instantly and before I could pose the obvious, I was beaten to the punch.

"It starts at six tomorrow, so get here at five. The lines will be long."

"I'll do that."

By the time I surfaced from my erotic playland and rejoined the summer nightlife outside the megastore, it was a certainty you would be greeted with two dozen red roses. Addicted and aroused, by the time I reached my apartment, a more daring decision was made. I wanted to seduce you.

Obsessed with turning fantasy into reality, an interesting blend of lust and curiosity held my head captive as it hit the cool side of my pillow. Visions of tomorrow dancing in my head, teasing me with an erotic guessing game, a myriad of questions flooded my senses as I wondered what it would actually be like to have sex with you. *Would it be so good I'd have to double back thrice for more and more of you? Would it have my name on it? Do you want to swing from the chandeliers in a frantic, frenzied, furious fuckfest? Or, in the alternative, would you prefer to savor a steamy, seductively sensual slow stroke session? How do you like your love served, Zane?*

How would I approach her with such a bold proposition? I thought. Could I accomplish my goal through verbal communication? Could I stand out among hundreds and create a magic from flowers alone? Dismissing that option immediately, I concluded that the best way to pique your interest would be to write a story. Rising from a restless sleep, I went to my computer, placed Alexander O'Neal's "The Morning After" on my MusicMatch, and lost myself in the thought of making love to you, Zane, after dark.

AFTER DARK

After dark is when the night is yours, Zane, for I would always come home to make love to you. Tonight, however, I want something different, baby. My arousal for your moist treasure is beyond reason this evening. I want you to remove yourself from writing and become my wench tonight.

The thought of you contracting around me is suffocating as I turn the key to the front door.

It's not gonna be a bedroom night tonight, I think.

Something is in the air on your end too, for the minute I enter, you ap-

proach me, nude, ready and wanting. Deep in passion from GO, the but-
tons fly off my shirt as you tear it open while avidly swallowing my lips with
a hungry kiss.

"Oh, shit!!!"

Trembling with pleasure from your aggression, my dick thickens instantly
as you rip open my trousers and lower yourself to my groin. Feeling the
nearness of your frame as you engulf my hardened tool, a low, prolonged
sound escapes my lips as your tongue dances hypnotic circles around its tip.

"Ooooh, Zane, that feels so good . . ."

Grabbing my base and licking me from stem to stern, then back again, I
swallow a soft moan as you gobble my hunger into your wet, warm mouth.
Oiling that special part of me with your oral liquid, you announce your intentions.

"Nice and sloppy is the way I want my dick tonight."

The exquisite torture of your lustful, lascivious lubrication of me tells me
so. My dick has never been harder. Experiencing a foreign stiffness, the intense, merciless throbbing of my shaft indicates the unleashing of a milk
flow is imminent. Where is it gonna go, Zane? On your shoulder, so it can
drip onto your ample cleavage? On your nose, so I can lick it clean with my
tongue? Or where it always goes?

My answer comes in your reaction. "Mm, Daddy, that was good . . ." Seeing you leave some of me on your index finger, I decide I want to taste what
you swallowed.

Extending your forefinger as you move to our sofa, the tender expression
in your eyes belies an animalistic craving for satisfaction. My heart pounding
in anticipation as I near the aroma of your femininity, I yearn to taste the
saucy-sweet insides of your pleasure zone as I fall to my knees. Pressing my
lips to your wetness, my tongue immediately darts into your secret place as I
send you spiraling into a pleasurable vortex of ecstasy. "Ooh, shit, please
don't stop . . ." Driving myself to the limit to satisfy you, delighting in the
near spell I have you under, faster and faster the object at my brim flutters.
Bravely, you try to control your reactions, but you can't.

"Lick this shit good, Daddy!" you scream between pants. Seductive, suc-
culent slurps sending sensuous sensations shooting through a shivering
body, I beg for a torrential flood of lust from your channel. The waterfall
flowing into my mouth is rich in substance, and the shit tastes good, Zane. It
really does.

But we're freaks tonight, I think as I drink from your intimate cavern. We must go deeper. *My face wet with your release, I make you sample yourself when ordering you to lick my aroused countenance. Emitting a soft moan with each breath, you slide a finger, then two into your canyon as I stroke my swollen manhood in preparation for your accommodation. My erection painfully hard, the urgency to fill your moistness is overwhelmingly intoxicating. Clenching your fists in anticipation of entry, your voice becomes deeper as a singular command comes from your throat.*

"NOW!"

Growing erect against your smooth, satiny hue, I rub my protrusion against a hungry clitoris. Writhing against you, then in you, I sigh as my eyes squeeze shut while driving deep, then deeper. Slowly lengthening my strokes with each movement, my rhythm next becomes circular as I fill all of you with all of me. "Keep it slow, Baby, all right?" *Blazing and burning, you are in a state of physical combustion as you contract around me.*

"Oh shit, Honey, hit it good!!!"

Free-falling into a passionate surrender, you moan uncontrollably with each thrust. Nearing simultaneous orgasms, the slowness of the buildup makes my release along the nexus of nerves in your walls that much better. Your eruptions escalate, then subside, as our bodies come together in love once more as we fall from the skies of contentment, eternally satisfied after dark.

Confidence oozed from my pores as I finished the story, then reviewed it. *She's gonna want me,* I thought. Dreaming of you opening wide, letting me sink in, stir and swirl in the secrets of your garden had me going crazy. *She's gonna want me,* I thought once more. The vision of you and me grunting and groaning, mixing and moaning, behaving like two untamed animals in the heat of passion made a warm solution escape me without a single hand stroke. The thought of engaging in a little bump and grind with you until the sun came up, signaling the onset of morning, drove me crazy. I would appease and tease, then please you, with the hopes that minds, hearts, bodies, and souls would fuse to the beats of ecstasy. Like a submarine torpedo locked in on a battleship, my fantasy would be fulfilled by feeling the moist cavern I craved. And after reading aloud my ode to you, Zane, my thoughts were simple, yet solid. *She's gonna want me.*

Arriving at the megastore at four forty-five, I was surprised to see a crowd of hundreds. Aligned in an orderly fashion by metal barricades, the awestruck gathering couldn't take their eyes off the vehicle parked directly in front.

And what a means of transportation it was. The size of a city bus and a half, it was big, beige, and beautiful. The tinted windows were accentuated by the books painted on the exterior. Live and in color, I saw *Addicted*, *Nervous*, *The Heat Seekers*, *Chocolate Flava*, and *Sistergirls.com*.

A feeling of pride enveloped me, temporarily replacing laserlike desire. Thinking of what our forefathers were subjected to: the dogs sicced on us, the hoses full-blast, the orchestration, infiltration, and systematic dissection of problack groups by an insecure, cross-dressing F.B.I. figurehead, and additional forms of racism, I realized their sacrifices were made so that another innovating trailblazer, Zane, could do her thing in unleashing the deepest passions of our women. Silently thanking those forefathers, I prayed that somehow, someway, my expression of gratitude to you would be delivered in the only way possible: by making love to you.

My militant musings were disrupted by the sounds of screams as the bus door opened. There you were. Wide, beautiful doe eyes captured my attention, not to mention rose-colored baby cheeks. Vibrant and voluptuous, you were everything I imagined in a queen. Feeling your humility from afar, I knew why you had been blessed. Tenderness etched across a confident countenance, I could feel the driven, determined ambition that belied your docile surface. The caring, protective spirit now filling my bones wanted to make sure you were okay with signing all of these books.

Making your way to the facility, you surveyed the crowd quickly and saw me standing there with my roses. Smiling ever so slightly, something buried deep in the pit of me spoke. Vibrations ran through me as its resonance was clear and direct.

She's curious. She wants to know if those are for her.

Your answer would come shortly.

I patiently stood in line; my CD player blared the seductive sounds of Prince. The song "Slow Love" had my head swinging back and forth, thinking of that man on the moon smiling at what would transpire if I were lucky.

Yeah, Zane, I thought. *It would be so much better if we took our time.*

The long wait would be spent in fantasy. Zane, I pictured us in a room filled with sexual devices. Properly attired in tight black leather, you were the dominatrix, and I was pretty much anything you wanted me to be. Offering to become your personal slave: your maid, your cook, your chauffeur, your typist and publicist and errand boy while you wrote your sex stories. You noted my compliance and left our erotic room of passion, then returned with pad and pen in hand.

Smiling mischievously, you told me that in order to become your full-time slave, I'd have to sign a contract. After I asked what it would entail, you politely responded by saying you get carte blanche permission to have your way with me, and that I couldn't object. If I breached the contract, you'd never see me again. Agreeing verbally to my subservience, you wrote our pact in neat, looping penmanship. The contract read as follows:

I will see Zane on a regular basis. Throughout this tryst I will accept and do anything and everything that is asked of me, without inhibitions or limitations. I am cognizant of the fact that Zane is my mistress, and she has complete ownership of my mind, body, and soul.

We both signed it, and after your direction, I lay on my stomach on a wooden table. Fully expecting ankles and wrists to be bound, to my surprise I was told to simply lie still. Feeling an open hand on a buttock, I flinched ever so slightly.

"Keep still, Lover," you demanded, "or you'll be in big trouble."

Next, I felt another smack, only this time it wasn't from your flesh. It was the impact of a wooden paddle against me. Howling loudly as I found each sharp, stinging blow arousing, the feeling my flesh felt almost made me cum.

To my amazement, this was only phase one of my indoctrination. Veering left, I saw you pulling a mysterious metal instrument from a drawer, then light a candle. Fear captured me as I watched you holding the object over the votive. Gulping to remove my heart from my throat, I asked what you were doing.

"You are now mine, and I'll ensure that by branding the letter Z on your ass. You will bear the mark of me forever."

When you thought the brand was hot enough, you motioned to the door, and in walked two of your assistants. Though their eyes were behind feline-shaped masks, the outline of the faces looked hauntingly familiar.

"Mistress Mary and Mistress Marissa, you want to hold him down for me?"

As Mistress Mary grabbed my arms, she tilted me slightly and noticed the length of my tool.

"He reminds me of Wellington in *Soul Mates Dissipate,* Marissa," she commented. "I want to fuck him."

Securing my ankles, Mistress Marissa's desires caught aflame as well.

"And it hooks too. I wanna ride on that *Chocolate Ship,* Zane. Can I make it cum?"

"Heel, ladies," you commanded. "I want to take him on a test drive."

"But somebody's gotta be on top," Mistress Mary reasoned.

"Yeah," Mistress Marissa echoed. "They all can't be addicted to you, Zane. I need a hot boy."

"We will all have fun the minute I leave my mark on his ass."

The verbal exchange made my dick as hard as granite, but I remained as cool as a poker chip. That is, until I felt a burning sensation. Searing my flesh, it was two inches wide and an inch high, I guessed. Within minutes, that scorching pain gave way to an enjoyable throbbing. To my credit, I'd been an obedient slave and would be rewarded with three lovers when I had expected only one.

"NEXT IN LINE, PLEASE!!!"

My imagination was jolted with the loud directive, and my reality was only a few feet away, at a nearby signing table. Though nervous, I was determined to make good on my promise. Wanting to fill your insides with me and set you free, that initial feeling of anxiety was replaced with one of poise. Fully composed, I picked up a copy of *Nervous* and approached you.

Surprisingly, you initiated the conversation.

"I hope your woman enjoys those beautiful roses."

Upon hearing that, an unfamiliar boldness surfaced.

"These are for you, Zane. I just started reading your books a couple of days ago, and I want to say that you captured my imagination in more ways than you'll ever know." Hoping that I wasn't rambling, I continued. "And I want you also to have this." Reaching into my back pocket, I handed her "After Dark." "If I never see you again, I want to thank you for being the object of my desires, if only for a moment in time."

Remarkably, you allowed me to finish my diatribe, and your beautiful face remained as cool as when I began.

"So to whom am I making this book out?"

"W-W-Willis," I stammered. "Shawn Willis."

After a couple of anxious seconds, you handed me the novel.

"Thank you, Shawn."

Feeling the air leave my balloon of desire, I took the book and ventured over to the bakery. Given the ambiguity of your facial expression, I was unsure as to whether security would be escorting me from the venue, or a dream of many a man would become a reality. Looking over my shoulder as I neared the bakery, I sighed when realizing that the former wasn't happening.

As far as what I hoped would occur, it was only after I was seated that I read your inscription: *"Someday is tonight. I'll see you later."*

Simple and succinct, the message was emphasized by the slow, secret smile I saw when looking your way. Sensing we shared an intense physical connection, the heated gaze was of the go-outside-before-I-fuck-the-shit-out-of-you-in-front-of-everyone-in-this-bookstore variety.

Blushing, I didn't know what to say. Or what my next move would be. My answer to the latter came quickly: once outside the megastore, I was greeted with a smile, courtesy of a female store attendant.

"My name is Sherry. Zane told me to let you on the bus."

Smiling, I remained polite with my introduction, but a helpless feeling came over me as I boarded the vehicle. Seeing the large, queen-size bedroom, the shower, minibar, and kitchen, a bead of sweat trickled off my brow as I found a seat in a recliner. Not knowing what was in store for me, now I knew the anxiety experienced by the men Janet Jackson kidnapped during her "Velvet Rope" tour. Aroused before her arrival yet fearful that I might be quick on the draw if nature ran its course, the wait was killing me.

Each passing second was turning me on. Drifting back into wonderland, I saw us making love on that bed. Michael Jackson's "Lady in My Life" enhanced the mood, and I was, once again, determined to please you. As you lay back in my tenderness, my will to rock you with my sweet caress was indomitable. Making slow harmony with the fluidity of your hips, I temporarily removed myself from you. Moaning with disappointment, I assured you that the urging for re-entry would not go unheeded.

The lips of your honey now distended, it was time for a slow submission.

"Here comes inch number one," I announced.

Gasping, you played along,

"One is for fun, but my hot spot needs more."

Laughing, I continued.

"Inch two, for you."

"Two makes me coo," you moaned.

"Do you want more, Zane?"

"Please."

"Here comes inch three," I said huskily, pushing a bit farther inside you.

Breathless with pleasure, your response made me harder than I had ever been in my life.

"Three makes me greedy. More, Sugar. Give me more."

Impaling you deeper with my iron-hard sword, "Four," I breathed.

"Four makes me . . ."

"Want more, right, Zane?"

"Yes, Shawn. Mama needs more!"

Your tunnel was wet and willing, ready to devour inch number five. Making it disappear within your thick walls, you hissed in appreciation of my appendage.

"Five makes my pussy alive!" Your pleasure escalating, you closed your eyes and let out a series of whimpers that reverberated through the vehicle. Humping on what was inside you, I demanded that you take the other half from me.

Obliging, your hands gripped my maximus and pushed me in slowly. Inch by inch, you seductively sliced those swollen lips and stabbed your watery well with my worthy, wealthy, wanton weapon of lust.

Breathing heavily as my nostrils flared in ecstasy, that our minds were one in this foray made me want to sink all of me inside all of you, dilate your honey delightfully, and make your legs kick in eternal ecstasy. However, restraint was in order, and with my self-control, so continued the game.

"Number six," you said breathlessly, "is for sex."

"Do you want to go to heaven?" I asked.

"Yes, Shawn. Yes."

"Then come get inch number seven."

Complying, you bucked into me and released a long, low moan of joy. Pushing your pelvis upward, the look on your face indicated that you, too, were in *that zone*. The neighborhood where bodies fuse into one and the sexual link of the chain is joined. The shared erogenous region where a woman's vagina is his sexual cure for deprivation, and his penis makes her forget all other lovers. A point where love organs are mutually numb in ecstasy; an awesome place where smiles and sighs of pleasure replace words, and facial expressions indicate complete and absolute gratification. You are thankful that for one moment in time, you have met your sexual equal. The connection, whether in a momentary diversion or consummation of a relationship, is spiritual, and though paths may separate after the encounter, you will remember the union with a smile shared only by one other person in the universe. The dick or pussy is that good.

Gripping my firm biceps, you got inch seven, then lurched upward once more.

"Eight is absolutely great. But I need to feel fine."

Not able to contain my control, I pushed in number nine.

"Mama feels fine with nine."

My mind spoke in tongues, you felt so good. Nobody handled my length and width the way your rivers of motion did, and the search for your spot would be complete with that final inch. Lunging forward to mingle bodies, I embedded myself completely.

Flinging your head back, I saw your eyes widen, then roll to the top of those cute lids.

"Ten . . . is . . . a . . . fucking . . . sin!"

Pumping furiously into a jouncing, juicy bliss, only the head of me remained inside of your spot with each outstroke as my arms slid behind spread, upthrust legs. Driving into you, I demanded that you open your eyes and see the man giving you such pleasure.

Doing so, you could barely keep them open.

"Damn, this dick feels good," you purred.

Squirming and screaming as the mattress shook and vibrated from the force of our fury, the transformation from strangers to sex-besotted lovers was complete.

"Do it, Shawn," was the request heard next from you. "Pump the fuck out of your pussy!"

Plunging and withdrawing, submerging, then retreating, I felt the sacs surrounding my pipe twitching. Majestically moving inside of you, going here, there, and all around the world with hypnotic hip motion, my voice went hoarse as you thrashed beneath me. Feeling my orgasm rise, my back stiffened as I prepared for its release.

"Daddy needs his pump primed," you calmly uttered. Clamping your walls around me, you milked all of my seed into the instrument worn. I couldn't take it. All I could say was, "Oh, shit!!" as you took care of my magic stick.

"Mmm, that's a good boy," you said after my peak. "Mama likes that."

There was an intrusion to my erotic trance: the bus engines. Peering outside the smoky windows, there you were, my hopeful dream come true. Discreetly surveying you, I liked what I saw. Your rose-carrying caramel silhouette was alluring, and the gorgeous, generous smile you possessed illuminated the twilight with its wattage. Your nylon-encased legs looked firm and appetizing, and though I had never been a breast man, something about seeing your ample cleavage accentuated by a red blouse and sexy black choker made me a convert.

Another fit of nervousness confined my senses as you boarded the vehicle and approached me.

"I see you've made yourself comfortable."

Blushing, I was speechless. Feeling my nervousness, you took hold of my hand and assured me that I wasn't a notch-in-your-belt sexual conquest.

"Shawn, forgive my aggression. I'm not usually this forward."

"Neither am I," I responded, alluding to the stunning arrangement you held. "Zane, I thought I would get my face slapped, or you would think of me as a deranged pervert."

Smiling as you searched the kitchen cabinet for a vase, I sensed that such was not the case. Confirmation came from your words.

"My gut told me you weren't, not to mention that erotic letter. By the way, are you sure that you don't have a blossoming career in writing?"

Chuckling, I was more than flattered by the compliment.

"No, I don't have literary pursuits. But I want you to know that you have a fan for life, Zane. And I will purchase every word you write."

My comments were met with a giggle I failed to recognize.

"Shawn, you are, and always will be, more than a fan to me. You and I are like spirits."

Purposely pausing, you left your thought in the air for me to ponder. But surprisingly, that action wasn't necessary. Fully comprehending the statement, heated blood was coursing through me, once again making me aware of the unique chemistry we shared as you continued.

"Shawn, there are people you come across in life where the physical attraction is so intense that you must act on it. Everything this person does, from the look in his eyes to the smooth gait of his walk, will arouse you. The inflection of his vocal tone seduces you as well. And if he, like you did in that store, invites the other party to share the attraction, then . . ."

"Everything falls into place easily. Am I correct, Zane?"

That I completed your sentence not only proved your theory on point but made you turn beet red as your eyes met the carpet of the vehicle.

"I guess so."

Those three words lifted the weight of nervous tension off my shoulders. Instantly, the sunshine of understanding the moment at hand completely lightened the mood. Sharing discreet flirtations, as the plush vehicle made its trip through the Lincoln Tunnel, then onto the New Jersey Turnpike, the conversation had more substance than the normal trivial banter reserved for two people just looking for a fuck.

Sharing your aspirations, you told me about Strebor Books, your self-made imprint that was picked up by a major distribution chain. But you weren't stopping there, you assured me; movies and lingerie lines were to follow.

Listening to your dreams and the methodical yet determined approach to bring everything to fruition, all I could do was sit in admiration. Never hearing a negative word from those pretty red lips of yours, I felt honored by the fact that you allowed me into your world if only for a moment.

This woman is powerful, I mused. *That she chose me to spend some time with means more than she could possibly imagine.*

When you inquired about my livelihood, instead of the awkward pause I receive from many a person disappointed with my corporate status, all I heard were words of encouragement.

"You can stay at my place if you need a new start," you suggested.

My legs turned to jelly and my stomach experienced knots like it does when I'm on the downslope of a speedy roller coaster. In this age of materialistic gain, I wonder if people fully understand the theory of standing and supporting a person through an impoverished winter in an effort to appreciate forthcoming spring prosperity. And here I was, riding on transportation supplied by an Oprah-like figure who wanted me as her naughty-naughty, and she opened her heart to my plight.

"Nah, Baby," I politely declined. "I'll be okay."

As if jolted by my words, I started to cover my lips.

Once again, your nurturing soul took over.

"I haven't been called Baby in such a long time. It's okay."

My head abuzz with arousal, at that precise moment the pole in my pants pitched a tent in my pants. I hoped you didn't notice the size as I rose from my chair for a glass of wine.

"Damn, I hope that's all mine, Shawn."

Embarrassed, how else could I respond?

"It sure is," I mumbled.

Returning to a heated gaze from exotic light brown eyes, we both knew where our chat was going next. Nightfall gripped the summer evening, and a full moon joined its place among the stars. Gone was the city and its bright lights. In its place came the low-key sparkles of a suburban skyline. While lacking the iridescence of its counterpart across the river, New Jersey was the perfect hideaway for lovers.

This was a point emphasized when the Madden-like cruiser stopped suddenly at a rest area. Rising quickly, you approached the driver, whispered something in his ear, and motioned to me with an extended forefinger.

"Let's go," you demanded as we left the motor coach for an inconspicuous black Mitsubishi Diamante, complete with tinted windows.

"No one needs to know my business," you uttered as we peeled out.

"This move is bold in itself," I countered.

You giggled again.

"I know, right?"

Speeding south along the freeway, our chatter took another turn, as the car seemed to take your mind to a mysteriously exciting place. Marques Houston's "Naked" had your head bobbing and your voice, once passive and demure, became deeper and more seductive. The transformation could also be seen in the subtle yet sexy change in your driving posture. Like a vampire lusting for red wine from the neck of its prey, I felt the aggression of your heat when you looked my way.

"I'm gonna have fun with you," you announced. Peering deep, I saw wide, piercing, possessing eye pupils, a sure sign of sexual hunger. In case my brain moved slowly, your free hand moved along the rising explosion in my slacks to catch me up to speed.

"Mmm, I like what I'm working with."

Blushing, your rubbing of my fire began the transport to a place I have been begging to be, a spot whose entrance is where tongues intertwine and discover each other's mouths, and life-producing body parts assemble to become one in a moist compartment built to accommodate all of my length. Or so I hoped.

Per my directions, we arrived at our destination: a discreet, luxurious lodge off of Exit 13.

"A place where no one knows your name," I joked.

"I see you've done this before."

How could I not be totally honest with you?

"Not in a while, Zane."

"No job means no pussy, huh?"

"Something like that."

"Well, I guess I can't have a handsome man like you walking around all clogged up, now can I?"

The wood between my thighs, now painfully stiff, could barely take the need for release of the salty, sticky sap it owned. My log needed to burn in your fiery hot oven, so that the heat of us could mix with the temperature of the late summer evening. I knew right at that moment your vagina would sing tonight. There would be no nuttin' up this evening. I would last longer than you ever experienced while searching your eyes for equal passion. Inhibitions wouldn't mean a damn thing tonight, for this was the collision of two sexual beings destined to come together in an all-nighter.

My eyes said this, but the only response to your comment would be, "No, Zane, you can't leave me this way."

"Mmm. Well, I guess I can help you with that." Smiling as you popped the trunk of your ride to retrieve a portable radio, you handed me two crisp Ben Franklins and ordered me to get the best space in the place.

Obliging, I returned to the stylish vehicle with a key to the most exotic room, which upon our entry only added to our building anticipation. Directly in view, a red, heart-shaped Jacuzzi made you purr "ooh" as you saw the elaborate fruit basket at its edge. In the mini–dining area was a stainless brass ice bucket with a bottle of Moët at its center.

The bed area had the feel of a jungle, compliments of the wax vines, branches, and exotic flowers that surrounded a large, circular mattress. Rotating fluorescent ceiling lights bordered the section of the suite, only adding to the already steamy setting.

The room was, in a word, awesome.

Dimming the lights as you made yourself comfortable, you fixed a glass of bubbly while I placed the radio on an adjacent night table. Removing a disk from my portable player, a slow, sensuous drumbeat filled the room the very second I placed it into the bigger model. Then, on came a saxophone riff that was all too common to me.

And upon looking your way to a sexy gleam, the groove was familiar to you as well.

"I thought I was the only one who knew about this record."

"Zane, I always wanted to have sex to this song," I said.

"So have I, Shawn. So have I."

By this point, you found the center of the mattress comfortable. I could tell from the sexy position you were in. The first sip of champagne relaxed your mind, and the music—"The Scandalous Sex Suite," a nineteen-minute lovemaking extravaganza—soothed your soul.

Your body, however, belonged to someone else that evening.

Me.

I watched you unfasten a button on your blouse, then raise your hand in a sensuous motion.

"Come closer," you mouthed as Prince serenaded those lyrics.

A nervous laugh escaped me as the spell your forefinger cast had me walking to you. Seeing the pinkness of your tongue when your mouth opened begged me to taste your oral dew with my own tongue. Obliging deeply, French-style, the scent of you intoxicated me, sending me spiraling into a special situation where fantasy and reality met, a place where you are so aroused by a person's kiss that you can barely tolerate the pleasure. You joined me there, Zane, as we entered a world where panoplies of sexual pleasures seemed to make anything you ever wrote about dull and pedestrian.

Admiring the activeness of my oral critter, you moaned, "I bet you could eat pussy real good."

"Can I break you off with some of my skills, Zane?"

"Don't ask, Shawn. Just do."

I would heed your command, but not right away, because I enjoyed kissing you so much. Returning my tongue into your oral haven, I licked your pearly whites, then sucked on your soft red lips.

Planting pecks all over your flesh, I proceeded south, slowly, however, for I wanted to savor every moment shared with the goddess of sex. Feeling privileged that you chose me to share a special part of you, with that honor was the ultimate responsibility of being the best lover you ever experienced. Every morsel of info I learned from those lonely nights at Times Square to the many books read on sexual techniques would be put to the test.

My patience would go through the checkpoint first; lord knows I wanted to part those gorgeous thighs and suck the sense out of your pussy. But, mmm, I had to taste the nape of your neck, then your luscious bosom. Inhaling the valley between your breasts, the steel between my legs twitched dangerously as it got harder than any calculus problems I faced in college. Rubbing and squeezing them, I heard your breathing get harsh and deep.

"You can write about it, Zane. But can you do it? Can you fuck, Baby?"

"You're about to find out, Shawn."

Your abundant cherries had large, protruding nipples that spoke to my lips, begging profusely for me to suck them. Obliging skillfully, I gave them their due attention, suctioning them like an infant searching for milk. Sensing my hunger, you cupped my head like a mother feeding her young.

"That's my spot, Baby," you moaned. "Get it, Shawn."

Hearing your request made me press your mounds together so that I could enjoy the taste of imaginary milk from both nipples simultaneously. That drove you crazy.

"Oh, God," you panted. "You just have to eat my pussy."

Lowering myself to your love zone, I removed your silk panties.

"I'm keeping these," I announced as I tossed them aside and slid one finger, then two, into your hot gateway. The sounds you were making left no doubt as to how much you enjoyed me. Feeling your body shimmer, then shake, brought a delicious, hungry grin from me. I hadn't even placed my lips on you, and you thrashed and experienced tremors.

I'm going to pulverize this pussy, I thought.

But first I had to eat some dinner. Needing to investigate each nook and cranny of where Wonder Dick would lead me later, my oral search was to find every responsive place your triangle possessed. Delicately kissing the opening of your offering, my nose playfully bounced against your clitoris while my lips and tongue danced a dervish around the lips leading to heaven.

"C'mon, Baby. Fuck my tongue," I demanded.

Entering you with my face, your hips moved in a circular motion as I grabbed your caramel backside. Pushing you close, then closer, you met my mouth with powerful thrusts. Feeling the dampness of you, I wasn't ready to give you my dick, so I inserted something else hard and solid into your sloppy, messy-wet pleasure zone. My chinny-chin-chin.

Guiding it slowly between your slippery, sensitive folds, I tilted my head ever so slightly, so that my oral paintbrush could dance against the pearl of your canvas. Guessing that you love to have the sides of it licked, the contented sigh received as I bathed your clit made me shudder once more.

My chin had enough exercise, so I relieved it of its duty by returning my flutter-brush deep inside your intimate cavern. Trying to extract every erotic nerve you possessed into my mouth as I consumed you, the intensity of my performance increased as you humped my face. Sucking on your shining labia, I let my tongue continue its exquisite exploration of your tunnel.

You were moaning and grinding your spot into my face so hard I thought you were trying to go through me. My tireless brim delightfully darting deep inside, I switched to a circular motion, touching and tasting each thick wall of you. Teasing and torturing your tunnel with the tantalizing talent of my tongue, damn, I loved the flavor of your pussy.

Squirming excitedly, you demanded, "Make it cum, Shawn."

How in the world could I refuse a request from a damsel in sexual distress?

Every crack and crevice of you deserved love, so I returned to your hooded clit, sucking on it with the upper portion of my mouth as my teeth munched on the inside of you. Savoring every sensation of my performance, you were moaning loudly as I scraped your clitoris lightly. Keeping my oral instrument active, I felt you jerk as the spasms of climax usurped your body.

As your kitty swelled, a river of salty hot juices poured from you, landing in my eager goblet. Quenching my insatiable thirst, you tasted like chocolate covered pretzels. It was tangy, yet syrupy.

"Enough," you gasped. "I want to taste you."

Kissing you, I noticed the clear look in your eyes. In case the swelling of your clit hadn't informed me, I knew you had joined me in *that zone*.

"You know I don't normally do this," you announced.

Too heated to care, I paraphrased my favorite rapper, The Notorious B. I. G.

"Whatever, Zane."

"Biggie, am I correct?"

We shared a laugh. As deep as I went mentally, you matched me. I knew we were meant to be.

Opening your mouth hungrily to accept my turgid stiffness, you shaped your mouth into a well-rounded O and feasted on my length. Relaxing the muscles of the back of your throat, you sucked me in slowly.

"Fuck!" I shrieked. Never before had a woman taken all of me, and that alone almost brought cum from me. Sliding and slurping, you made me clench my fists as you bobbed up and down on my joystick. I was moaning loudly when your next request floored me.

"Stand up and dick-feed me that pickle, Shawn. I want to show you something."

Rising, I received warm kisses on my pole, causing the slit of it to drip precum. Mixing my dew ever so sweetly with your saliva, you paused slightly.

"What's wrong, Zane?"

"Nothing, Baby. I just want to kiss you."

There we stood, in the middle of the mattress, sharing a deep, special mouth merger. To say our shared kiss cooked in degrees is a gross under-statement; we became arsonists, for the deliciously long embrace set the walls ablaze. Forgetting all prior rendezvous, the room's walls would talk about this collaboration forever.

Drinking your saliva, as if my thirst were unquenchable, we danced hun-grily, tasting every recess. The kiss would last a full ten minutes. Then you moved to my neck, causing me to shiver. I never had a woman find the erog-enous zone on my body, so I was pleasantly surprised when your mouth traced, then devoured my right nipple.

"Damn, Zane," is all I could say. My breathing became irregular as my core shook and shivered from the pleasure you brought me. A wicked grin encompassed you as you lowered yourself to my groin. Thinking re-entry into you oral nastiness, I was pleasantly surprised when you let your breasts separate.

"Do you want to put that nice piece of meat here?" you asked, while licking your lips.

Delightfully dunking my rod into your cleavage, a bit of excitement es-caped me and found your décolletage.

"Shawn, you have got to give me all of your cum, not just a sampling." Your voice, bold and salacious, had my knees sagging. Moving my massive heat along, and in between your mounds, you squeezed them together to envelop me into your world, shaking as you did so. If toenails could shimmy, I knew I had you.

My dick found every nerve ending between your breasts, but that wasn't sufficient for you; you guided my dick into your mouth. That you gagged while slurping and sliding up and down on my hook made me that much harder. Tenderly cupping my tightened balls, you tickled them with your long fingernails as you seductively sucked my stiffness.

After about five minutes, I received the shock of a lifetime when you slipped a rubber band around the base of my manhood as a makeshift dick ring.

"Yeah, Sugar. Mama's gonna make you explode just like a lover in one of my stories." Repoising your mouth over my swollen arousal, you lubricated me with your own arousal. I felt the wetness of your tongue mingle with my balls.

"Damn, I'm glad they're not sweaty," you said.

I laughed.

"Does Shawn want to cum now?"

"Yes, Zane."

"Mmm, my pussy muscles are clenching."

With that, you continued with your oral escapade. Working me over for another twenty minutes, I was piston-whipped, in and out of your mouth. Grabbing the back of your head as you pulled as much of my length as you could muster, you made me flinch with desire as you held your mouth there on eight inches. Gripping the bottom to hold it steady, you took the last two, hook and all.

"Shit," was all I could say. Bobbing up and down, you submerged my dick entirely, then withdrew until just the tip was inside. After nibbling on it, you shoved me all the way into something wet, watery, and warm. The fusion of image and sensation was getting to me. You wrapped your lips around my fatness like a velvet vise and ran your mouth down the length of me until we were playing tonsil hockey.

"Mmm," you said. "I could feel your dick veins pulsating."

You were right, and the intensity of my orgasm would be stronger than ever before. It wasn't the rubber band around the base that turned my arousal up a notch. It was you, Zane.

Peering downward, I noticed that a pool of juices had gushed from you, drenching the sheets. I figured that the wetness was temporary, because the heat between us would not only dry, but singe and scorch them.

As you continued your lustful lubrication of my well-greased metal, a shiver ran up and down my spine. I felt you reshaping your face so that the length of me could touch your esophagus. Moaning and whimpering like a puppy as my body tensed, I could hold back no longer.

"Fuck, I'm gonna cum!" I screamed as my vision blurred. Shuddering intensely, as a gallon of my seed left me, I heard you gulping, then swallowing my erotic eruption. That only brought more from me.

Peering down breathlessly, I noticed some of me on your chin and your chest. That I licked it off surprised you. Or so I thought.

"It came from me, Zane," I said between ragged breaths.

"I expected you to clean up your mess."

Mental and sexual fusion complete, we laughed together as we collapsed arm in arm onto the mattress. No, I wasn't hallucinating. My dreams were now a reality.

Recovering quickly, I knew that you were a woman who took complete care of your man sexually, for you nibbled on my reawakened dick. Not one to be ungrateful, I clamped your thighs around my face and resumed dining on you. Sixty-nine was a wonderful number for us.

But not for long; we both needed penetration. Just in case I wasn't cognizant of your urgency, you begged, "I need you right now." Bringing your mouth to mine, we shared a furious kiss as our hips quivered. Hardening once more, I prayed that your thick sugar walls were accommodating. Some men like their honey nice and tight. However, because of my size I'm an exception. I love big, juicy pussy, so I can do a dance in it. The search to find the G-spot with my strokes is tons of fun, not to mention the variety of pumps you can utilize in an effort to please. The need to hit all corners, crevices, and angles of you made me even harder as my head poked against your entrance.

"Do you want it hard and fast, Zane? Or slow and—"

"Shawn, fuck the shit out of me in every way." You paused, then smirked. "Please."

Your cervix was welcoming as I levered Wonder Dick inside of you. Thrusting deep, you took all of my manhood easily. Initially moving my hips in tiny circles, you met my movements with small waves. It felt so good being inside of you.

Mercilessly rhythmic, I increased the beat of my gyrations as your newly inducted passage got familiar with my steel. Inserting, then quickly retreating, there was something about trying to make your love come down that was extremely erotic. As the strokes increased in ferocity, I couldn't help myself when leaning down to kiss you.

Not shying away, as we danced, your tongue met mine with reckless abandon. Zoning into a place where emotions existed, I knew that this moment in time meant more to you than satisfying a need. The desire you wrote about needed to be acted out, if but for a moment in time.

Varying the speed of my strokes, I slammed against your pelvis one moment, then gently glided in and out of you the next. Making around-the-world circles with my hips, your cries of passion became louder and louder.

"This dick is so fucking good!" you screamed. "Please keep fucking me!"

Picking up the pace once more, my wrists and forearms clasped your ankles as I hammered away. Fervent, forceful strokes filled you as you anticipated, then met my fury with equal vigor. My hook was hitting previously undiscovered spots, and the bed rocked from the shared passion between us.

"Hurt me, Shawn," you urged. "Hurt this pussy good."

Giving you deep, then deeper penetration, our fused flesh was a blur as the body slapping became animalistic. Instead of words, over the next hour or so, pleasurable grunts and wonderful groans escaped us. Affectionate, yet animalistic, our bodies sweated as if we were drowning in a vat of scented oil. Leaning down from the missionary, I couldn't help but taste your perspiration. Mmmmm.

As if on cue, you stuck a long, juicy index finger into my ass, sending ripples of delight through me as I hammered away. Your alive, wet pussy clinched around my heat as if it were part of you.

Trembling as you grabbed the sheets, your eyes were screwed shut as you tried to fight the orgasms. You lost, big-time. Your moans matched the slurping sounds of your cunny as you crashed and convulsed in ecstasy. Quivering as you squeezed my diamond-hard masculinity, a gusher of milk traveled through my shaft and flooded my condom as I lost my breath.

"That's right, Baby. Give it all to Mama," you said.

Wincing with light-headed pleasure, more juice left me with your words. Both of us now panting, our eyes met with wonder and amazement. Nodding, you knew what I knew. We were sexual soul mates.

Throughout the night, we revisited our lovemaking course, mastering different angles and positions as if we had made love in a prior existence. But as nightfall turned to dawn, we knew that our suspended time in passion would cease.

And suddenly, it did. Midday came, and your next city was Atlanta, nineteen hours away on your bus. Driving me back into the city, you held my hand as if you never wanted to let go.

Somehow, I summoned the courage to speak.

"We'll never see each other again," I said.

I predicted the response, given your ambiguity.

As the car stopped at the megastore, you smiled.

"This isn't good-bye, Shawn. It's so long."

Pecking my lips slowly, heat rose between us for the last time as the kiss turned erotic.

"Zane, thanks."

You handed me an envelope.

"Open this after I pull off."

As the shiny Diamante sped away, I opened the envelope. It contained a thousand dollars and a note.

Something to help you until your feet are planted on solid ground.

Thank you for being so special to me.

Zane.

All I could do is smile. Some moments in life you feel eager to share; others, like the one I just experienced, are compartmentalized in that room of secrets. This one would forever reside at the forefront of those memories.

So there you have it, Zane: my gift to you by way of paper and pen. I will continue to read your stories and say to myself, *Sock it to me*. By the way, isn't that the title of your video?

Lustfully yours,

A Fan